THE REPUBLIC OF
VIRTUE

HOW WE TRIED TO BAN CORRUPTION, FAILED, AND WHAT WE CAN DO ABOUT IT

F.H. BUCKLEY

ENCOUNTER BOOKS   NEW YORK · LONDON

First American edition published in 2017 by Encounter Books,
an activity of Encounter for Culture and Education, Inc.,
a nonprofit, tax exempt corporation.
Encounter Books website address: www.encounterbooks.com

Manufactured in the United States and printed on
acid-free paper. The paper used in this publication meets
the minimum requirements of ANSI/NISO Z39.48—1992
(R 1997) (Permanence of Paper).

FIRST AMERICAN EDITION

LIBRARY OF CONGRESS CATALOGING-IN-PUBLICATION DATA

TK

For Esther, Sarah,
Nick & Benjamin Herbert

Contents

PART ONE

THE UNITED STATES
OF CORRUPTION

All plans of government, which suppose great reformation in the manners of mankind, are plainly imaginary.

—David Hume

Our Machiavellian Moment

FOR FOREIGN INVESTORS, America is always a good bet, and that's especially true when they come from corrupt countries, as Kambir Abdul Rahman and Yassir Habib did. Together the two formed Abdul Enterprises and deposited a million dollars in Chase Manhattan Bank to give themselves credibility. Then they hired Melvin Weinberg to approach American politicians for their support. If this is beginning to sound familiar, that's because it's the Abscam sting of 1978–80, and the basis for the 2013 film *American Hustle*.

Kambir Abdul Rahman and Yassir Habib didn't exist. The entire operation was an FBI plan to entrap corrupt politicians, and before it was over it led to the conviction of six U.S. congressmen as well as Senator Harrison Williams (D-NJ). Melvin Weinberg was all too real, an elementary school dropout and ne'er-do-well who once took $10,000 from a doctor on a promise to kill his wife and then simply kept the money without doing the job. He subsequently moved on to bigger stings, making $500,000 a year and never paying income tax. In time the feds caught up with him, and after being convicted of wire fraud he agreed to work for the FBI to entrap corrupt politicians. Beginning with low-level New Jersey pols, he quickly moved up to Washington officials as word spread that he had money to hand out. The first congressman he caught in his web was Michael Myers (D-NJ), who was persuaded to introduce a private bill that would have permitted "Rahman" and "Habib" to remain in the United States. "I'm no Boy Scout," he told Weinberg. Truer words were never spoken, but Myers might have been less candid had he known that he was being taped and the FBI was listening in.[1]

It made for a good movie, but it was only garden-variety corruption, where public officials take money under the table in exchange for an official act and are sentenced to jail. In such cases, the FBI and the local police seem entirely up to the job of ferreting out the grifter, the pol on the take. What they miss are the nudges and winks that fall short of an official act, the way in which campaign donors and lobbyists support candidates and thereafter enjoy a privileged relationship with them. The donors and lobbyists will expect to have their calls returned and their opinions respected, and that's not a crime. "Ingratiation and access . . . are not corruption," ruled Justice Kennedy in *Citizens United*.[2] In a subsequent case, Chief Justice Roberts took it one step further. There's nothing wrong with campaign donors not only gaining access but expecting that the officials they support will respond to their interests, he thought. Rather, it's "a central feature of democracy."[3] That sounds like a heavy dose of realism.

Pay-for-Play Networks

There are worse things in the annals of government than donors who influence elected officials. But that isn't an endorsement of America's pay-for-play networks, in which officials exchange public favors for campaign contributions, book contracts, media hires, charitable gifts, and the like. Then we get the shady dealings of Bill and Hillary Clinton that were detailed by Peter Schweizer in *Clinton Cash*.[4]

What "ingratiation and access" might look like became clear from Clinton Foundation emails to the State Department, made public only after protracted Freedom of Information Act litigation forced their disclosure. In 2009, Salman bin Hamad al-Khalifa, the crown prince of Bahrain, sought a private meeting with Hillary Clinton, the newly appointed secretary of state. The request went through normal diplomatic channels, but that didn't work. Bahrain wasn't on the State Department's best-friends list, and little wonder, since Human Rights Watch says that the little sheikdom regularly practices torture and that its human rights record is "dismal." Nothing daunted, the crown prince turned to the Clinton Foundation, which had received $32 million from him. The foundation's chief executive, Doug Band, then reached out to Huma Abedin, Mrs. Clinton's chief aide. The two were so close that Clinton saw Huma as her surrogate daughter (but would demote her to "one of my staffers" after the Anthony Weiner scandal broke).[5] Abedin's job at the State Department included taking care of "Clinton family matters," and while working at State she was also on retainer with both the Clinton Foundation and Band's advisory firm.[6] And when Band wrote her, "Cp of Bahrein in tomorrow to Friday Asking to see Good friend of ours," that did the trick.[7] Secretary Clinton met with the prince, and then, between 2010 and 2012, Clinton's State Department approved major arms sales to Bahrain, including chemical weapons that would be used to crush pro-democracy protests.[8]

In another case, Secretary Clinton brokered a deal that helped the Swiss banking giant UBS, which the IRS had sued to force disclosure of the names of the 52,000 Americans with secret bank accounts. UBS had stalled on releasing the names, pleading that this would violate Swiss secrecy laws. Within months of taking office Clinton took the unusual step of personally announcing that UBS would have to turn over the names of only 4,500 depositors. Thereafter, UBS donations to the Clinton Foundation swelled: from $60,000 by the end of 2008, to a total of $600,000 at the end of 2014. The bank also made a $32 million donation to the foundation's inner-city loan program, and paid Bill Clinton $1.5 million to participate in a series of question-and-answer sessions with a UBS executive. Secretaries of state are sometimes called on to tout major U.S. businesses, but this was a foreign corporation, and a bank at that.[9]

In surveying the pattern of fees and donations to the Clinton Foundation, Schweizer suggested that the Clintons had put America's foreign policy up for sale. The foreign countries that supported the foundation, many of them human rights abusers such as Saudi Arabia, were presumably more interested in seeking Secretary Clinton's favor than in foundation issues such as empowering women and improving LGBT rights. And if it was favors they wanted, favors they got. Foreign dignitaries, such as Salman bin Hamad al-Khalifa, were more likely to score a meeting with Secretary Clinton if they supported the foundation, and this was true of private individuals as well. More than half the private people who met with her were foundation donors, either personally or through their businesses. Eighty-five private donors in all gave a total of $156 million.[10]

That's a lot of money, but some donors seemed to get their money's worth. In one example, Hillary Clinton's State Department approved the transfer of 20 percent of U.S. uranium production capacity to the Russian government at the same time that businessmen involved in the transfer donated $145 million to the Clinton Foundation. Simply a coincidence, claimed Clinton, who said she wasn't aware of what was happening.[11] Another foundation donor, Rajiv Fernando, a securities trader, was appointed to the International Security Advisory Board, which provides the State Department with advice on arms control, disarmament, nonproliferation, and international security. Its members typically include past cabinet secretaries, nuclear scientists and distinguished diplomats. They have access to the most secret government information, and none of the others had a clue what Fernando was doing there. When ABC News started asking questions about him, Fernando promptly resigned and the State Department stonewalled requests for information about how he was appointed.[12]

All of this looked very much like a quid pro quo, a contribution to the Clinton Foundation (the quid) in return for a government favor (the quo). There isn't direct evidence of a bribe, however, but only a suspicious pattern of favors granted against contributions given. So Clinton loyalists say it's not proved, it's all innuendo. But in such cases it's never really proved, unless somebody is wired or the phones are tapped, and even those measures don't catch the pattern of reciprocal gifts that make up the pay-for-play networks of corruption. As it is, we are permitted to wonder if we'd have learned more about corrupt dealings had Hillary Clinton not taken the extraordinary step of wiping her private emails from her hard drive with a software program from a company that afterward boasted it had "stifled" the FBI's investigation of Clinton.[13]

In a very short time, the Clinton Foundation had become fabulously wealthy. It took in $2 billion, with a significant bump after Hillary became secretary of state. Part of this came from speaking fees, $150 million between 2001, when Bill Clinton left the White House, and 2015.[14] Often the speeches were made in Third World dictatorships. Speaking fees for former presidents generally decline over time, but Bill Clinton's fees doubled or tripled after his wife became secretary of state. In one case, he declined to speak at a charity devoted to building schools in countries devastated by the 2004 Indian Ocean tsunami unless he was paid $500,000. That was a quarter of what the event brought in, and it would have been enough to build ten preschools in Indonesia.[15] When Hillary Clinton left office as secretary of state, she got into the act. After she quoted a fee of $300,000 for a speech, UCLA officials asked whether they might get a reduced rate as a public university. That *was* the special university rate, they were told.[16]

Then there's the way the foundation was run. It wasn't a normal grantmaking foundation that acted as a conduit for passing money to worthy causes. Instead, it was more of an operating foundation, which organized events where others were encouraged to donate money. Its work involved the high-level schmoozing at which the Clintons have been so adept: international conferences, speeches, prizes, and the like. In 2013 the foundation took in $140 million but spent only $9 million on direct aid. The rest went toward administrative expenses— salaries, bonuses, conferences, travel, and development. Bill Allison, a senior fellow at the Sunlight Foundation, a nonpartisan watchdog group, looked at the financials in 2015 and concluded that the foundation appeared to be run as a slush fund for the Clintons.[17]

As if to demonstrate how the Clinton Foundation had become a pay-for-play network, contributions began to dry up as soon as Donald Trump defeated Mrs. Clinton. The Australian government, which had given the foundation $66 million over a ten-year period, announced plans to zero out the payments a few weeks after the election. As for the speaking fees, a wag announced that Mrs. Clinton had agreed to give a speech to Goldman Sachs executives in return for a brand-new toaster.

The more reputable media outlets found the whole affair disturbing. The *New York Times*, for example, agreed with Donald Trump that "it was hard to tell where the foundation ended and the State Department began."[18] To veteran Clinton-watchers, it was all just the latest in a long list of scandals, from the commodity futures trading, Whitewater, Travelgate, Troopergate, Chinagate, Filegate, Pardongate, the impeachment, on up to the private email server. In the past, a record like this would have disqualified a person from candidacy for higher office. That it didn't do so today, that Hillary Clinton became the Democratic nominee for the presidency, that there were furious apologists for every new scandal—all this seemed to tell us that we now live in a country where corruption is of little concern. With the Trump victory, we may be permitted to wonder if we were wrong, if Mrs. Clinton's defeat was a popular repudiation of public corruption. But then it was a near-run thing, as she racked up nearly three million more votes than Trump.

Republican Virtue

In the presidential election season of 2015–16, Hillary Clinton's ethical lapses drove millions of voters to support the campaign of a self-proclaimed socialist, Bernie Sanders, or of a business mogul, Donald Trump. All our professional pundits were astonished, but was it really that surprising? Sanders and Trump had one thing in common, which voters appreciated: they weren't Hillary Clinton. On economics, they were both to the left of their respective party's establishment, but that didn't hurt them with primary voters. The conservatives who faulted Trump for his lack of entitlement-reform plans didn't understand the much greater cost that corruption imposes on our economy. The voters got it, however. The old liberal-conservative ideological axis appears increasingly irrelevant as a corruption-virtue axis bids to take its place.

We've been here before. Two hundred and forty-one years ago. You might not think of "corruption" as the burning issue of the day in the American colonies in 1776. What about taxation without representation? Well, the tax in question was the price of today's dinner date. What about restrictions on liberty? But Britain and its American colonies were the freest places on earth (if you didn't count the slaves, of course). Ordinary Britons couldn't understand these complaints, and they thought the American Patriots needed to chill. But what they missed was the colonists' ire over corruption in the British government—the King's Friends in Parliament, the showering of gifts on royal favorites, the patronage machines of prime ministers and of royal governors in the colonies.

The Patriots thought they could do better. They had studied John Locke and were steeped in theories of natural rights. But they had also read Livy and thought that monarchies were necessarily corrupt, whether in ancient Rome or contemporary Britain. Kingly rule would breed a race of tyrants who surrounded themselves with a swarm of courtiers, who in turn would milk the public purse. The Patriots said we needed a republic instead, one from which selfish dealings and corrupt bargains would be banished—a government founded on the rock of republican virtue, the virtue shown by citizens who champion the general welfare in a personally disinterested manner.[19]

What the Patriots were experiencing is what the historian J. G. A. Pocock called a "Machiavellian Moment." Today, Niccolò Machiavelli is not well known as an exponent of republican virtue, but he was in fact a loyal servant of the Florentine Republic and the author of extended reflections on political morality. In his *Discourses on the First Ten Books of Livy*, he praised the public-spirited Lucius Junius Brutus, who expelled the last Roman king, Tarquin the Proud, and founded the Roman Republic. The American Patriots of the revolutionary period were also steeped in classical Roman history and celebrated the republican heroes of ancient Rome. They quoted Latin epigrams, sometimes accurately, while pamphleteers such as James Madison and Alexander Hamilton adopted the names of Roman republicans as pseudonyms. Patrick Henry ominously warned that "Tarquin had his Brutus, Charles the First his Cromwell, and George III . . . may profit by their example." The language of republican virtue provided the Patriots with a justification for breaking away from their corrupt British overlords.

But just how long did republican virtue persist in America? There wasn't much left of it by 1829, when Andrew Jackson introduced the spoils system and gave plum government jobs to his supporters. As for today, the lobbyists of K Street, the hundreds of special-interest associations in Alexandria, and the dense network of political donors in America have created what Pocock characterized as "the greatest empire of patronage and influence the world has known." Our government, he wrote, is "dedicated to the principle that politics cannot work unless politicians do things for their friends and their friends know where to find them."[20]

The dream of a government free of corruption never dies, however, and in the passions excited by the 2016 electoral campaign we experienced another Machiavellian Moment. Voters noticed that government policies were tilted in favor of powerful interest groups and the wealthiest Americans, and they demanded a change. When Martin Gilens and Benjamin Page looked at survey evidence on voting preferences, they found that the wishes of the average voter don't correlate with those of influential interest groups such as the U.S. Chamber of Commerce.[21] Instead, there's a negative correlation: what business groups want—subsidies for their industries, for example—is what the average voter *doesn't* want. It's the same for economic elites generally: their preferences diverge from those of the average voter. And they pay more attention to politics, are more likely to vote, and contribute more money to candidates.[22] They're also more likely to belong to the same social circle as the candidates they support financially. So they get the things they want—funding for National Public Radio, money for Planned Parenthood, favorable tax loopholes.

In the election, Clinton was the candidate of the status quo, of cozying up to Wall Street. In a speech to Goldman Sachs, as revealed by WikiLeaks, she told the bankers that she would let them write the banking regulations: "How do you get to the golden key, how do we figure out what works? And the people that know the industry better than anybody are the people who work in the industry."[23] She refused to release her speeches, and we now know why. As if to remove any doubt, she told another group that when it comes to policy questions "you need both a public and a private position."[24]

On the other side, Trump was the candidate of change, a challenge to politics as usual, to the whole political culture that accepted Clintonian corruption. The Democratic campaign focused almost entirely on his ethical lapses. And his supporters knew he was human, all too human. What they didn't understand was why Hillary Clinton's supporters didn't seem to care about *her* lapses. She had left a trail of public corruption in her wake, and the Trump supporters wondered why that didn't seem to matter.

— 2 —

Excusing Corruption

I N NEW YORK CIRCLES, it's not hard to come across a Clinton Foundation donor. They're honorable men, for the most part, and simply playing the game as it's played in America. Unlike suspect donors such as Rajiv Fernando, they aren't seeking personal favors for themselves, but they might at some point want to recommend a worthy friend or suggest a benign policy change. It's rather like the old-boy network of days gone by, populated by members of the Cosmos or Harvard clubs. The difference is that today's network has been monetized.

That wouldn't have surprised Alexis de Tocqueville. His *Democracy in America*, according to Harvey Mansfield and Delba Winthrop, "is at once the best book ever written on democracy and the best book ever written on America."[1] Reading it today, many Americans have been led to believe that Tocqueville actually liked America, but that's because they weren't paying attention. Tocqueville was astonished by what he saw here, bowled over, and while he was able to see positive features that had eluded other visitors such as Captain Marryat and Mrs. Trollope, what the unwary reader might take as praise was often meant as blame.[2]

Tocqueville preferred France's family-centered aristocracy to what he saw as America's selfish individualism. Say what you want about aristocracy, he thought, but it ties people to past and future generations and makes them more caring. In a democracy, by contrast, one generation is cut off from those that preceded it and those that will follow. What remains is a radical autonomy, with little connection even to one's own generation. At first, individualism merely saps the virtues of public life, "but in the long run it attacks and destroys all the others and will finally be absorbed in selfishness." It throws one "back toward himself alone and threatens finally to confine him wholly in the solitude of his own heart."[3]

Tocqueville saw an answer to individualism, however, in America's free institutions. With greater accuracy, he would have identified American politics as the remedy, for what he had in mind was how we have an incentive to join a political party. "When the public governs," he said, "there is no man who does not feel the value of public benevolence and who does not seek to capture it by attracting the esteem and affection of those in the midst of whom he must live."[4] In short, politics will rescue us from individualism, and Americans have bought into politics with a vengeance. By one count, there are more than half a million elected officials in this country,[5] from the president all the way down to the local dogcatcher.

I saw how far politics might extend when I first moved to the United States and rented a new house in Chevy Chase, D.C. As the house was new, it didn't have a garbage can, so I phoned the city to ask for one. And phoned and phoned. Finally a neighbor, observing the plastic bags I kept putting out on garbage day, took pity on me. "Don't call the city," he told me. "Call your councilman." That's what I did, and the garbage can arrived a few days later. Not long after that came the first fundraising flyer from the councilman. I had learned how I might be able to "attract the esteem" of my local city councilor, but it didn't seem much like a virtue. It felt more like a shakedown, as though I might not expect such prompt service in the future if I failed to make a donation. I might have preferred to live in a city where it sufficed to pay my taxes, and where I could have cultivated my individualism without knowing who was on city council. What I wanted was less of politics and more of an honest and impersonal administrative state, one in which garbage cans are delivered without being followed by a solicitation for money. That was the very point of administrative law and civil service reform, which were meant to replace the realm of politics with that of law, with equal justice rendered to all, without special payoffs to the well connected or to campaign donors. If Tocqueville's politics made Americans less individualistic, they also made us more corrupt.

The Mutual Protection Association

What happens when the state recedes and people are left to their own devices? That's more like freedom, and it's where one finds the clubs and associations that Tocqueville discovered in America and which he so much admired. We'll find them in the PTA, the Red Cross and the groups that pick up litter along the roadways. They are formed around individuals united in a common goal, often doing things the government can't or won't do. To the extent they're effective, voluntary associations permit us to shrink the state, an insight that won Elinor Ostrom a Nobel Prize in economics in 2009.[6] Conversely, the expansion of the government plausibly explains Robert Putnam's claim in *Bowling Alone* that Americans are less likely to join an association today than they were fifty years ago, or in Tocqueville's day.[7]

People who join a voluntary association become less individualistic, and that's all to the good. At the same time, the associations can be seen as what the philosopher Robert Nozick called a "mutual protection association."[8] What Nozick had in mind was an association that would do all the things in the state of nature that we would normally expect the government to do: provide a justice system, a police force, a fire department and so on. But even where there's a government, there are things the state won't do but which an association of private individuals might do. Sometimes it benefits most of us and sometimes only a narrow interest group. The League of Women Voters, the trade union, the special interest cartel—they're all mutual protection associations.

Even if Putnam is right about a declining disposition to join up, we'll still find more voluntary associations in America than in other countries. People here feel they should lend a hand, and joining a group for that purpose makes people more sociable, more concerned about the opinions of others, more like a little politician. It smooths the corners and wears away sharp edges, which is often a good thing, but it also sacrifices the *je m'en fiche* individualism of the eccentric, of the Christopher Hitchens who takes a savage delight in eviscerating sacred cows. The desire to please others civilizes us, but taken to the extreme it may smile at corruption.

There can be material incentives to join up and pay our dues, particularly when noncontributing free riders can be excluded from participation. If an organization is creating its own baseball diamond, for example, we may want to contribute our share if that's the only way we get to play. Pay for play, in other words. Even if free riders can't be excluded—from what economists call public goods—we might still want to chip in if a failure to do so would be noticed and we'd be stigmatized as a freeloader, and perhaps excluded from other goodies that might be tossed our way.

That, of course, is the secret of the Clinton Foundation. Taken at face value, the Clinton Global Initiative provides public goods on a worldwide basis. There's no pressure to donate, but there are strong incentives for doing so, especially while Mrs. Clinton was the secretary of state and then widely expected to be the next president. A major donor such as Rajiv Fernando didn't have to wait for the next world for his reward, but instead got a government position for which he was not obviously qualified. It's nothing like bribery, but only the expectation of return favors. Without contracts, without promises, a settled pattern of cooperation easily develops when one person gives to another, who then gives a return gift, and this is repeated over time.

Marcel Mauss and Lewis Hyde called this a gift economy, as opposed to the market economy of legally enforceable bargains, and they regarded it as a worthy alternative to market transactions.[9] And all it requires to get started is the very human instinct of gratitude, the readiness to repay gifts with return gifts. Stable forms of cooperation can emerge when parties deal with each other over a period of time, as W. D. Hamilton and Robert Axelrod have shown, borrowing from the work of evolutionary biologist Robert Trivers on "reciprocal altruism" in animals.[10] When gifts are exchanged again and again, the parties come to expect that the relationship will be maintained in good faith, and that's as good as a promise. The historian René Girard called it mimetic rivalry, with good paid back for good, and ill for ill.[11] One sees this everywhere, and it might sound uplifting. But grafted onto the institutions of public authority it creates a pay-for-play nexus, and in America it has produced the thickest form of crony capitalism in any First World country.

The Polemarchist

To understand corruption in America, it seems that all one need do is follow the Clintons around and take notes. And yet Hillary emerged as her party's candidate for the presidency, supported by voters who cared less about her character than about the causes she espoused. She was buoyed up by a media that draws a discreet veil between the public policies and private acts of the candidates it favors. After the Monica Lewinsky story broke, for example, *Time* magazine's Nina Burleigh said that she'd be happy to give Bill Clinton oral sex "just to thank him for keeping abortion legal."[12] More recently, as a *Newsweek* correspondent, Burleigh labeled Peter Schweizer a "right wing hatchet" man when asked to comment on *Clinton Cash*.[13]

There's nothing dishonorable about supporting a corrupt official if his opponent is still worse. Louisiana's Edwin Edwards was one of the most ethically challenged governors in that state's colorful history, but in 1991 he had the good chance to find himself opposed by the former Ku Klux Klan grand wizard and neo-Nazi David Duke. "Vote for the Crook" bumper stickers began to appear, as well as "Vote for the Lizard, not the Wizard," and Edwards handily won the election. Doubtless, many Democrats supported Hillary Clinton because they thought Donald Trump little better than David Duke. It's different, however, when the supporter ignores the evidence of corruption, winks at it, and absolves her of blame, for then he becomes an enabler and accomplice of corruption.

A bit of that is to be expected. Just as we are biased in favor of our personal friends, we'll tend to ignore the lapses of political friends—those who are advancing causes we believe in—while denouncing those of political enemies. But at the extreme, with the Nina Burleighs, politics is everything and personal morality becomes irrelevant. We'll see the mote in the eye of an enemy while ignoring the beam in a friend's eye.

This double standard might be labeled Polemarchism, from a character in Plato's *Republic*. On his way home from Piraeus, Socrates encounters several people with whom he debates the meaning of justice. Polemarchus tells him that justice requires doing good to one's friends and evil to one's enemies. Socrates replies that doing evil to anyone doesn't sound much like justice. Moreover, he says, you might think your friends are good, but what if they're not? You wouldn't want to do good to an evil person whom you mistakenly think good. Justice requires doing good to the truly good person, not to the friend who in fact is evil. Friendship therefore is not the proper basis of justice.

Polemarchism is the crudest of ethical theories, but it's how American politics is increasingly conducted. It's in the newspapers we read and the shows we watch on TV, where partisan hacks are given a respectful hearing. One finds them on both sides of the debate, though David Brock stands out as an attack dog. It doesn't get more partisan than Brock's Media Matters, but he's still taken seriously as a political commentator by the mainstream media.[14]

For an example of Polemarchism at work, consider the media reaction to the firing of Gerald Walpin, the congressionally appointed inspector general of the Corporation for National and Community Service (AmeriCorps). Inspectors general are charged with overseeing government moneys, and after Walpin uncovered that the mayor of Sacramento had improperly spent AmeriCorps funds he referred the matter to the Justice Department for prosecution. The mayor was an Obama donor and friend, however, and AmeriCorps was a favored Obama program. A White House lawyer asked Walpin to resign in June 2009, and when Walpin refused to do so he was summarily fired, in violation of the rules for dismissing inspectors general. The White House spread the word that Walpin was incompetent, and for most of the media that was the end of the story.[15] In other First World countries, that would have been a major scandal, but not in today's America. Subsequently, the Obama administration doubled down on its obstructionism by denying inspectors general unfettered access to the documents they need to do their job.[16]

Let's suppose that Obama believed he was doing good, defending the work of AmeriCorps while returning a favor to a friend and ally. In the seventeenth century, Pascal wrote that men never do evil so completely and cheerfully as when they believe they are following their conscience.[17] They can then enjoy that most delicious of sensations, the feeling of justified hatred toward enemies. When it's one tribe against another, Republicans against Democrats, when everyone is a Polemarchist, public virtue shrivels and everything is permitted.

The more divided we are, the greater the appeal of Polemarchism. In recent years, partisan divisions have become more pronounced, through what journalist Bill Bishop has called "the big sort."[18] We don't care to live on streets where our neighbors despise us, and this self-segregation further intensifies the polarization of American politics. Liberals become more liberal, conservatives more conservative, and what we're left with is a country in which the grimly serious business of politics becomes all-consuming. But if it's all a matter of supporting your friends and beating up your enemies, then complaints about a politician's corruption are hypocritical when leveled at an enemy, and naïve if directed at a friend. Indeed, the more a country is politicized, the more it is corrupt.

This isn't to say that political loyalties should be irrelevant, that one shouldn't show a partiality to political friends. There's something repellant about the paragon of virtue who is indifferent as between allies and opponents. The German philosopher Carl Schmitt was not entirely wrong when he wrote in 1932 that "the specific political distinction . . . is that between friend and enemy."[19] The political fray is necessarily agonistic, pitting one party against another, and it demands that people take sides. But there's a limit to the merits of loyalty, which is something that Schmitt appears not to have learned. He joined the Nazi Party in 1933, rejoiced in the burning of books by Jewish authors, and then resisted every effort at de-Nazification after the war.

The Apologist

In his more candid moments, the Clinton loyalist will admit that all is not right with the Clinton Foundation, and that Mrs. Clinton's venality embarrasses him. He might nonetheless ridicule the prissiness of those who are too quick to see corruption in others, who recoil from the rough-and-tumble of political engagement. "It ain't beanbag," said Mr. Dooley (the Finley Peter Dunne character) in response to the good government "goo-goos" who looked down their noses at Chicago's machine politics. With their patrician WASP scorn for the Catholic underclass, the goo-goos didn't come across very well in *The Last Hurrah*, the Edwin O'Connor novel and later the Spencer Tracy movie. Moral prissiness can even seem ridiculous. In 1950, a story went around that Senator George Smathers (D-FL) had made some shocking claims about a challenger for his Senate seat:

> Are you aware that Claude Pepper is known all over Washington as a shameless extrovert? Not only that, but this man is reliably reported to practice nepotism with his sister-in-law, he has a brother who is a known homo sapiens, and he has a sister who was once a thespian in wicked New York. Worst of all, it is an established fact that Mr. Pepper, before his marriage, habitually practiced celibacy.

Most probably this began as a joke, demonstrating that even a politician can recognize the absurdity in trying to paint his opponent as the lowest form of life.[20] Still, our experience with the Clintons suggests that the punctilio of an honor the most sensitive mightn't be such a bad thing. The person who says politics ain't beanbag is telling you that corruption doesn't much bother him, and we might wish that it did.

The Apologist can also be heard to plead that corruption is the way of the world, that everyone does it. The deeper question, he will argue, is whether corrupt means may be employed to arrive at the desired end of a virtuous state. That's what the French philosopher Maurice Merleau-Ponty wondered when he complained of the hypocrisy of the anticommunist liberal who objected to Stalinist violence: "He forgets that communism does not invent violence but finds it already established, that for the moment the question is not to know whether one accepts or rejects violence, but whether the violence with which one is allied is 'progressive' and tends towards its own suppression or towards self-perpetuation."[21] The same thinking brought Rubashov, in Arthur Koestler's *Darkness at Noon*, to confess to crimes of which he was innocent in a Stalinist show trial. As a Soviet high official, Rubashov had recognized that in order to defend his communist faith he must acquiesce in his own execution. For Western liberals, Koestler's book was an exposé of communism's falsity and inhumanity, but in 1947 Merleau-Ponty saw it differently. As a proponent of a "Third Way" between America and the Soviet Union, he thought there was little to choose between what he saw as liberalism's institutional violence (colonialism, capitalism) and the legalized violence of communism. While not a Stalinist, he nevertheless sympathized with those who had believed that a reign of truth and justice might at last emerge from communism's charnel house of lies and violence.

Similarly, the Apologist for Clinton Cash argues that Mrs. Clinton's sins are trivial by comparison with the institutional corruption of our present system of politics, where wealthy campaign donors have an outsized voice in government policies. What matters, he thinks, is not whether she enriched her family by corrupt means, but whether her administration would have been more likely to lead in time to a virtuous, progressive state. More progressive it might be, in the Apologist's eyes, but did he give us any reason to believe that virtue might emerge from so corrupt a vessel?

Finally, the Apologist is apt to rely on the hoariest of procedural tools to avoid substantive moral questions: the legal burden of proof. Unless one can prove a quid pro quo beyond a shadow of a doubt, he says, the Clintons are entitled to a presumption of innocence. And indeed no one has ever proved that Hillary Clinton was corrupt, as her defenders are quick to note. But that's a long way from saying that the charges against her have been discredited, and the very American tendency to turn all moral questions into legal ones—to insist on moral innocence unless legal guilt is proved to the hilt—encourages corruption. We might not wish to charge the Clintons with crimes, but we may still wish to blame them for their disregard of the proprieties, and to hope that Hillary Clinton has paid a political price for it. We might also want a tougher set of anticorruption laws, of the kind we'll see later in this book.

— 3 —

The Silent Killer

So just how corrupt is America? What we're interested in is public corruption, where public officials abuse the public trust, and not the private chiseling where one individual cheats another. To measure public corruption, we need something more than the number of criminal indictments for bribery. These might sometimes be without foundation, and themselves a corrupt method of silencing political opponents. That's how they do things in Russia—and also at times in the United States, as we'll see. In addition, corruption is mostly a game played under the radar, through the patterns of pay-for-play, of reciprocal gifts that escape detection or, if detected, don't ascend to the level of crime.

Today there is a relation of mutual dependence between America's largest firms and the political class, one in which deals are made and favors are traded, and it kicked into high gear with the Troubled Asset Relief Program (TARP) bailouts during the Great Recession of 2007–9. Senior financial executives found themselves traveling to Washington for the first time, and the former assistant treasury secretary Richard Clarida saw how the relationship between Wall Street and the federal government had fundamentally changed: "It's often said that Wall Street is no longer the financial capital, that it's Washington, D.C., and that's certainly true. I don't think this is destined to change. I think this is going to be a fact of life."[1]

From TARP, to the Export-Import Bank, to the tariff protections offered to favored industries, there is a growing concern that the federal government has become a necessary business partner, and that the (imagined but not entirely imaginary) free-market capitalism of the past has been transformed into a wasteful crony capitalism that favors well-connected special interests. The fact that 81 percent of the government's green-energy grants went to Obama's 2008 campaign donors should be troubling regardless of one's stance on climate change.[2] Or take the support given to America's sugar producers, who benefit from tariffs that raise sugar prices 64 to 92 percent above the world average.[3] A strategic sugar stockpile isn't exactly in America's national interest, but for the industry the tariffs represent money well spent on lobbyists and campaign contributions. And the problem is bipartisan. Rajhuram Rajan and Luigi Zingales calculate that the trade barriers introduced during the Reagan-Bush 1980s amounted to a $30 billion subsidy to industry, and that those subsidies cost consumers $6.8 billion.[4]

Are trade barriers necessarily harmful, though? Do they always favor powerful interest groups at the expense of average Americans? Many people believe it's the opposite: that we're hurting ourselves as a nation with our current trade deals, and that our free-trade policies transfer wealth from the poor to the rich within America. Donald Trump has brought the issue of trade policy to the front burner, arguing that free trade ships jobs overseas and impoverishes many working Americans, who then have even more difficulty buying the consumer goods that free trade is supposed to make affordable. On the other hand, tariffs may impose costs disproportionately on low-income Americans, and the support given to sugar producers is a good example. Poorer Americans spend a greater share of their earnings on food, so a sweet tooth will hurt them in the pocketbook more than rich Americans. If we erect higher trade barriers, then, might we possibly be making things worse for the poorest? Consider, too, that trade barriers would be set in Washington, where the thumbs of donors and lobbyists weigh heavily on the scales, and they won't be representing America's underclass. It's easy to imagine shiny new policy gizmos, but before they're enacted the same old tools of influence will be applied.

Rent-Seeking

Spending resources to shape legal rules—through campaign contributions, government—relations departments and lobbyists—is called *rent-seeking*, a phenomenon first described by Gordon Tullock in the 1960s.[5] A business seeks rents when it expends resources in the pursuit of politically driven business gains, through government bailouts,[6] tariff protections[7] or favorable tax treatment.[8] The efforts to secure these advantages may bring some public benefit by informing voters and overburdened officials about the consequences of burdensome laws.[9] But there are costs that must be deducted from any such gains. In fact, rent-seeking will often represent a net deadweight loss, either because the firm or industry proposes inefficient rules, or because any social benefits are exceeded by the costs of rent-seeking. It dissipates resources by shifting investments away from core business functions, drawing talent, technology, and capital away from their most productive uses.[10]

The rent-seeking firm or industry will seek to create a semipermanent relationship with a politician.[11] We're most likely to find this happening in regulated industries, and the relationship between regulator and regulated can become very cozy. It's what George Stigler, an economist at the University of Chicago, called "regulatory capture," where the regulated industry captures the regulator, who then sides with the industry more than with the public he's supposed to protect.[12] That would seem to be the only explanation for the Agriculture Department's love affair with the domestic sugar industry, and the same might be said for federal peanut programs, which guarantee farmers high prices and result in overproduction. The Agriculture Department buys the surplus peanuts and then dumps them on poor countries such as Haiti, which further impoverishes the desperately poor peanut farmers there.[13]

Regulatory capture also helps explain the government's stimulus programs during the Great Recession. The Federal Reserve's near-zero interest rates were meant to restart the economy, but it's been calculated that they cost U.S. savers—many of them retirees on a fixed income—$500 billion in interest income.[14] When the zero-interest policy didn't produce a healthy recovery, the government pumped trillions of dollars into the economy through the TARP bailouts and a quantitative easing program of buying long-term government bonds. Politically connected banks received larger bailouts than financial institutions that spent less on lobbying or political contributions.[15] Senator Elizabeth Warren (D-MA) has pointed to a chummy relationship between major banks such as Goldman Sachs and the Federal Reserve, which is supposed to monitor them.[16]

As the number of government regulations has increased, so too have the rewards from having a hand in shaping them. Our regulatory regime, ostensibly designed to help middle-class buyers, begins to resemble a form of consumer protection for billionaires that cartelizes our economy and squeezes out competition from below.[17] Even the burdens of regulation can turn out to be an anticompetitive blessing for the major firms that enjoy economies of scale in coping with them. For a large firm, with its battery of lawyers and compliance experts, it's simply a cost of doing business. For smaller firms, however, the startup costs of conforming with the regulations can be prohibitive. To mention but one example, the Dodd-Frank Wall Street Reform and Consumer Protection Act of 2010, itself 1,000 pages in length, has already spun off 22,000 pages of regulations. Imagine a new entrant into the market trying to work its way through all of that before it can open its doors for business.

Lee Drutman of the New America foundation describes how a seemingly simple rule can become a regulatory nightmare. Dodd-Frank's "Volcker Rule" began as a three-page proposal to prevent banks from engaging in proprietary trading (where a firm invests its own money rather than that of its depositors). When enacted, this had turned into ten pages, but it soon became 298 pages of rules. That left too many questions unanswered, however, and when finally released the rules were nearly 1,000 pages long. Even then the Federal Reserve criticized the rule's lack of specificity.[18]

Complexity in government advantages the large firm that can invest in the legal resources to work its way around the plethora of rules, and that's especially true if the firm invests in lobbying. One of the largest companies in the world, General Electric, paid no taxes in 2010. At the same time, it spent tens of millions of dollars to lobby for changes to the tax code.[19] GE wasn't alone in this arena, either. The Sunlight Foundation reported that the ten Fortune 100 companies that lobbied on fifty or more bills over 2008–11 paid an average effective tax rate of 17.1 percent, while the publicly traded companies that lobbied on fewer than twenty-five bills paid a rate of 26.0 percent.[20] What complexity offers to large firms is not only economies of scale in regulatory compliance, but also the ability to bend the rules in a way that's hidden from public view.[21]

Rent-seeking and crony capitalism may bring benefits to particular companies or industries, but they are drags on the overall economy. They're also highly unjust, for they amount to a transfer of wealth from those who lack access, to those who have it—from the outsider to the corporate welfare bum. The new man without connections is less likely to start a firm or expand an existing one when the scales are weighted against him. Rent-seeking and crony capitalism explain much of America's problem with corruption. Because these practices are wasteful and unfair, people on both sides of the political fence have condemned them, yet they also find beneficiaries and therefore defenders on both sides, too.

Measuring Corruption

Objective measures of corruption are hard to come by, and generally unreliable. But a subjective measurement is readily available and quite useful. Transparency International, a highly regarded German

NGO, produces a Corruption Perceptions Index (CPI) every year, rating countries on the basis of reporting by respected observers, including businessmen and experts from the country itself.[22] People are asked such questions as:

- Are misbehaving public officeholders prosecuted or penalized?
- Are there effective public auditors?
- Is corruption a problem in the court system? The tax bureau? Inspection bodies?
- Is the executive accountable to oversight institutions?
- Has the government been captured by special interests?

The responses to these questions are used to score each country on a scale of 0 to 100, with higher scores meaning less corruption. The CPI has been criticized for its subjectivity,[23] but any ranking system of this nature must inevitably rely on judgment calls, and the CPI is in fact the most widely followed measure of public corruption.

How does the United States do? In 2014 it scored 74 out of 100, giving it a rank of 17th place behind higher-scoring countries.

As Table 1 shows, Denmark beats us hands down on government integrity, with a score of 92.

TABLE I
Transparency International's Corruption Perceptions Index 2014

Country	Rank	Score	Country	Rank	Score
Denmark	1	92	Australia	1	92
New Zealand	2	91	Germany	2	91
Finland	3	89	Iceland	3	89
Sweden	4	87	United Kingdom	4	87
Norway	5	86	Belgium	5	86
Switzerland	5	86	Japan	5	86
Singapore	7	84	Barbados	7	84
Netherlands	8	83	Hong Kong	8	83
Luxembourg	9	82	Ireland	9	82
Canada	10	81	**United States**	10	81

Frank Fukuyama has said that "getting to Denmark" should be the goal of public policy.[24] That might seem an impossible dream, though, since Denmark is much more ethnically homogeneous, and societies where people are more alike have been shown to be generally more trusting[25] and less corrupt.[26] But we couldn't turn America into Denmark, and we wouldn't even want to do so. As a self-styled "nation of immigrants," America prides itself on its diversity, and we're not about to change that. Moreover, some countries that beat us in the CPI rankings are far more welcoming to immigrants. While 14 percent of American residents (legal and undocumented) are foreign-born, the figure is 20 percent in Canada and 26 percent in Australia, the true nation of immigrants. Canada scores 81 on the CPI, and Australia comes in at 80. Evidently, ethnic diversity isn't an excuse to throw up our hands over corruption.

The Cost of Corruption

Corruption is a silent killer of the U.S. economy, and it's possible to put a number on this. The dots in Figure 1 represent 107 countries, with their 2014 CPI score on the horizontal axis and their 2015 per capita gross domestic product on the vertical axis.[27] Through a standard econometric estimation technique described in Appendix A, the diagonal straight line estimates how corruption affects a country's wealth (per capita gross domestic product). From corrupt and poor Afghanistan up to honest and rich Luxembourg and Singapore, less corruption means a higher GDP.

The model tells us that if America's CPI score were to rise to Canada's score of 81, its per capita GDP would increase from $54,629 to $59,914. Were the CPI score to increase, *per impossibilia*, to the level of Denmark at 92, per capita GDP would rise to $68,219. For America as a whole, that would amount to an 18 percent or $3.2 trillion increase in the country's wealth. Think of that missing wealth as the tax that corrupt politicians, regulators, and judges impose on all Americans.

The results shown in Figure 1 are consistent with the many cross-country, empirical studies on how public corruption impover-

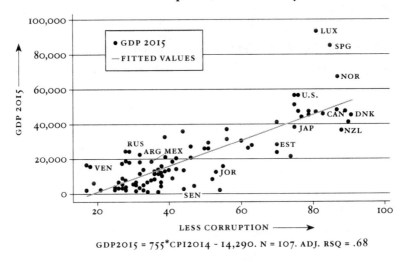

FIGURE I

More Corruption, More Poverty

GDP2015 = 755*CPI2014 - 14,290. N = 107. ADJ. RSQ = .68

Source: GDP per capita, PPP International Monetary Fund World Economic Outlook (April 2015); Transparency International Corruption Perceptions Index 2014.

ishes people.[28] Within the United States as well, there's a penalty for living in corrupt states. Measuring differences in corruption state by state is tricky: looking at the numbers of state prosecutions of government officials might not be very helpful, since fewer prosecutions could mean either that officials are more honest or that state prosecutors are themselves corrupt. The way around this problem is to look at prosecutions brought by the federal government, since the Justice Department can be presumed to employ uniform standards across the country. With federal prosecutions as a proxy for levels of corruption, it has been shown that corrupt states have significantly lower economic growth.[29] Another study found that corrupt states have lower bond ratings, which means they pay higher interest rates on their public debt, and these costs are passed on to taxpayers in those states.[30] As a matter of common observation, Louisiana and Mississippi (first and second, respectively, in federal corruption prosecutions per capita) aren't exactly economic dynamos.

It's easy to see how public corruption can impose costs on a country's or state's economy. The fraudulent or criminally irresponsible firm that escapes prosecution harms everyone touched by its actions. The honest and efficient firm might fail in the market, while the corrupt, inefficient one flourishes. Even if he plays by the rules, the crony capitalist who milks the system will draw resources from better firms that fail to invest in politics. By schmoozing with Obama and his green energy appointees, Solyndra was able to score a $570 million loan guarantee from the federal government. The company manufactured solar panels and lost money on every panel it sold. It was like the old garment industry joke where the boss's son wonders how they stay afloat when they lose money on every suit they sell. "We make it up on volume," says the boss. For Solyndra, making it up on volume meant passing the loss on to the American taxpayer.

The Rule of Law

If Transparency International isn't terribly impressed with American integrity, the World Justice Project (WJP) has no better opinion of us. The WJP, cofounded by a former head of the American Bar Association, collects data from the general public and from legal professionals to rank countries according to their adherence to the rule of law.[31] Among the factors considered are equality before the law, an efficient and honest judicial system and the absence of corruption. Russia came in at 75th place out of 102 countries on the Rule of Law Index in 2015, way behind former communist countries that invested more heavily in the rule of law: Estonia (15), the Czech Republic (20), and Poland (21). What about America? It's not Russia, not by a long shot, but it still doesn't rank all that high, coming in at number 19. On the particular measure of an absence of corruption, the United States ranks 20th.

Until fairly recently, the rule of law wasn't on economists' radar screens. To explain why some countries were wealthy and some not, they would refer to natural endowments, such as valuable minerals or oil; or point to a country's infrastructure or to human capital investments, such as those provided by a public education system; or note differences in culture or religion. Over the last forty years, however, economists have increasingly pointed to the role of institutions, such as a legal regime that protects property rights and enforces contracts, in explaining a country's wealth. That's the difference between North Korea and South Korea, one country desperately poor and the other rich, but alike in all respects except for their political and legal institutions.[32]

A corrupt country might be rich in natural assets such as farmland, or oil and minerals, or in capital assets such as plant and machinery, but these aren't the most important sources of wealth. The World Bank estimates that natural and capital assets amount to only 23 percent of a country's riches. The other 77 percent is composed of intangible assets, the difference in institutions, of which the most important element is adherence to the rule of law. Remarkably, this accounts for 44 percent of a country's total wealth, according to the World Bank.[33]

The United States may be one of the richest countries in the world, but we still pay a price for corruption. If we could somehow make the country more honest, we'd want to do so, and if the cost of corruption is as high as it appears, we should make it one of our chief goals—ahead of changes to the tax code, entitlement reform or fixing our health-care system. But just how might this be done?

— 4 —

The Dream of a Virtuous Republic

THE IDEAL of a corruption-free republic is an old one. It lay behind Socrates' answer to Polemarchus and the design of a virtuous government set out in Plato's *Republic*. It inspired John Winthrop's vision of a City on a Hill, which he described aboard the *Arbella* in 1630 during its voyage to the new land. Once there, he imagined, the settlers could begin building a country whose citizens would be "knitt together . . . as one man." There can be no corruption, he said, where people

> delight in eache other, make others Condicions our owne rejoyce
> together, mourne together, labour, and suffer together, allwayes
> haveing before our eyes our Commission and Community in the
> worke, our Community as members of the same body, soe shall
> wee keepe the unitie of the spirit in the bond of peace, the Lord
> will be our God and delight to dwell among us.[1]

A century and a half later, Maximilien Robespierre proposed a dechristianized but not dissimilar republic of virtue for revolutionary France:

> In our country we want to substitute morality for egoism, honesty
> for honor, principles for customs, duties for propriety, the empire
> of reason for the tyranny of custom, the contempt of vice for the
> contempt of misfortune, pride for insolence, greatness of soul for
> vanity, love of glory for love of money, good people for fashion-
> able people, merit for intrigue, genius for wit, truth for showiness,
> warmth of happiness for boredom of sensuality, greatness of man
> for pettiness of the great; a magnanimous, powerful, happy people
> for a polite, frivolous, despicable people, that is to say, all the virtues
> and all the miracles of the Republic for all the vices and all the ab-
> surdities of the monarchy.[2]

Who could reject this happy harmony, universal honesty and magnanimity? Who would not wish to banish all insolence, intrigue, pettiness, all the vices we find annoying in our neighbors? Well, some people wouldn't, and the question is what to do with those who fail to live up to the dictates of the most exacting virtue. For Plato, the answer in *The Republic* lay in a fantastically illiberal tyranny of virtue, under the rule of philosopher kings. In John Winthrop's Puritan Massachusetts, dissenters from Dissent such as Anne Hutchinson and Roger Williams were simply driven from the colony. For his part, Robespierre believed that the republic of virtue required stern measures of protection from internal enemies, and thus the Terror. Virtue is impotent without the guillotine, he said. "Terror is nothing but prompt, severe, inflexible justice; it is therefore an emanation of virtue."[3]

In the pursuit of virtue, there are things we wouldn't do, such as abandon the principles of a liberal society. There are also things we *can't* do, insofar as corruption is driven by cultural norms, by what is socially accepted. Andrew Breitbart memorably said that politics is downstream from culture. But what is upstream from culture? How might the culture itself be changed? We might want to make Americans less willing to accept sordid backroom deals. But just how is that to be done without sacrificing personal liberties? David Hume was not far off the mark when he observed that "all plans of government, which suppose great reformation in the manners of mankind, are plainly imaginary."[4]

The Framers of our Constitution were hard-nosed realists about the manners of mankind, and they weren't about to launch a moral rearmament crusade when they set out to design a corruption-free government in the summer of 1787. The notes of their deliberations at the Constitutional Convention in Philadelphia were kept secret and not published until all the delegates had died, which allowed them to state their opinions of their fellow citizens with remarkable candor. "Take mankind in general," said Alexander Hamilton, "they are vicious—their passions may be operated upon."[5] That was a little over-the-top, but not a few of the delegates must have nodded their heads in agreement, given their general suspicion of democracy and mob rule.

The Framers' solution was to turn things on their head. The republic of virtue would not be erected from below, from Winthrop's moral community knit together as one man, but constructed from above upon a fallen humanity. The new government would accept the reality of our ordinary vices, but would make it harder for them to infect the body politic. By dividing powers and asking one branch to check another, the Framers sought to restrain those who would use the means of government to serve wasteful private ends. And this could be done without employing Plato's oppressive restrictions on personal freedom. That was the vision of the Framers, at once noble-minded and liberal.

It didn't last. If we were ever a republic of virtue, we're not that to-day, as evidence by how we rank on Transparency Internationals CPI. Wholly corrupt politicians such as Louisiana's Edwin Edwards might find themselves charged with bribery, and backroom deal-makers like Virginia's Eric Cantor might be dumped by the voters. But it's easy to point to successful politicians who've raised pay-for-play to a fine art while avoiding the threat of criminal liability. Along the way something went wrong. The Framers meant to produce a corruption-free government, but like a boomerang their Constitution flew back and hit us on the head.

The Separation of Powers

In *The Federalist Papers*, the selling document for our Constitution, James Madison described a government in which the different branches—executive, legislative, and judicial—would be set in equipoise, in a regime of separated powers. The separation of powers means several different things, but all of the convention delegates including Madison thought it would check the possibility of public corruption. That's not how it turned out, however, for two reasons.

First, the grim logic of the separation of powers ensures that over time the preponderance of power will come to reside in the executive branch.[6] That's what has happened in nearly every other presidential regime and it's happening apace in the United States. The president has slipped off many of the constraints that were meant to curb his authority through the separation of powers. He makes laws by regulatory fiat and executive order, and unmakes them by refusing to enforce properly enacted legislation. He can reward friends and punish enemies in ways the Framers would not have anticipated.

It turns out that presidential regimes are significantly more corrupt than parliamentary ones. And that's to be expected. For one thing, the president's role as his country's head of state clothes him with a moral authority that prime ministers wholly lack in parliamentary governments. If presidents are the symbols of their countries, prime ministers are more apt to be figures of fun, and ridicule is a sovereign remedy against the abuse of authority. Then there's the ability of an opposition party in Parliament to hold a government's feet to the fire when there's a scandal. By convention, a prime minister is required to attend a daily question period in Parliament, when he must answer his critics, and the opposition can prolong debate over government weaknesses. "No better method has ever been devised for keeping administration up to the mark," observed Harold Laski.[7]

Parliamentary governments have far more effective ways to discipline a misbehaving chief executive. It's a great deal easier to remove an inconvenient prime minister through a simple no-confidence motion or party vote than it is to impeach a sitting president. Not merely are the requirements of a trial in the House of Representatives and a two-thirds majority in the Senate virtually impossible to achieve, but a President may cover up his tracks through his control of information and his ability to delay the proceedings. The separation of powers in the American Constitution was designed to discipline a misbehaving executive, but instead has had the opposite effect, insulating him from criticism.

The separation of powers also introduced another kind of corruption, in which members of Congress demand wasteful benefits for their districts as a condition for supporting a bill. This became glaringly obvious in the debate that led to the enactment of the Affordable Care Act (Obamacare) in 2010, in a frenzied atmosphere of last-minute deal-making. To get his filibuster-proof sixty votes, Senator Harry Reid (D-NV), the majority leader, had to bargain with the members of his caucus who demanded special earmarks. Among these, the "Louisiana Purchase" gave $100 million in extra Medicaid funding to the Bayou State to help get Senator Mary Landrieu (D-LA) re-elected. Then came the "Cornhusker Kickback" for Senator Ben Nelson (D-NE), a permanent exemption from his state's share of Medicaid expansion that would cost taxpayers an additional $45 million in the first decade. Next came "Gator Aid" for Senator Bill Nelson (D-FL), a grandfather clause that would allow Floridians to preserve their pricey Medicare Advantage program. The list went on and on.[8] In the final bill, the Cornhusker Kickback was stripped out, but many other goodies were so well hidden in the one-thousand-page document that they went undetected. Seven years later, we're still finding out what's in it.

The Framers' republic of virtue has evolved into a very different country, one that is more corrupt than those it most resembles, the "settler" societies of Canada, Australia, and New Zealand. We share a similar heritage and legal system, but unlike those other countries we have a presidential form of government with a separation of powers, and those features of our Constitution have, over time, made the United States more corrupt. We shaped our institutions, and then our institutions shaped us.

Federalism

In addition to dividing powers laterally among the branches in the national government, our Constitution disperses power vertically, between Washington and the states. American federalism was not so much a conscious choice by the Framers, however, as a necessity imposed upon them by the states, a legacy of the many years of self-government in each of the thirteen colonies. In Albany, Trenton, and other state capitals, Americans had created their own state constitutions and governmental institutions, and were loath to give them up. At the Constitutional Convention, the smaller states, as a condition for joining in the union, rejected the idea of an all-powerful central government, and that is why we have a federal form of government. This division served to check corruption by bringing government closer to the voters most affected by its actions. Federalism also allows people to move from corrupt states to more honest ones. With fewer people and businesses to prey on, the corrupt state is made to pay for its lack of integrity.

Over time, however, the federal government has assumed control over more and more powers originally left to the states. This happened partly because the Supreme Court gave an expansive definition to the federal commerce power, permitting Washington to overrule the states on purely local matters. Then, through the spending power, the federal government was permitted to condition grants to the states on compliance with federal mandates, which is how state policies on transportation, health care and education came to be often set by Washington.[9]

On the other hand, states have been exercising powers that should be assigned to the federal government. In particular, state courts have been permitted to rule on interstate civil actions, where the plaintiffs and defendants are in different states, under a strained interpretation of the Constitution by the Supreme Court. These cases more properly belong in federal courts, since the home-state bias of state courts allows in-state plaintiffs to impose wasteful costs on out-of-state defendants. One might think this a trivial matter, but one would be wrong. A wise reform would ensure that all such cases are turned over to federal judges, as the Framers intended.

Money

Mention corruption to a highly educated American, and chances are that he'll complain about the baneful effects of money in politics. Pressed further, he might mention the 2010 Supreme Court decision in *Citizens United*[10] and denounce big-bucks conservative donors such as the Koch brothers. He'll say that we would get more honest government by eliminating the scandal of money in politics, but his actual aim may be to disarm those he disagrees with and prevent a successful challenge to the incumbents he favors. Instead of making government more honest, restrictions on campaign spending may help protect corrupt incumbents from the wrath of fed-up voters.

What democracy offers as a cure for corruption is competition and the chance to throw the bums out. What the bums want to do, therefore, is neutralize the opposition by restricting its spending and therefore its ability to make its voice heard. That can't happen here, since the Supreme Court ruled in the seminal case of *Buckley v. Valeo* (1976) that campaign spending caps would trench on First Amendment rights.[11] It's true that some other countries, lacking the equivalent of our First Amendment, have enacted campaign spending caps without making their political races less competitive. And it's true that our own elections don't appear all that competitive, since few seats are ever seriously in play in congressional races. But that doesn't mean we could adopt stricter spending limits here at no cost in competitiveness, for laws that work elsewhere cannot simply be copied in the United States with the same results. Each country must work out its own compromise between corrupt and competitive politics. If spending in American elections were capped, the result might well be less competition in politics and more corruption in government, given the particular dynamics at work here.

The campaign finance laws we have now are mostly worse than useless. They don't get in the way of clever donors or officials who know how to skirt the rules, but they're a snare for the little guy. They're like a fisherman's net with the curious feature that the big fish escape while the small ones are caught. Worse still, they're an invitation for flint-eyed ideologues, ambitious prosecutors, and partisan officials to criminalize political differences.

Rather than imagine a fanciful scenario of politics without money or corruption, we should begin by recognizing that Draconian reforms that restrict our freedoms might actually make things worse. When countries already have a certain amount of corruption, there's a tipping point where stronger anticorruption laws produce more corruption, particularly when they are exploited as partisan political weapons. As Justice Scalia noted, "nothing is so politically effective as the ability to charge that one's opponent and his associates are not merely wrongheaded, naïve, ineffective, but, in all probability, 'crooks.'"[12] And politically motivated prosecutions for corruption can themselves be a form of corruption. In the United States, this problem may not reach the level of the old Soviet Union, where the prosecutor Lavrenti Beria infamously said, "Show me the man and I'll show you the crime." But some of those facing politically charged prosecution here may be forgiven for feeling that it isn't much different.

Three Proposals

If stricter campaign finance limits and more anticorruption laws won't help, what can we do? Some things, such as our basic constitutional structures, can't be changed. Nor can we rely upon the innate wisdom and goodness of the voters. The Framers, with their awareness of human fallibility, believed that a purely democratic government isn't always a good government, and that a virtue-driven constitution must at times blunt the voters' desires. This wisdom has sadly been forgotten by today's campaign finance reformers, whose vision of good government resembles John Winthrop's close-knit Puritan community, in which corruption is simply a departure from the popular will. The Framers had the better of the argument, for the most corrupt officials are often those most attentive to what the voters want. Broad democratic reforms will not ring in a reign of virtue, and the work of combatting corruption is rather a matter of smaller rules here and there.

Here are three proposals for election law reform that would curb corruption rather than aggravate it:

- Unless they are lobbyists, donors should have an unimpeded ability to contribute anonymously to campaign committees and political parties without fear of intimidation or harassment. But when the money is paid into the official's pockets, that changes things, and a bribery charge properly applies if pay-for-play is promised or given.

- While they can give useful information about proposed rules to overworked congressional staffers, lobbyists should be barred from leveraging their influence through campaign contributions and fundraising for elected officials.

- Lobbyists should not be permitted to "capture" a legislator or congressional staffer with the promise of a high-paying job after he leaves government. To prevent this practice, a Chinese Wall should be erected between lobbying and legislating to close off the revolving door between the two activities.

And that's it. The existing set of contribution limits and disclosure requirements should be repealed. As we'll see, they haven't done anything except made our government more corrupt.

We needn't tolerate America's mediocre ranking on cross-country measures of government integrity if we can do something about it. But the optimal level of corruption is not zero, for achieving it would require a Robespierre to weed out those who fail to live up to the most exacting standards of republican virtue. Nor should we subscribe to the sociological fallacy which supposes that pathologies such as corruption can be attributed entirely to deep and immutable social causes. If culture matters, so do the legal rules and institutions that shape our culture and behavior. To understand America's problems with corruption, we'll look more closely at some of those institutions, beginning with the most fundamental one of all, the Constitution.

PART TWO

THE SEPARATION
OF POWERS

If the Legislature elect, it will be the work of intrigue, of cabal, and of faction.

—*Gouverneur Morris*

An Anticorruption Covenant

I N 1789, Thomas Jefferson returned from Paris to become America's first secretary of state. As neither he nor President Washington wanted entangling alliances with other countries, he would have
time on his hands, but soon he became something more than a cabinet member. He also led a growing political movement that was troubled by a centralizing Federalist Party. Jefferson's party came to be
called Democratic-Republicans, and he would run as their candidate
for president in 1796 and win the highest office in 1800.

In Paris, Jefferson had witnessed the eruption of the French Revolution—the Tennis Court Oath, the Storming of the Bastille, the Declaration of the Rights of Man. He returned "in the fervor of natural rights,
and zeal for reformation" to what seemed to him a sadly conservative
country.[1] In France the aristocracy had lost its feudal privileges, but in
postrevolutionary America a new hereditary aristocracy appeared to be
emerging around the Society of the Cincinnati's officer class. Writing
from France, Jefferson warned Washington that so much as a single fi-
ber of the society left in existence "will produce an hereditary aristocracy which will change the form of our governments from the best to the
worst in the world."[2] There was also a rising moneyed aristocracy, based
in New York and Philadelphia, composed of urban merchants whom
the agrarian Democratic-Republicans saw as their natural enemy. The
new financial class was led by Washington's brilliant but imprudent secretary of the treasury, Alexander Hamilton, who would shortly become
a leader of the High Federalists and Jefferson's principal opponent.

Jefferson was dismayed to find himself surrounded by monarchists
in Hamilton's New York, the new country's capital. "I cannot describe the wonder and mortification with which the table conversation filled me. Politics was the chief topic, and a preference for kingly,
over republican, government was evidently the favored sentiment."[3]

The country was already abandoning the republican principles of its founding, and some people hankered for a return to court government, with its attendant corruption.

Jefferson also objected to the federal assumption of state public debt, which Hamilton had negotiated in 1790. Southern republicans weren't happy with how this measure was shifting the locus of financial power from the states to the federal government. Worse, those being paid off weren't the farmer-patriots who had purchased state-issued bonds during the revolution. These bonds had mostly been sold off to a set of "speculators" and "stock-jobbers" who bought them at deep discount. The federal assumption of the debt was nothing other than a bailout of Hamilton's friends, a moneyed class of wealthy investors (not unlike the 2008–9 bailout of Wall Street bailout by another treasury secretary). What Hamilton's scheming came down to, said Jefferson, was monarchism, and not just the desire for a king but "a monarchy bottomed on corruption."

Corruption was a favorite topic for Jefferson, and he returned to it at a private dinner with Hamilton and John Adams in 1791. He wasn't especially inclined to socialize with either of them, but Washington had left for Mount Vernon and had asked his cabinet and his vice president to deal with important matters that might arise during his absence. So the three met over dinner, and after the tablecloth was removed and the port produced, the conversation drifted to general matters. The anglophile Adams praised the British constitution. Could it only be purged of its corruption, he said, it would be "the most perfect constitution ever devised by the wit of man." For Jefferson that was anathema: Britain was so corrupt that nothing could save it. Then Hamilton spoke up. Corruption was inseparable from what he admired in the British constitution. "Purge it of its corruption, and give to its popular branch equality of representation, & it would become an impracticable government," he said, but "as it stands at present, with all its supposed defects, it is the most perfect government which ever existed."[4]

Among the Framers, Hamilton wasn't alone in his admiration for the British form of government. At the Philadelphia Convention, many of the other delegates had gone out of their way to praise the British constitution. But they had just fought a revolution to free themselves from it, and they wanted something better for America. Theirs would be a different kind of constitution, an anticorruption covenant.

The Constitutional Convention

The crucial moment in American history was not the Revolutionary War but the Philadelphia Convention of 1787, when fifty-five delegates from twelve states assembled to frame a new constitution for the country. (Rhode Island sent no delegates.) It may now seem inevitable that the delegates would agree on a constitution, but at various points in the proceedings they were at full stop. Several of the delegates threatened to walk out, and not a few thought the country might split into two or three parts.[5] In that case, said Gouverneur Morris of Pennsylvania, they should prepare for civil war. "The Country must be united," he warned. "If persuasion does not unite us, the sword will. . . . The stronger party will then make traytors of the weaker; and the Gallows and Halter will finish the work of the sword." Moreover, foreign powers might have been happy to take advantage of the confusion.[6] A formal return to the British Empire, with a right of American self-government, was not beyond the realm of possibility, in which case the revolution would have been undone.

Even after the delegates agreed on the new Constitution, on September 17, it still had to be ratified by the states. But the outcome was then in little doubt, because the Framers presented the states with a take-it-or-leave-it document. It would be this or nothing, and the second option was not in the cards, since remaining under the Articles of Confederation might have resulted in a breakup of the new country. In the end, even corrupt little Rhode Island came around and ratified the Constitution in May 1790, a year after George Washington had been inaugurated as the first president. The state may have earned its label of "Rogue Island" by the convention delegates, but trying to make a country of itself just wouldn't make sense.

So we got our Constitution. The debates along the way were filled with high drama and extended argument among an extraordinary group of politically astute leaders. But that isn't to say they were all high-minded great men. "There is nothing less true," said George Mason. "From [New England] there were knaves and fools and from the states southward of Virginia they were a parcel of coxcombs and from the middle states office hunters not a few."[7] It's all the more striking, then, to see how often the delegates expressed their concerns about corruption, and some of the strongest voices for virtue came from the strangest places.

When Mason spoke of the middle-state "office hunters," he likely let his eye fall upon Benjamin Franklin from Pennsylvania. At the age of eighty-one, Franklin was the oldest person at the convention, and next to Washington he was the most famous, the author of *Poor Richard's Almanac* and a member of the Royal Academy. As a politician and a diplomat he had first asked the British to expel the French from North America and then persuaded the French to kick the British out of the United States, a triumph unmatched in U.S. diplomatic history. He was the indispensable American as much as Washington was. And he had built a career by securing lucrative public positions for himself and his family, beginning with his appointment as postmaster of Philadelphia in 1737.

The delegates may therefore have suspected that Franklin was less than sincere in his statements about the corrupting effects of payment for high office. In proposing that presidents should serve without pay, Franklin argued that men are moved by their passions for money and power, and that the worst candidates will seek office when the two are combined. The result would be British-style corruption, with vast numbers of *placemen* appointed to government office in reward for services to their party. "The struggles for [government places] are the true sources of all those factions which are perpetually dividing the [British] Nation, distracting its councils, hurrying sometimes into fruitless & mischievous wars, and often compelling a submission to dishonorable terms of peace."[8] It would be the same in America if the posts of honor became places of profit.

When he finished speaking, there was silence among the delegates. Perhaps they were thinking of how effectively Franklin had sought profitable places himself, and how much he had enjoyed the *salon*s of Paris. They may also have been recalling the services he had done for America and wondering if it might be a mistake to discourage people like Franklin from taking public office. Finally, Hamilton seconded the motion for an unpaid presidency. Few delegates had less sympathy for the proposal, but Hamilton did not want to see the older man embarrassed. No one wished to debate Franklin's proposal, wrote Madison in his convention notes, but "it was treated with great respect, but rather for the author of it, than from any apparent conviction of its expediency or practicability."[9] And so it went nowhere.

Hamilton wasn't particularly troubled by corruption, as we have seen, but if any delegate was more cynical still it was Gouverneur Morris. While the story that he owed his peg leg to a jump from a window to escape a jealous husband is probably apocryphal, we do know something of his many affairs, thanks to his candid diary.[10] When he went to Paris on banking business, he quickly adapted to local customs and shared a mistress—the comtesse de Flahaut—with Talleyrand, the bishop of Autun. With a touch of envy, a French diplomat described Morris as a man "without morals and, if one believes his enemies, without principles."[11]

At the convention, Morris was the master of the adroit suggestion, the strategic compromise, the art of the deal. Though he was present at the start, in mid-May, he left after a few days, returning only on July 2, and then he wasted no time in launching into a patronizing speech in favor of an aristocratic senate, composed only of those who could serve without pay. The "aristocratic interest" would then be set against the "popular interest," so that the two would check and control each other. Morris hoped the delegates had "strength of mind eno' . . . to look truth in the face" and acknowledge what really motivates people, rich and poor. "He did not hesitate therefore to say that loaves & fishes must bribe the Demagogues."[12] In his brashness, Morris failed to take the measure of the delegates, and Madison was especially annoyed. On July 11, he admonished Morris for continually insisting on the "political depravity of men, and the necessity of checking one vice and interest" against another.[13] Within a short time, however, the two had made up, and Morris persuaded Madison to support the idea of a popularly elected president in a system of checks and balances.

Filtering Virtue

Up to this point, Madison had subscribed to a very different theory for restraining corruption. The voters, he thought, might be made to elect their betters through a process of *filtration*, an idea first proposed by David Hume. Madison would have read Hume's essays as a student at Princeton and would have come across his "Idea of a Perfect Commonwealth." There, Hume proposed a highly artificial scheme of government that began with a division of Great Britain and Ireland into one hundred counties, and each of these into one hundred parishes, and then built up from there with county-town assemblies, county magistrates, and senators.[14] Ordinary voters would elect local representatives, who in turn would elect a higher level of representatives, and so on up the ladder. At each rising level, the electors would presumably have better judgment than those who elected them, resulting in a superior set of representatives at the highest levels. The cream would rise to the top.

Madison suggested this concept of filtration or refinement of representatives in "Vices of the Political System of the United States," his essay on the defects of the Articles of Confederation. What he envisaged was "a process of elections" designed to ensure that the most senior places in government would be occupied by "the purest and noblest characters" in society.[15] Such a system would "extract from the mass of the Society" those who "feel most strongly the proper motives to pursue the end of their appointment, and be most capable to devise the proper means of attaining it." People like Washington, in short. People like Madison himself, come to think of it! And so he proposed a constitution in which the voters would directly elect the House of Representatives, which would then choose the Senate, and both bodies jointly would pick the president. At the convention he described this as a "policy of refining the popular appointments by successive filtrations."[16]

This process would be a remedy for the defects of democracy, argued Madison. Ordinary voters would have little information about candidates and wouldn't know how to choose wisely. They could easily become pawns in the hands of a corrupt demagogue "veiling his selfish views under the professions of public good, and varnishing his sophistical arguments with the glowing colours of popular eloquence." In addition, self-interest would blind people to the common good. Washington, himself the paragon of virtue, privately agreed that governments could not rely upon a disinterested citizenry, for as he wrote to Madison's father, "the motives which predominate most in human affairs" are "self-love and self-interest."[17]

Many politicians since Madison have questioned whether the voters, unaided, choose well. After the 1994 Republican landslide, Rep. Barney Frank was asked what he thought of the election's message to his fellow Democrats. "The voters," he exploded. "They're nothing to write home about either!" When the Framers looked at the American electorate of 1787, they also didn't see much virtue. They saw the confederation falling apart through an "excess of democracy," with its "turbulence and follies."[18] In George Mason's view, "it would be as unnatural to refer the choice of a proper character for chief Magistrate to the people, as it would, to refer a trial of colours to a blind man."[19]

In parliamentary systems of government, the voters do not choose the chief magistrate. The voters in Britain do not elect the prime minister. Only the voters of the Maidenhead constituency have the privilege of voting for or against Theresa May. What makes her prime minister is the support of Conservative MPs in the House of Commons, and that's a form of filtration. It might be a minimal kind of filtration, since the MPs who chose May have run for election as members of her party in modern media campaigns. But Madison wanted this type of parliamentary or congressional government for the United States. He didn't get what he wanted at Philadelphia.

On July 16, 1787, the delegates voted for the Connecticut Compromise, under which the state legislatures would appoint U.S. senators, and the states would have equal representation in the Senate. There would be filtration, but the states would do the filtering. As a strong nationalist, Madison hated this plan. The next morning, the dispirited nationalists from the large states of Virginia and Pennsylvania met over breakfast to consider their options. Some thought they should make the best of the situation. Others argued for a walkout, and as Madison more than anyone else wanted to draw power from the states, he was likely of this number. The Connecticut Compromise had caused "serious anxiety," he wrote,[20] but the group of nationalists came to no decision. "The time was wasted in vague conversation."[21]

Virtually all of Madison's ideas had been rejected. He had lost, and he knew it.[22] He must have wondered whether anything could still be rescued of the convention.

That breakfast meeting was on July 17, arguably the most important day in American history. There would be no walkout, and the convention would produce a constitution. The delegates had settled on how to choose the House of Representatives and the Senate, but they had yet to decide on the executive branch, and that would turn out to be the most important question of all. The debate over how the president would be chosen is the most fascinating story of the convention, and it began with a speech about corruption that Gouverneur Morris made that day.

Choosing a Virtuous President

Madison doesn't tell us who attended the July 17 breakfast meeting. Morris was likely there, as a representative of a large state and as one who spoke more than anyone else during the convention. He must have argued against a walkout, for he had a fresh card to play, and later that morning he would deliver one of the most consequential speeches in American political history. Over the following weeks it would be Morris's convention more than anyone else's, as he rallied his side, stick-handled the puck, and polished the language of the text. The convention would have another two months to go, and during that time Morris returned again and again to the danger of corruption.

By the time Morris made his speech, the structure of the new government had largely been agreed upon. The states would not be abolished, as Hamilton would have wished. Instead, they would retain broad powers in their internal affairs, and would be represented on an equal basis at the heart of the federal government, in its Senate. Seats in the House of Representatives would be allocated by population, and the members elected by the people. Still to be decided was how the president would be chosen. "This subject has greatly divided the House," said James Wilson, "and will also divide people out of doors. It is in truth the most difficult of all on which we have had to decide."[23] It was also the most consequential, for today we have a government that is dominated by the presidency.

Over the course of the convention, the delegates voted six times for a congressionally appointed president, once unanimously, and they also voted once for a president chosen by state legislatures. (The convention didn't follow strict rules of procedure, so the delegates returned again and again to matters previously voted on.) We would have a president appointed by Congress today, but for the way Morris cleverly turned the delegates by appealing to their fear of corruption. He had initially wanted a congressionally appointed president, for like Madison he was suspicious of democracy. Also like Madison, he was a nationalist who wanted to draw power to the new federal government. And he was a quicker thinker than Madison. After the Connecticut Compromise had passed on July 16, Morris was the first to recognize that a congressional appointment of the president would weaken the national government. If senators were appointed by state legislatures, and small states were given equal representation in the senior branch of Congress, then a congressionally appointed presidency would empower the states. When Morris realized this, his nationalism trumped his fear of democracy, and he promptly began to argue for a popularly elected president.

First he sidled up to the small-state delegates by opposing Madison's pet project, a federal veto power over state legislation. I am "more and more opposed to the [federal] negative. The proposal of it would disgust all the States."[24] Having thus positioned himself as a moderate on the issue of federal power, Morris then made his masterstroke in a speech designed to persuade the small-state delegates to support a popularly elected president as a means of combatting corruption. Two weeks earlier he had told the delegates that bribery of demagogues with loaves and fishes was to be expected, but now he presented himself as corruption's implacable foe. He argued that a congressionally appointed executive would be "the mere creature of the Legis[lature] if appointed & impeachable by that body." Instead, said Morris,

> He ought to be elected by the people at large, by the freeholders of the Country. That difficulties attend this mode, he admits. But they have been found superable in N.Y. & in [Connecticut] and would he believed be found so, in the case of an Executive for the U. States. If the people should elect, they will never fail to prefer some man of distinguished character, or services; some man, if he might so speak, of continental reputation. If the Legislature elect, it will be the work of intrigue, of cabal, and of faction: it will be like the election of a pope by a conclave of cardinals; real merit will rarely be the title of the appointment.[25]

This was catnip to the small-state delegates, with their aversion to corruption. But would the Virginia nationalists recognize that having a popularly elected president would mean a shift of power to the federal government? Not at first. When the matter was put to a vote shortly thereafter, only the Pennsylvania delegates voted with Morris, while Madison's Virginia joined the other states in the majority. But then Morris returned to the fray on July 19 with new arguments for a popular election. As the country was large, he said, it would require a vigorous executive to govern it, and a president who was popularly elected would be more powerful than one who owed his election to Congress. Also, the government would be less corrupt with a popularly elected president. Were Congress to appoint him, it would become the dominant branch, and its members would be chosen from among the "Great &

the wealthy." Corruption would be the result, for "wealth tends to corrupt the mind & to nourish its love of power, and to stimulate it to oppression."[26] That would be avoided with a popularly elected president, for he would be the tribune of the people, especially of the lower classes.

The delegates weren't buying this argument, but Morris succeeded in one thing: he turned Madison around. For Madison, the penny finally dropped on that day, and he was persuaded to support a popularly elected president. His speech on the subject is frequently quoted:

> If it be a fundamental principle of free Govt. that the Legislative, Executive & Judiciary powers should be *separately* exercised; it equally so that they be *independently* exercised. . . . This could not be if [the president] was to be appointable from time to time by the Legislature. . . . Certain it was that the appointment would be attended with intrigues and contentions that ought not to be unnecessarily admitted.[27]

Of course, it wasn't Madison's idea that the separation of powers required a popularly elected president. It came from Morris, as did the idea that this measure was necessary to avoid the corruption that would follow upon a congressional appointment of the president.

In following Morris's lead, Madison abandoned the filtration theory he had brought to the convention. What changed his mind was realizing the implications of the way senators would be chosen under the Connecticut Compromise. If state legislatures chose senators, and then Congress chose the president, this would empower the states. For Madison, as with Morris, nationalism trumped filtration, and with it the dream of virtuous leaders chosen by Congress. Thereafter the nationalists from Pennsylvania and Virginia, the two largest states, would unite around the principle of a popularly elected president, though the other delegations still opposed it.

On July 26 the delegates turned over a draft constitution, with an appointed president, to a Committee of Detail for fine-tuning, and then they adjourned for ten days. The committee reported back on August 6 with a new draft that had significant changes but retained a congressionally elected president.[28] That question, it was thought, had been settled. It wasn't, though. A motion for a popularly elected president was brought forward once more, on August 24, winning only two votes against nine.[29] Then Morris spoke up again to warn of corruption if the president were to be chosen by Congress. "Cabal & corruption are attached to that mode of election," he said.[30] His proposal for a popular election of the president did better, but still failed, with five votes against six.[31] That was as close as the Philadelphia Convention came to giving us a popularly elected president. Not once did the delegates ever vote for it.

On August 31 the delegates referred the question of presidential elections to the Committee on Unfinished Parts, with one delegate for each state. The committee was dominated by delegates who supported a popularly elected president, including Morris. Four days later, on September 4, they presented a plan for the president to be chosen by electors appointed in a manner determined by each state's legislature. Today that means a popular election in every state, but in 1787 the delegates would have expected state legislatures to pick the electors. They also expected that presidential candidates after George Washington would usually not have nationwide support, and with no candidate winning a majority of electoral votes, the decision would be thrown to the House of Representatives (originally, to the Senate), voting by state. This is what would happen in the elections of 1800 and 1824, and most of the Framers thought it would almost always be that way. In essence, they thought they had agreed on a congressionally chosen president.

The deliberations of the Committee on Unfinished Parts were kept secret, but the plan for selecting a president seems to have come mainly from the pen of Gouverneur Morris, who was the foremost advocate of a popular election and who had the strongest strategic sense of any of the delegates. He was also the committee's chief spokesman in explaining the new plan to the other delegates. The new system for choosing a president was designed to address the possibility of corruption, he said. "The principal advantage aimed at was that of taking away the opportunity for cabal," which the delegates would have taken as a reference to corruption. A legislative appointment would have introduced "the danger of intrigue & faction." [32]

In accepting the new plan, the delegates did not anticipate the extension of the franchise to all adults or the direct election of senators under the Seventeenth Amendment. They didn't think the presidential electors would be chosen by the voters, and they did expect that electors would exercise independent discretion in picking a president. Most of the delegates didn't even realize they had effectively abandoned the idea of a congressionally appointed president, since they expected that few candidates would ever secure a majority of votes in the Electoral College. Nor did they think the nationalists had won. But over time, power shifted from the states to Washington, and in Washington it shifted to the executive office; and the cumbersome machinery of the Constitution's Article II has given America its strong presidential form of government.

All of this began with Morris's little-known speech on July 17. And when his proposals were put to a vote, it was the fear of corruption that tipped the scales.

— 6 —

What Corruption Meant to the Framers

THE U.S. CONSTITUTION, with its presidential system and separation of powers, was sold as an anticorruption covenant, and that is how the convention delegates understood it. But just what did the Framers think corruption meant? The answer is several quite different things, but the simplest explanation is that it referred to how the British were governed.

The Framers may have recalled, for example, how James I plundered the Royal Treasury to give presents to his favorites. David Hume tells how James once observed a porter bearing £3,000 on his way to the Treasury. "How happy would that money make me!" said one of James's handsome courtiers, whereupon the king gave it to him. "You think yourself very happy in obtaining so large a sum," said James. "But I am more happy, in having an opportunity of obliging a worthy man, whom I love."[1] James subsequently ennobled the favorite as the Earl of Holland, a title he would bear until he died on the scaffold in 1649 at the hands of a vengeful Puritan Parliament.

Not all the gifts were so conspicuously without merit, however. One cannot read Johnson's *Lives of the Poets* without being struck by how many of England's greatest writers were sustained by the patronage of the king or the nobility. When he wrote *The Old Bachelor*, the twenty-three-year-old William Congreve was made one of the commissioners for licensing coaches, and soon afterward he was given places in the Pipe Office and the Custom House. Johnson himself held a pension from the king. Nor did contemporary Britons see themselves as especially corrupt. When George III ascended to the throne in 1760 promising a reign of virtue, free of corruption, no one thought he meant a government from which the tools of influence had been banished. Whig politicians, beginning with Robert Walpole (prime minister 1721–42) and continuing with the Pelham brothers (Henry Pelham, prime minister 1743–54; Thomas Pelham, 1st Duke of Newcastle, prime minister 1754–56, 1756–57), had perfected a patronage machine through which the government could rely on the support of a majority in the House of Commons. The king held important cards as well, in his control of the civil list of paid government appointees and his ability as the fount of honor to ennoble his supporters. With these instruments at his disposal, he could rely upon his allies in the House of Commons, the "King's Friends."

All sides thought it legitimate to offer plums to political friends and to feast on whatever was sent their way. "Men . . . no more dreamt of a seat in the House in order to benefit humanity," observed Sir Lewis Namier, "than a child dreams of a birthday cake that others may eat it."[2] David Hume thought the king's patronage powers had even served a useful purpose in preserving the balanced British constitution, which had been undermined by the rising power of the House of Commons. Formally, the king could veto legislation, but his power to do so had fallen into abeyance and could not be revived. What he retained was the ability to rally the King's Friends in Parliament through the favors he could grant, and this permitted him to shape ministries to his liking. "The crown has so many offices at its disposal, that, when assisted by the honest and dis-interested part of the house, it will always command the resolutions of the whole; so far, at least, to preserve the ancient constitution from dan-ger." Call this "*corruption* and *dependence*" if you will, said Hume, but it was "necessary to the preservation of our mixed government."[3]

In America, the Patriots weren't buying this. They had read of British corruption from John Trenchard and Thomas Gordon (*Cato's Letters*, 1720–23) and from Henry St. John, 1st Viscount Bolingbroke (1678–1751), and they wanted no part of it. American visitors to Brit-ain had brought back reports of the mother country's appalling level of public vice. As John Adams saw it, both electors and elected in Britain had "become one mass of corruption."[4] John Dickinson, "the penman of the American Revolution,"[5] was the strongest Anglophile at the Philadelphia Convention, but when he had visited England earlier he was shocked by how the British conducted their elections.

> It is astonishing to think what impudence & villainy are practizd on this occasion. If a man cannot be brought to vote as he is desird, he is made dead drunk & kept in that state, never heard of by his family or friends till all is over & he can do no harm. The oath of their not being bribd is as strict & solemn as language can form it, but is so little regarded that few people can refrain from laughing while they take it. I think the character of Rome will equally suit this nation: "Easy to be bought, if there was but a purchaser."[6]

It was bad enough that Britain was so corrupt, but worse still that the British were exporting their corruption to America through the officers they appointed. Royal governors such as Thomas Hutchin-son of Massachusetts (Anne's great-great-grandson) had created a system of dependents through their placemen, which John Adams thought amounted to a tyranny.[7] "Cæsar, by destroying the Roman Republic, made himself perpetual dictator," and likewise "Hutchinson, by countenancing and supporting a System of Corruption and all Tyranny, has made himself Governor."[8] Adams's obsession with Hutchinson bordered on neurosis, but it wasn't entirely divorced from reality. At one point Hutchinson was simultaneously the colony's lieutenant governor, a member of its house of representatives, and its chief justice. The tea that the Sons of Liberty threw into Boston Harbor had been intended for delivery to Hutchinson's sons.

Whether or not the British system of government and the royal governors it gave America were as corrupt as all that, many of the colonists (anticipating Henry James) subscribed to a notion of American innocence versus European experience. Like George Mason,[9] they may have admired the British constitution but detested British corruption, and that was an argument for Americans to have a different kind of government.[10] They would build a republic of virtue.

Republican Virtue

In the eighteenth century there was a special understanding of disinterested republican virtue, the virtue of patriots who scorned corruption and championed the general good. In Britain it was represented by a "Country party," whose members detested Walpole and were avid readers of *Cato's Letters* and of Bolingbroke, and who stood in opposition to a "Court party" that was more comfortable with corruption. In France, republican virtue found its most striking expression in the paintings of Jefferson's friend Jacques-Louis David (1748–1825), where it reached repellant heights.

Jefferson and David belonged to the same radical-chic set, the seedbed of revolution in a Paris where the line between art and politics was thin.[11] Just a few years after Jefferson returned from France, David would sign the death order for Louis XVI and would become a close political ally of the sea-green incorruptible Robespierre. Jefferson greatly admired *The Oath of the Horatii* when he was in Paris. "I do not feel an interest in any pencil but that of David," he wrote.[12]

It wasn't simply the stunning tableaux that drew him to the artist, for both men shared Robespierre's belief that "immorality is the basis of despotism, as virtue is the essence of a republic."[13] Both yearned for a reign of virtue clothed in classical republican garb, as seen in the painter's subversive *The Lictors Bring to Brutus the Bodies of His Sons.*

David took his inspiration from Livy's account of how Lucius Junius Brutus established a Roman Republic by expelling the last king in 509 BC. The king, Tarquin the Proud, had outraged his subjects but was nevertheless supported by a class of courtiers who knew that "as long as there was a king, there was a person from whom they could get what they wanted, whether lawful or not."[14] That didn't save him, however. After the revolt had succeeded and Brutus became the first leader of the Republic, he provided the supreme example of self-sacrifice and republican virtue by having two of his own sons executed for conspiring to restore the monarchy. David's painting portrays the moment when the bodies are brought home. Brutus sits in the shadows, his back to his sons, his face stern and grim, the picture of republican self-sacrifice and a reproach to the weeping women of the family on his left. If the symbol of the frivolous *ancien régime* was the feminine *salon*, republican virtue was a distinctly masculine trait.

The Country party and the ideal of republican virtue were well represented at the Philadelphia Convention, in delegates such as Roger Sherman and George Mason.[15] These were the people to whom Gouverneur Morris appealed in his speeches on corruption. But Morris privately belonged to a Court party that scoffed at the idea of a special kind of republican virtue. Hamilton might also be counted a member of the Court party. So too can Madison, who in "Vices of the Political System of the United States" had argued that self-interest would blind voters to the common good: "Place three individuals in a situation wherein the interest of each depends on the voice of the others, and give to two of them an interest opposed to the rights of the third? Will the latter be secure?"[16] Later, in *Federalist* 51, he famously expanded on the limits of republican virtue. Men are not angels, he said, but seekers of private gain, and government should channel self-interest in such a way that it serves the public good. "Ambition must be made to counteract ambition," so that the overweening pursuit of advantage by one group is checked by other groups in the competition for power.

While the Country party had a stronger aversion to government corruption than did the Court party, all the Framers shared Madison's skepticism about the innate goodness of the people. None would have agreed with Robespierre, or Jean-Jacques Rousseau, that social ills never stem from *le peuple* freely pursuing their own interest. "To be good, people have only to prefer their interests to that which is not in their interest," wrote Robespierre. "To be good, the magistrate has only to sacrifice himself (*s'immoler*) to the people."[17] No one in Philadelphia would have spoken like that—not Madison, certainly not Hamilton or Morris, and not the Country party members either. As Hamilton observed, "the members most tenacious of republicanism . . . were as loud as any in declaiming against the vices of democracy."[18] Robespierre defended the *jacquerie* that burned down castles in the French Revolution, but the Framers took a different view. They had witnessed mob violence at home, with Shay's Rebellion in western Massachusetts still a fresh memory, and they wanted none of it. Jefferson might perhaps have agreed with Robespierre about the innate goodness of the people, but happily he was in Paris and did not attend the Constitutional Convention.

The Framers understood that democracy was not a cure for corruption. While they sought to restrain the kind of self-seeking they saw at royal and aristocratic courts, they also knew that popular rule brought its own varieties of corruption. Voters often choose unwisely and politicians often take questionable actions to curry favor with their constituents. This is a problem that Madison sought to address with his idea of extensive virtue in a large polity.

Extensive Virtue

The Patriots of 1776 saw corruption emanating from London, and they aimed to foster civic virtue by drawing power away from the imperial capital to the periphery. Eleven years later, the Framers thought corruption had migrated to America and now was to be found at the periphery, in the state legislatures. For the nationalists in 1787, the concern about corruption had become an argument to shift power back to the center, this time to the new federal government whose constitution they were drafting.

Among the problems they saw in the states were shortsighted trade policies and a penny-pinching refusal to fund the national government. Under the Articles of Confederation (1781–88), Congress lacked a taxing power and therefore relied upon requisitions made to the state governments, which were paid tardily or not at all. A Virginia delegate, William Grayson, complained to James Monroe that New Hampshire "has not paid a shilling, since peace, & does not ever mean to pay one to all eternity." In New York, on the other hand, "they pay well because they can do it by plundering [New] Jersey and Connecticut."[19] By plundering, he meant the practice of levying tariffs on goods passing through from one state to another. States had also devalued their currencies as a means of paying off creditors on the cheap, with the result that it was difficult to borrow money. "In every point of view," wrote Madison in 1785, "the trade of this Country is in a deplorable Condition."[20]

The Framers thought these problems came from the mercenary new men who now inhabited the state houses in America, a second string of ill-educated populists who were deaf to the national interest and all too ready to advance wasteful local interests.[21] Not long before, the Patriots had fought against corruption by shifting power closer to the people. Now, in an ironic twist, the remedy for corruption would be to concentrate power in the central government. To remedy state corruption, Madison proposed a federal veto power over state laws—the same power that the British Board of Trade in Westminster had exercised before the revolution. This was a matter of some embarrassment for Madison, but he argued that there was a crucial difference, for the new federal government would be faithful to *American* national interests.[22]

Nationalists such as Madison had come to regard a beggar-thy-neighbor preference for one's particular state as a form of corruption. The true patriot was a person of "enlarged" or "extensive" views, with "a real concern for the welfare of our whole country in general," as one preacher put it.[23] George Washington, the very model of republican virtue, had learned the new language of extensive virtue during the revolution and had come to despise the narrowness of state "demagogues" in Congress. Writing to Jefferson as the convention began, he prophesied the ruin of America unless a stronger central government were created. "The situation of the general government, if it can be called a government, is shaken to its foundation, and liable to be overturned by every blast. In a word, it is at an end."[24] The disorder could be laid at the feet of the self-interested state politicians who, lacking patriotism, were guided only by local attachments and would "not yield to a more enlarged scale of politics."[25]

Madison took up the new definition of enlarged civic virtue and employed it in a second theory about the need for a strong national government. He had abandoned the idea of filtration, but now he argued that corruption might be checked by the *extended republic* of the federal government. Again, he borrowed his ideas from David Hume, who had turned Montesquieu's argument for small republics on its head. In a large republic, Montesquieu had said, powerful interest groups would promote their corrupt, private ends, while smaller states would not allow as much scope for such interest groups to grow.[26] Hume said it was just the opposite, that a large republic is protected from "tumult and faction," since the very size of the country makes it harder for factions or interest groups to unite in a common plan. "The parts are so distant and remote, that it is very difficult, either by intrigue, prejudice, or passion, to hurry them into any measures against the public interest."[27]

At the convention, Madison promoted the idea of extensive virtue in response to Roger Sherman's claim that people seemed happier in small states and that this was a reason for a weak national government. Not so, said Madison. Large states would be better able to keep "Sects, factions, & interests" in check.[28] He returned to the idea in *Federalist* 10, where he argued that an extended republic would set interests and factions against each other, so that each would be restrained. "Extend the sphere, " he said, "and you take in a greater variety of parties and interests; you make it less probable that a majority of the whole will have a common motive to invade the rights of other citizens; or if such a common motive exists, it will be more difficult for all who feel it to discover their own strength, and to act in unison with each other."

This argument represented a change in the way civic virtue was understood between the revolutionary period, when colonial Horatii were called to arms against the British, and the 1787 convention, when the delegates were charged with the lawyer's task of framing a constitution and the prosaic search for what Madison called an "efficient government."[29] One doesn't find paeans to Brutus or Cato in the notes of their deliberations, but instead a quest for the proper balance of power among the branches of the federal government, and between the federal and state governments. The nationalists appropriated the language of civic virtue to argue for a strengthened federal power in an extended republic, laying the blame for corruption upon narrow state interests. At the same time, the proponents of states' rights would have recalled the earlier language of republican virtue, and Morris's brilliant July 17 speech succeeded in fusing both senses of civic virtue in an argument that ultimately gave us our strong presidential form of government.

Governing Above Faction

In his Farewell Address, George Washington famously warned against "factions," by which he meant party politics, or "the baneful effects of the spirit of party." Madison expected factions and political parties to arise, but he trusted in an extensive republic and the constitutional machinery to keep them in check and prevent them from oppressing minorities. "Among the numerous advantages promised by a well constructed Union," he wrote in *Federalist* 10, "none deserves to be more accurately developed than its tendency to break and control the violence of faction." But other eighteenth-century patriots in both Britain and America, like Washington, appealed to a pre-political order in which the common good was easily understood and not much in dispute.

Back then, it was easier to think like that. By the time George III acceded to the throne in 1760, the Tories had made their peace with the Hanoverian usurpers and British party differences had dissolved. In America too, party differences diminished after the revolution, since the more vocal Loyalists had been driven into exile—which was one way of avoiding the baneful effects of politics. It was therefore possible, in both countries, to imagine enlightened rulers who would serve the general welfare rather than particular interests.

For Bolingbroke, the virtuous ruler would be a "patriot king" who would "espouse no Party, but . . . govern like the common father of his people . . . where the head and all the members are united by one common interest, and animated by one common spirit."[30] George III was happy to see himself as just that person, reigning virtuously above parties for the common good. Unlike his great-grandfather and grandfather, George I and II, he was also a British patriot who said "I glory in the name of Briton" when he ascended to the throne. There was something new in the air, and his subjects reacted to the youthful monarch with enthusiasm. "The King seems resolved to bring all things back to their original principles, and to stop the torrent of corruption and laziness," wrote Laurence Sterne.[31]

In America, enthusiasm for George III soon wore off, and when the Framers assembled in Philadelphia to draft a new constitution, they knew that America must be a republic. Would it be virtuous, though? Would its citizens and leaders place the good of the country above their private interests? The convention delegates didn't have far to look for an example of disinterested republican virtue, with Washington sitting before them on the dais, the likely first president of the United States. When he retired to his farm after two terms in office rather than seek a third, George III was told of this and pronounced Washington "the greatest character of the age."[32]

The yearning for a virtuous leader who rules above parties never entirely dies. It lies behind the question "What would Washington do," and it is the ideal to which American presidents appeal when they claim to speak for the common good as against a corrupt Congress and partisan politics. Under our strong presidential form of government, with power concentrated in the executive branch, a president can too easily see himself as a patriot king. This is not what the Framers envisioned, however. They wanted the president to have the virtue of Bolingbroke's patriot king but not the ambitions or pretentions of a monarch who rules above Congress. The search for republican virtue in a virtuous but all-powerful president is always a betrayal of republicanism.

Private Virtue

While the republic of virtue could not be founded upon the character of the president, the Framers agreed that he should be a model of private as well as civic virtue, like George Washington. And while they had human corruptibility firmly in mind when they designed their constitution, they agreed that the public virtue needed for good government required private virtue in the citizenry. "To suppose that any form of government will secure liberty or happiness without any virtue in the people is a chimerical idea," argued Madison in the Virginia ratifying debates.[33]

The Framers saw a corruption of private as well as public virtue in Old World capitals. Most of them would have agreed with the prim John Adams that Franklin's long stay in Paris had done nothing to improve his morals, private or civic. After spending six weeks with him as a fellow ambassador, Adams wrote in his diary that Franklin's life was "a Scene of continual discipation." By Adams's account,

> Mr. Franklin kept a horn book always in his Pockett in which he minuted all his invitations to dinner, and [fellow ambassador Arthur Lee] said it was the only thing in which he was punctual. . . . He went to his Invitation to his Dinner and after that went sometimes to his Play, sometimes to the Philosophers but most commonly to visit those Ladies who were complaisant enough . . . to make Tea for him. . . . After Tea the Evening was spent, in hearing the Ladies sing and play upon their Piano Fortes and other instruments of Musick, and in various games as Cards, Chess, Backgammon, etc., etc.[34]

With his plain clothes and fur cap, Franklin was lionized as the representative of New World simplicity, while ladies of the court vied with each other to bring him to their *salons*. Rustic garb notwithstanding, Franklin had settled into Parisian *douceur de vie* as comfortably as one might step into a warm bath.[35] Adams found it all inconsistent with republican principles. "What Absurdities, Inconsistencies, Distractions, and Horrors would these Manners introduce into our Republican Governments in America," he said. "No kind of Republican Government can exist with such national manners as these. Cavete Americani."[36] Needless to say, Franklin was a good deal more successful than Adams as an ambassador to the French court.

For Adams and other Patriots, private virtue was a political issue, since the manner in which we live our lives has an effect on the country as a whole. Public or civic virtue, the willingness to sacrifice oneself for the country, could not be expected from those who lacked private virtue. Such men would seek luxuries and become venal, and this would lead to corruption. Any government that encouraged luxuries must therefore be a bad government.[37] Writing from London, the young John Dickinson prophesied what would become of a wealthy British Empire whose subjects had lost their virtue.

> It is grown a vice here to be virtuous. . . . People are grown too polite to have an old-fashioned religion, and are too weak to find out a new, from whence follows the most unbounded licentiousness and utter disregard of virtue, which is the unfailing cause of the destruction of all empires.[38]

The delegates agreed that some type of private virtue was needed to guard against corruption, but they couldn't agree on what kind. Some, like Charles Pinckney, had a distinctly premodern cast of mind, thinking that commercial men should have little influence on politics. Rather it was the "landed interest," such as the planter class in his native South Carolina, "who are and who ought ever to be the governing spring in the system."[39] There is an echo here of Jefferson's belief that agrarian virtues must be the moral underpinning of the republic. In his *Notes on the State of Virginia* he had written that "those who labour in the earth are the chosen people of God, if ever he had a chosen people, whose breast he has made his peculiar deposit for substantial and genuine virtue. Corruption of morals in the mass of cultivators is a phaenomenon of which no age nor nation has furnished an example." By contrast, the "mobs" in the cities were like a "canker" that subverted the manners and laws of society.[40]

For the agrarians among the delegates, private virtue meant a voluntary simplicity and the avoidance of unnecessary expense. In that spirit, Mason proposed that Congress be given the power to enact sumptuary laws against luxury goods. Frugality was admirable for its own sake and as a foundation of public-spiritedness in the citizenry. "No Government can be maintained unless the manners be made consonant to it," he argued.[41] Where there are great disparities in wealth, people will compete for luxuries to signal their superiority, and will employ corrupt means to do so. The love of distinction is natural, Mason admitted, but it should be channeled into desires more conducive to the public welfare. His motion for sumptuary laws failed, though it received support from three states.[42] Four days before the convention ended, Mason tried once more, suggesting that a committee be formed "to report articles of Association for encouraging by the advice and influence of the members of the convention, œconomy, frugality and American manufacturers."[43] This motion was agreed to without debate, and the members appointed to the committee included Franklin.

The resolution was without force, so everyone went along with it. Some of the delegates simply liked the idea of restrictions on luxury goods.[44] Others must have been acutely aware of the need to placate Mason, who threatened to walk out of the convention—and would shortly do so in order to oppose the ratification of the new Constitution. Mason's proposal would also have brought back memories of the nonimportation movement of twenty years earlier, when the colonists boycotted British goods as a way of protesting taxes imposed by Westminster. For Virginians such as Mason, the appeal to frugality had a special meaning, as they would have recalled the planters' debt crisis of the 1770s when fortunes were lost.[45]

However the delegates might have felt about luxuries, they shared a conviction that the new country's leaders should adhere to the highest standards of private virtue. Indeed, this sense of virtue had caused George Washington much anxiety two years earlier when he was asked to accept shares in a private company formed to make the Potomac more navigable. Washington had served without pay as the commander of American forces during the revolution, and by giving up his command in 1783 he also abandoned the opportunity to cash in afterward. Returning to his plantation on the Potomac, he saw the river as the gateway to the West, and became what his biographer Ron Chernow describes as "something of a monomaniac" on the subject.[46] He lobbied Virginia to back the project, and the state offered him the gift of 150 shares in the company. Perhaps the grateful legislators recalled how Parliament had awarded Blenheim Palace to the Duke of Marlborough as a gift from the nation.

While that was how the British rewarded victorious generals, Washington feared that the gift of shares might be less seemly in an American republic. In a lengthy and tortured letter to Governor Benjamin Harrison, he confessed that "no circumstance has happened to me since I left the walks of public life, which has so much embarrassed me."[47] It might be churlish to decline so generous an offer, he said, but he did not want anyone to think he had private motives for promoting the river project. He was severely tempted, however, and took the unusual step of asking his friends whether he might with propriety accept the gift, hoping they'd say he could. All agreed that he must of course do so, with the exception of the priggish Jefferson.[48] In the end, Washington solved the dilemma by accepting the shares but holding them in trust for the public.[49]

The convention, took place at a moment of change, however, when agrarian sensibilities began to give way to a more modern understanding of virtue. The new republic the delegates were creating would, in the fullness of time, be commercial rather than agrarian, and this was anticipated by delegates such as Hamilton, Morris, and the Franklin of *Poor Richard's Almanac*. What this would entail was a very different kind of morality—not an aristocratic code of honor or a classical republican one of stern self-denial, but rather the bourgeois ethic that Montesquieu described in *The Spirit of the Laws*, the gentler virtues of the *doux commerce*.[50] The bourgeois virtues of honesty, trustworthiness and industry would temper the competition for political positions that Montesquieu saw as the seedbed of corruption. Members of the rising merchant class would be satisfied to pursue wealth in trade, and would not be tempted to bribe the voters for political power. At the convention, it was Morris who spoke for this way of thinking. "Take away commerce," he said, "and the democracy will triumph,"[51] by which he meant demagogues and corruption. But then Morris was no prude, and might privately have agreed with Danton's retort to Robespierre that "virtue is what I do every night with my wife."[52]

Religious Virtue—and Vice

Republican virtue drew its inspiration from writers of pagan antiquity such as Plutarch and Sallust, or from contemporary Enlightenment writers such as Edward Gibbon. But its emphasis on self-denial in the country's service echoed the Reformed Protestant ethic of self-renunciation. Jonathan Edwards, the first president of Princeton and a leading Calvinist theologian, told his readers that the Christian was called upon to deny "his worldly inclinations, . . . forsaking and renouncing all worldly objects and enjoyments . . . so that he does freely, and from his very heart, as it were renounce and annihilate himself."[53] The devout American Christian would, along with renouncing Satan, deaden himself to luxuries and the lure of royal courts.[54]

This rather dour ethic was not for everyone, and some of the Framers had a more practical sense of the virtue needed in a commercial republic. Still, we should not underestimate the influence of Calvinist teaching on them. Visitors to the nation's capital may be puzzled by the statue of John Witherspoon, the sixth president of Princeton, when they see it on Connecticut Avenue, but Witherspoon's importance in his day can scarcely be overstated. He signed the Declaration of Independence and taught six of the Framers, including Madison, and his students would have absorbed something of his beliefs about fallen humanity. "Others may, if they please, treat the corruption of our nature as a chimera," Witherspoon wrote. "For my part I see it everywhere, and I feel it every day."[55] This view of human nature informs the distrust of popular democracy that Madison expressed in *The Federalist Papers*, where he wrote: "In all very numerous assemblies, of whatever character composed, passion never fails to wrest the sceptre from reason. Had every Athenian citizen been a Socrates, every Athenian assembly would still have been a mob."[56] For this reason, governments should be designed to blunt the voters' passions, as the complicated machinery outlined in the Constitution was meant to do.

Religious institutions would play their part in fostering virtue, but they also brought the danger of contention between sects, or of the larger ones oppressing the smaller. In Madison's view, this problem would be mitigated an extended republic where no denomination would have the power that comes from majority status. The Anglicans might be dominant in tidewater Virginia, the Congregationalists in Connecticut, but in the country as a whole no denomination would be in the majority. And this was another argument for transferring power from the states to the federal government.

Protestants might be content to coexist with other brands of Protestants in that way, but Catholics were another matter. Many Americans saw Catholicism not as a font of moral teaching but as a glaring example of man's natural depravity. (Morris's analogy to "the election of a pope by a conclave of cardinals" in his July 17 speech was a clever dog whistle to anti-Catholic sentiment.) *Cato's Letters*, whose defense of liberty profoundly influenced the Patriots, described a "catastrophe of popery" which "depopulates nations, destroys industry, overturns law and justice, . . . discourages trade, drives out merchants, enervates states, and renders the race of mankind feeble, lazy, and miserable."[57] During the Revolutionary War, the sermons of New England Protestant divines explicitly identified the cause of liberty with the repudiation of what was routinely called the Whore of Babylon.[58] What Catholicism had done, John Adams concluded, was to reduce its adherents "to a state of sordid ignorance and staring timidity . . . in a cruel, shameful and deplorable servitude, to [the Pope] and his subordinate tyrants."[59] Had Charles II gotten his way, he would have "established the Romish religion, and a despotism as wild as any in the world." In that case, "the light of science would have been extinguished, and mankind drawn back to a state of darkness and misery like that which prevailed from the fourth to the fourteenth century."[60]

In Catholicism, Americans saw a fatal conjunction of corruption and tyranny, of sly Jesuits and *éminences grises*, of Stuart pretenders and the Inquisition. The Patriot party spied the specter of popery in the Quebec Act of 1774, which was listed as one of the "intolerable acts" in the Declaration of Independence.[61] This act, in which Britain ceded the Ohio Valley to Quebec and to aboriginal Americans, was a thumb in the eye of American land speculators in the colonial assemblies. But what especially provoked their ire was the toleration of the Catholic religion in Quebec. In the paranoid style of the conspiracy theorist, American pamphleteers saw the generous treatment of 65,000 French Canadians as a threat to force Catholicism down the throats of three million American Protestants.[63] During the debates over the Quebec Act, it was always Loyalists such as Jonathan Boucher and Daniel Leonard (Massachusettensis) who argued for religious toleration, and bigoted Patriots such as John Adams who saw a menace to American liberty from a province with a population one-fiftieth that of the thirteen colonies.[64]

The Framers rejected religious tests as a condition of holding office in the Constitution's Article VI, § 3, and four years later the First Amendment guaranteed all citizens the free exercise of their religion. Catholics had also fought on the Patriot side in the revolution, and the war might have ended very differently but for the intervention of Catholic France. There were two Catholics among the delegates to the Constitutional Convention. That might seem to absolve the Framers from the charge of bigotry, but then they identified religious freedom with Protestantism. If Catholicism by its nature was intolerant of other religions, then religious freedom must imply its rejection. That was why Madison, in pleading for religious toleration in his "Memorial and Remonstrance against Religious Assessments," reminded Virginians of the Inquisition and complained of Catholic "superstition, bigotry and persecution."[65]

Law is one thing, popular sentiment another. When waves of Irish immigrants began arriving in the 1840s, nativist groups saw them as a threat to republican institutions. In Massachusetts, for example, the nativist American Party, a.k.a. the Know-Nothings, won the governorship and every statewide race in 1854, as well as 379 out of 381 seats in the state house of representatives. The newly elected governor pledged to "Americanize America" by barring naturalized citizens from public office and imposing a twenty-one-year residency requirement before they were allowed to vote. Although Catholics could not be specifically singled out, they were obviously the main target.

Catholics were widely identified with corruption, and not entirely without reason, since Irish immigrants used their voting clout to gain elective office and then proceeded to staff city halls and police stations with other Irish Catholics. Marginalized socially and economically in a Protestant society, they fought back by employing their political skills to create New York City's Tammany Hall and the big-city political machines portrayed in Edwin O'Connor's *The Last Hurrah*. There is little left of those old machines, or of the good-government "goo-goos" who opposed them, but today new minority groups use the same political tools to gain influence, help each other out, and thereby ascend the economic ladder. In a second-best world, a modicum of corruption might even be defended if it permits a disfavored group to surmount indefensible barriers of discrimination.

Some of the Framers' comments on the subject of corruption seem naïve and even rebarbative today, but there was a good measure of sober realism at the Constitutional Convention, too. Mason's attempt to introduce sumptuary laws went nowhere. None of the delegates sought to ban factions or political parties, a notion that Madison dismissed as inimical to liberty in *Federalist* 10: "Liberty is to faction what air is to fire, an aliment without which it instantly expires." As we would not abolish liberty, we must therefore learn to live with faction, but Madison thought the new Constitution would ensure that no faction could win absolutely in the competition for power. We might wish to live in a harmoniously virtuous world, free of corruption, but that is not the only desideratum. And in the hands of a Robespierre the single-minded crusade for civic virtue can produce monsters.

And what of today? We have made our peace with luxuries and with partisan politics, yet the Framers' vision of a virtuous republic, shorn of the prejudices of the day, remains a worthy ideal, the more so as Madison's competition among factions has served not to neutralize them but instead to create the thickest network of interest groups and lobbyists to be found in any country, at any time.

— 7 —

The Promise of Virtuous Government

THE BEST-KNOWN ANECDOTE from the Constitutional Convention happened on the day it ended, September 17, as the delegates filed from the Pennsylvania State House. A woman—Mrs. Powell, it is said—asked Franklin: What kind of government have you given us? He replied, "A republic, if you can keep it."[1] But that raises the question, if it wasn't going to remain a republic, what did he think it would become? The answer, almost certainly, was a monarchy. Not a democracy. Democracy wasn't on the table anywhere in the world, but there were monarchies everywhere. "There is a natural inclination in mankind to Kingly Government," Franklin observed at the convention.[2] Jefferson had been alarmed to find so many crypto-monarchists in New York, and they weren't alone.

The Framers, as Gordon Wood notes, took very seriously "the possibility of some sort of monarchy developing in America."[3] In proposing a new constitution, they aimed to close off the avenues by which a president might acquire quasi-monarchical powers. And when they had to decide on a method of choosing a president, and what his powers and term of office would be, it was always the fear of corruption that swayed them.

Reining In the Presidency

The new federal government was going to be a republic, but that wouldn't eliminate the possibility of corruption if the president had all the instruments of persuasion that the British monarch possessed. So the delegates tried to ensure that the president would not have the sorts of tools that George III had employed to assemble his King's Friends in Parliament. They did this through the Incompatibility, Appointments, and Appropriation clauses of the Constitution, and the ban on titles of nobility.

The Incompatibility Clause (Article I, § 6, cl. 2) sets out the core principle of the separation of powers:

> No Senator or Representative shall, during the time for which he was elected, be appointed to any civil office under the authority of the United States . . . : and no person holding any office under the United States, shall be a member of either House during his continuance in office.

The goal was to prevent the kind of corruption that the delegates saw in the British government, where the king could build a group of supporters in Parliament with the promise of lucrative executive offices.[4] The principal effect of the Incompatibility Clause is to close the door to parliamentary government by making it impossible for a congressman to accept a cabinet position or serve as president at the same time. (North Americans are sometimes surprised to find, for example, that a member of the French Chamber of Deputies is also a mayor back home.) Thus, John Kerry had to resign his Senate seat before he could become Obama's secretary of state. But in an era of crony capitalism, this rule doesn't seem to make our government any more virtuous.

Eighteenth-century British monarchs had another means of persuasion in the funds they controlled under the *civil list*. This was a grant of money intended to keep the king in regal style, but there was always enough left over for grants and pensions to favorite supporters.[5] In America too, the colonists had observed how royal governors such as Thomas Hutchison had created a network of supporters by conferring profitable offices on their allies. The 1776 Pennsylvania Constitution explicitly linked the multiplication of government placemen with corruption: "There can be no necessity for, nor use in establishing offices of profit, the usual effects of which are dependence and servility unbecoming freemen, in the possessors and expectants; faction, contention, corruption, and disorder among the people."[6]

The concern about a president's ability to buy influence by bestowing offices explains the fetters that the Framers placed on presidential powers under the Appointments Clause (Article II, § 2, cl. 2).[7] Under this clause, the president

> shall nominate, and, by and with the Advice and Consent of the Senate, shall appoint Ambassadors, other public Ministers and Consuls, Judges of the supreme Court, and all other Officers of the United States, whose Appointments are not herein otherwise provided for.

With the need for Senate approval, the president would hesitate before appointing mere cronies to office, argued Hamilton. He "would be both ashamed and afraid to bring forward, for the most distinguished or lucrative stations, candidates . . . personally allied to him, or . . . of possessing the necessary insignificance and pliancy to render them obsequious instruments of his pleasure."[8]

In addition, there would be no secret bribes by the president, for the Constitution's Appropriation Clause (Article II, § 9, cl. 7) required congressional appropriation for all expenditures as well as a regular public accounting of moneys spent.

> No Money shall be drawn from the Treasury, but in Consequence of Appropriations made by Law; and a regular Statement and Account of the Receipts and Expenditures of all public Money shall be published from time to time.

The Appropriation Clause has its origins in seventeenth-century British constitutional history and Parliament's efforts to rein in free-spending Stuart monarchs. But if the principle that the House of Commons controlled the purse was well established in the eighteenth century, the king still had more discretionary authority than the Framers were willing to accord to the president. They wanted the appropriation power to be set down in detail so that, as Hamilton explained, "no money can be expended, but for an *object*, to an *extent*, and *out of a fund*, which the laws have prescribed."[9] Further, the president had to account for his expenditures, a requirement added at the suggestion of George Mason,[10] who more than any other delegate feared that the Constitution would give excessive powers to the president, and that this would result in tyranny and corruption. Beginning with the first Appropriations Act in 1789, allocations were based on accounts presented by the Treasury Department that showed every individual salary or pension payment.

Finally, the Constitution bans *titles of nobility*. In today's Britain, decisions about knighthoods and peerages are made by the prime minister, and only the Order of Merit remains within the sovereign's sole discretion. In the late eighteenth century, however, all titles of nobility were the king's choice alone, so George III could use the promise of a title to prop up a favored ministry. An American president might similarly have used titles of nobility to strengthen his hand, had this been possible in America.

There had never been an American nobility, of course, and it was too late to introduce one in 1787. Nobility was "the growth of ages," as John Dickinson said, "and could only arise under a complication of circumstances none of which existed in the Country."[11] Nor would ordinary Americans have stood for the creation of a nobility. There was another thing, too: the possibility of corruption, which is why the ban on titles of nobility is coupled with the prohibition on accepting "any present, Emolument, Office, or Title, of any kind, from any King, Prince, or foreign State."[12] An American republic, said Charles Lee, would still have places of honor, but these would "be obtain'd without court favor; or the rascally talents of servility."[13] That was how the prohibition on titles of nobility should be understood, said Hamilton in *Federalist* 69: as a barrier to presidential corruption.

Electing a President

Some of the Framers saw popular elections as a cure for corruption. Gouverneur Morris, for example, thought that the necessity of facing the voters every four years would suffice to keep presidents honest, so he argued for a weak impeachment power.[14] Most delegates were more mistrustful of democracy, however. The voters, they thought, were foolishly ignorant and would be the pawns of demagogues. The Constitution's cumbersome method of choosing a president was designed to prevent corrupt demagogues from assuming the highest office.

Although Madison had abandoned the idea of a congressionally appointed president, the filtration theory survived to the extent that the delegates expected the choice of president to fall to the House of Representatives in most cases. And before that happened, the choice would also be filtered by an Electoral College under Article II, § 1, cl. 2:

> Each State shall appoint, in such Manner as the Legislature thereof may direct, a Number of Electors, equal to the whole Number of Senators and Representatives to which the State may be entitled in the Congress . . . .

The Electoral College represented a double filtration in the republic's early years, as most state legislatures simply picked the electors themselves, and electors were expected to exercise independent discretion. That's what helped bring Madison on board, since he thought the electors would be "more judicious" than voters in a popular election.[15] In *Federalist* 64, John Jay agreed with him, as did Hamilton in *Federalist* 68:

> It was equally desirable, that the immediate election should be made by men most capable of analyzing the qualities adapted to the station, and acting under circumstances favorable to deliberation, and to a judicious combination of all the reasons and inducements which were proper to govern their choice. A small number of persons, selected by their fellow citizens from the general mass, will be most likely to possess the information and discernment requisite to so complicated an investigation.

That was the plan. Today, the presidential electors in each state are chosen in accordance with the popular vote for president, and they are pledged to vote for their party's candidate. With few exceptions they do so, like robots, instead of exercising their own discretion. In fifty-nine presidential elections, only 167 electors have failed to vote as they promised, and just sixteen in the last fifty years, according to the Center for Voting and Democracy.[16] People generally like to keep their promises, and party loyalty supplies a further motive to do so. In addition, half the states impose criminal sanctions on a "faithless elector" who doesn't vote for the party's candidate as pledged.[17] But even if he ends up in jail, a vote based on his own judgment would still be valid.

After the 2016 election, a group called the "Hamilton Electors" trotted out Hamilton's *Federalist* 68 and urged electors to vote for a Republican other than Trump. They didn't get very far. Others argued that Hillary Clinton deserved to win because she had garnered more votes than Trump, which was certainly an un-Hamiltonian argument. Critics of the Electoral College complain that it gives individual voters in small states more voting power than those in large states, because each state has a number of electors equal to the number of its representatives plus its two senators. But that's what the Framers wanted. They distrusted democracy, so they gave us a federal republic instead, and they sought to reduce the relative voting strength of the most populous states through the Electoral College. If that means the vote of someone in North Dakota has more weight than the vote of someone in California, it's all according to plan. Moreover, it would have been deeply unfair to take the victory from Trump on the basis of the popular vote, since he had played the *Moneyball* game of looking for votes in close states such as Ohio, Michigan, and Pennsylvania, rather than in vote-rich states such as California that he was bound to lose. The rules of the game shouldn't be changed after it's over.

Today, Hamilton's argument in *Federalist* 68 for the independent discretion of the electors is very dated. In his day, electors might indeed have had more "information and discernment" than ordinary voters, who wouldn't know much about candidates from other states. News traveled slowly, if at all, and even Madison confessed to having little knowledge of other states: "Of the affairs of Georgia, I know as little as those of Kamskatska."[18] How different things are today, especially with a national celebrity such as Trump. The millions of voters who cast their ballots knew all they needed to know about him.

That's not to say that presidential electors should never be permitted to use independent discretion. Imagine that the winning presidential candidate is found to have committed a dreadful offense the day after the election. In the honeymoon after the 2008 election, *The Onion* published a satirical story entitled "Media Having Trouble Finding Right Angle on Obama's Double-Homicide," an apt comment on the press's adulation of the new president. Suppose, however, that the president-elect had actually committed a crime so heinous (a triple-homicide?) that everyone agreed he should never take office. He might be arrested and jailed, but the electors would still be required to hold their vote as scheduled, and if they picked him he might try to pardon himself. Or we might have to wait until after his inauguration to impeach and remove him, which would leave the nation in limbo for six months or more. Instead of that, we might ask the electors to solve the problem for us.

In such a case, the electors would most likely vote for the vice-president-elect, which is what the Twentieth Amendment requires if the president-elect dies between the election and the inauguration. But nothing in the Constitution requires them to do the same if the president-elect is facing a murder charge, so they could pick anyone at all, provided he be a natural-born citizen at least thirty-five years of age and a U.S. resident for at least fourteen years. Consider, then, how tempting it might be to bribe 270 electors in order to win the most important office in the world.

The Framers saw this problem too. They were alive to the possibility of a corrupt Electoral College, and they addressed the issue in three ways. First, Article II, § 1, cl. 2 bans congressmen from sitting as electors. Second, the electors vote "by ballot," meaning by secret ballot, the only place in the Constitution that mandates this method of preserving the independence of voters—and it would be many years before secret ballots became commonplace in popular elections. "Ballot has been called the silent assertor of liberty," said James Wilson. "With equal justness, it may be called the silent assertor of honesty."[19] Third, the electors all meet on the same day but in their separate states, which the Framers thought would eliminate the possibility of a corrupt bargain among them. "How can cabal and intrigue extend or combine their influence at the same time, in many different places, separated by one another by the distances of hundreds or thousands of miles?" asked Wilson.[20] Physical distance is obviously less of an impediment to corrupt bargaining in an age of instant messages, but in their day the Framers thought it would do the trick.

On the question of the president's term of office, the Framers, surprisingly, took seriously the idea of a lifetime appointment of a president selected by Congress rather than elected by the people.

That would have made the presidency what Mason called an "elective monarchy."[21] When Hamilton proposed this idea on June 18, he felt himself so marginalized that he left town. Nevertheless, it's what Madison supported on July 17.

Twenty years later, when Madison edited his notes of the convention, he felt a need to explain away a vote for what his republican friends would have seen as monarchism. The proposal for a lifetime appointment had been made by a naïve friend of his, Madison recollected, and he didn't want to embarrass the friend by rejecting his idea. As for his own aims, Madison really didn't want a lifetime appointment for the president; the proposal was a strategic one, he wrote, with the real goal being term limits. Supporting a lifetime appointment was his way of telling the delegates what would be needed *without* term limits and with a president appointed by Congress, because the president could then make corrupt bargains with Congress in order to keep getting reappointed.[22]

That might sound like an argument for a popular election of the president, so why had Madison earlier in the day opposed Morris's proposal for just that? The simplest explanation is that Madison had not put it all together. He had not realized, as Morris had, that a popularly elected president would draw power from the states to the national government, which was something that Madison favored. Moreover, a lifetime appointment of the president would not have seemed a foolish idea to those who, like Madison, had a fear of democracy. When the motion was put to the delegates, in fact, it was supported by Madison's Virginia, Morris's Pennsylvania, Dickinson's Delaware, and New Jersey, while six states opposed it.[23] In the end, the Framers rejected both a lifetime appointment and a limit on the number of terms a president could serve. It was only in 1951 that the Twenty-second Amendment set a limit of two terms.

Impeachment

What if a president proved to be unfit before his term ended? If America was to be a virtuous republic, the legislature would need the power to remove a corrupt president from office. The Framers would have known that a British monarch could, technically, be removed. Under the British constitution, the monarchy was hereditary but defeasible: as it was hereditary it would ordinarily descend from parents to children; but as it was defeasible the line of succession could be broken by an act of Parliament. An act of Parliament, however, required the king's assent to be lawful, so this was an empty power. In the dynastic change of 1689, Parliament had to justify its recognition of the new monarchs by invoking the legal fiction that James II had voluntarily surrendered his crown—just ahead of an invading army. With that precedent before them, the Framers wanted to give Congress the power to impeach and remove a president without his consent.

As for what would constitute grounds for removal, two possibilities presented themselves. The first was for "maladministration," a term taken from Mason's 1776 Virginia Constitution. This was broad enough to cover any act to which Congress objected, and it would have been equivalent to a vote of no confidence in a modern parliamentary system. The delegates unanimously agreed to this on June 2.[24] Then the Committee on Unfinished Parts, in its September 4 report, substituted a narrower standard specifying treason or bribery. Mason tried to reintroduce maladministration as grounds for removal, but backed down in the face of objections from Madison and Morris, who as nationalists wanted a strong presidency. At Mason's suggestion, the Framers then adopted the explicit anticorruption standard of "Treason, Bribery, or other high Crimes and Misdemeanors" in Article II, § 4 of the Constitution.[25]

The meaning of those words has been much debated, particularly during the impeachment of Andrew Johnson and more recently during the Nixon and Clinton presidencies. In a practical sense, the words might mean whatever Congress says they mean, since there is no appeal from an impeachment and removal. Nevertheless, what the Framers had in mind was something narrower than that, something different from a no-confidence motion in Parliament. Impeachment was designed specifically to punish presidential corruption.

Once again, it is impossible to read the notes of the Framers' deliberations without being struck by how worried they were about corruption in the government, and how much of the Constitution was designed to curb it.

— 8 —

How Did That Work Out?

WITHIN A FEW GENERATIONS, the Framers' vision for a republic of virtue had faded, and by Andrew Jackson's time, American politics had begun to resemble Sir Robert Walpole's patronage machine. At nearly the same time, the British reformed their system of government and put paid to Hume's balanced British constitution and its separation of powers. In its place was the "efficient secret" that Walter Bagehot identified in *The English Constitution,*[1] as the House of Commons became all-powerful and the crown prerogative was transferred from kings to prime ministers. Such corruption as existed was exposed to sunlight in the debates during the Prime Minister's Questions in the Commons. The two countries had traded places, with corruption finding a comfortable home in America's presidential system.

Interest-group lobbying is present in both democracies and dictatorships, in presidential and parliamentary governments. What the United States Constitution has given us, however, is a form of government that is particularly susceptible to corruption, in ways the Framers could not have imagined. First, the separation of powers created a novel form of corruption in which congressional leaders wastefully earmark moneys for their local districts. Second, technological change and the rise of democracy broke down the election processes that were expected to filter out ignoble politicians. Finally, the concentration of power in the executive branch has increased the possibility of corruption at the highest level.

Minoritarian Misbehavior

Madison, as we saw, wanted a strong federal government because he believed that majorities would be less able to oppress minorities in a large, "extended" state. *Majoritarian misbehavior*, whether racial or religious, would be seen more at the state level, he thought. Yet bigness gives rise to the opposite problem: *minoritarian misbehavior*. This happens when legislators favor their own districts at the expense of the majority of Americans, as they did in their indecent scramble for special treatment in passing Obamacare, and we're more likely to see this behavior in an "extended" republic. It has given us "the work of intrigue, of cabal, and of faction," in Gouverneur Morris's words—the corrupt bargains by which congressmen seek to benefit their districts at a cost to the country as a whole.

We all hate Congress, pollsters tell us, but we love our individual congressman. We love his ability to bring home the bacon, even if we recognize the corruption in the system that permits him to do so. Corrupt and wasteful though it may be, the system continues because the costs are spread out among all American taxpayers while the benefits are concentrated on the residents of the congressman's own state or district, who have the power to re-elect him. The cost won't be much noticed, but the benefits will. And it's harder to get the dispersed, nationwide group to organize against the smaller, concentrated group. The structure of government therefore tends to shift wealth from dispersed losers to concentrated winners.[2] It's the same collective-action problem that explains why the small sugar lobby can get away with imposing wasteful costs on dispersed American sugar consumers.

The most glaring examples of minoritarian misbehavior are the budget items that directly or indirectly specify the recipient, that are directed to a particular district and that circumvent the otherwise applicable merit-based or competitive allocation processes. These are the *earmarks* that gave us the pork in Obamacare and the fifty-odd Robert Byrd Centers for This or That in West Virginia. Those who defend earmarks are apt to note that they empower Congress as against the executive branch, which would otherwise decide how the funds are to be spent. They also point out that earmarks account for only a small percentage of the federal budget, and grease the wheels to get things done. Nevertheless, it's a form of corruption much less evident in parliamentary regimes.

The Tea Party Congress of 2011 reined them in, but earmarks are still there, and efforts to measure them won't include the artfully opaque provisions that benefit a particular local community. For example, the lobbyist Jack Abramoff protected his client's Indian casino by getting an obscure clause added to the Help America Vote Act of 2002, an anodyne reform measure. The clause reads: "Public Law 100-89 is amended by striking section 207 (101 Stat. 668, 672)."[3] Even the committee chairman didn't know what that meant. Nor would an earmarks ban catch the horse-trading whereby Congressman Smith proposes to allocate funds in Congressman Jones's district in return for Congressman Jones's allocating funds in Congressman Smith's district. We might try to curb this practice, but reform efforts will always spark a race between reformers on the one hand and lobbyists and individual congressmen on the other, a race in which one side keeps trying new measures to constrain corruption while the other side keeps looking for ways to sidestep the new laws. It's what the Red Queen said in *Alice in Wonderland*: "Here we must run as fast as we can, just to stay in place. And if you wish to go anywhere you must run twice as fast as that."

Madison argued that we'd see fewer interest groups and less minoritarian misbehavior in an extended republic. That may have been true in 1787, given the limits of transportation and communication at the time, but it's flat-out wrong today. The theory amounts to a prediction that we'd see more lobbyists at the state level than at the federal level, but that's obviously not the case, and a comparison of costs and benefits explains why. Given today's technology, the costs of organizing a group at the national level aren't much greater than they are at the state level, and the benefits of countrywide rules vastly exceed those restricted to a single state. There's more bang for your lobbyist buck if you legislate for the entire country, not just for Rhode Island. And the bigger the country, the less noticed are the costs of an earmark for one state.

If we could, we'd write a contract to ban this, but we're already bound by a contract that fosters it: the Constitution. Minoritarian misbehavior, is worsened with a presidential system, with its separation of powers, in which people are asked to vote separately for the president and for their individual congressmen. One result is bifurcated political parties, divided into national and local levels, which makes the national parties weaker than the more unified parties in parliamentary systems.[4] In America, a Robert Byrd might get elected again and again by West Virginia voters who value the federal moneys he wastefully brings to the state. By contrast, a parliamentary party will generally require broad, countrywide support to be elected, and will therefore have a greater incentive to acquire a reputation for putting the common, national good ahead of corrupt local interests. Robert Byrds are not to be found in Westminster or Ottawa, whose parliaments more closely resemble the idealized assembly described by Edmund Burke in his "Speech to the Electors of Bristol," an assembly "of *one* nation, with *one* interest, that of the whole; where, not local purposes, not local prejudices, ought to guide, but the general good, resulting from the general reason of the whole."

Then too, a parliamentary government can choose when to go to the people, within a five-year window from the last election, and the writs for a new election are generally dropped only two months out. That gives relatively little time for political action committees (PACs) to gear up. By contrast, the dates for American elections are set in stone, and PACs will know just how to plan their activities to best effect. That's why PACs are stronger in presidential regimes than in parliamentary countries, while parties are weaker.[5]

The greater strength of parties in parliamentary systems leads to greater responsibility, while the separation of powers, with its weaker political parties, breeds finger-pointing and irresponsibility. If legislation isn't passed when the different branches of the government are in different hands, who's to blame? In the tortuous 2011 negotiations over the debt ceiling, when Republicans held the House and Democrats the presidency and the Senate, each side said the other was responsible for the holdup. But if everyone is responsible, then no one is responsible. We wouldn't see that in a parliamentary regime, where a unitary government is in charge and will be blamed if things don't get done. When there's a scandal we'll know better whose fault it is, and when reforms are needed we'll understand who is charged with enacting them. These differences between the two kinds of systems help explain my findings in Appendix I that presidential regimes are more corrupt than parliamentary ones.

The Democratic Presidency

Our government initially resembled a parliamentary regime, with a president selected by the House of Representatives or by electors exercising their own discretion. Within a few decades, the revolution in transportation and communication had begun to transform the government into our modern presidential system, with voters across the country electing the president. This is something that few of the Framers would have expected. They thought the barriers of distance would in most cases prevent a national candidate for the presidency from emerging, so the House of Representatives would choose from among the top candidates. That's what happens under Article II when no candidate gets a majority of votes in the Electoral College, and George Mason thought it would occur 95 percent of the time.[6]

That was a plausible expectation in 1787, when it took George Washington five days in his new carriage to cover the 151 miles from Philadelphia's Independence Hall back home to Mount Vernon at the end of the Constitutional Convention.[7] (He might have done better on a Roman road two thousand years earlier, when a carriage could travel as much as forty miles a day.)[8] Traveling times would shorten somewhat with the building of turnpikes, but would not greatly change until the arrival of steamboats and railways many years later.[9] News traveled no more quickly in 1787 than Washington's carriage.

We might have assumed that *The Federalist Papers*, printed in New York between October 1787 and the following April, greatly influenced the ratification debates, but they were little read in other states.[10] Samuel Morse's telegraph was more than fifty years in the future, and until then the means of communication had changed little in millennia.

Given the limits of eighteenth-century technology, the Framers expected that each section of the country would present its particular candidate, each of whom would be unknown in other parts of the country, so none would receive a majority of the electoral votes. The election of 1824 followed this pattern, with four sectional candidates, none of whom secured a majority of votes in the Electoral College. Andrew Jackson won 41 percent of the popular vote and 38 percent of the electors, more than any of the other candidates—William Crawford, Henry Clay, and John Quincy Adams—but not enough to make him president. The decision went to the House of Representatives, and Clay then threw the support of his western states behind Adams, who already had New York and the New England states.

When President Adams appointed "Henry of the West" as his secretary of state, this was widely thought to be a payoff for Clay's support in the election. Jackson supporters called it the "Corrupt Bargain," since the winner of the popular vote had lost the election. It wouldn't seem corrupt to people in parliamentary systems, where parties not infrequently win the most seats without winning the most votes. And it wouldn't have seemed corrupt to the Framers, who gave us the Article II method of choosing a president. It would also have been expected that Clay and his supporters would prefer Adams to Jackson.[11] Clay and Jackson had quarreled over the latter's lawless conquest of Florida, and the two men loathed each other.[12] Jackson would not support Clay's "American System" of roads and canals, as Adams did. Nor was there anything remarkable in the choice of Clay as secretary of state. He was a skilled diplomat who had worked with Adams to negotiate the Treaty of Ghent that ended the War of 1812, and was eminently qualified for the office.

It would be Jackson's administration, in fact, that began the spoils system to bestow government positions on political supporters.[13] If we could ask the Framers what was the point of filtration in elections, they might tell us that it was to exclude fantastic brawlers like Jackson from office. After 1824, however, filtration was little heard of, washed away by the tide of democracy. In 1828, Jackson won a majority of both popular and electoral votes, running as the democratic candidate of the people against the Corrupt Bargain.

Democracy transformed the Framers' Constitution and eliminated the last vestiges of filtration. Presidential electors lost their independence and were themselves increasingly elected by the people rather than appointed by state legislatures. By 1812, half the states held popular elections for the electors, and three-quarters did so in 1824. By 1860, only South Carolina continued to appoint its electors through a vote in the state legislature.

Democracy had been a dirty word at the Philadelphia Convention, and the Framers' Constitution was designed to guard against it. In the age of Andrew Jackson, however, it was the barriers to democracy that were seen as illegitimate, and even Madison had to adapt to the times. At Philadelphia in 1787 he had supported restrictive property qualifications for voting, but by the time of the Virginia Constitutional Convention of 1829 he conceded that the country had changed and his state needed to change along with it.[14]

Where filtration survives as a cure for corruption is in British-style parliamentary regimes. Prime ministers are chosen by their caucus, which tends to exclude unworthy candidates. The imperious leader who might flourish as a president, and who might be willing to cut corners, would fare poorly in a parliament, where his pretentions are more easily mocked and his shortcomings more clearly on view.

Power and Corruption

The delegates to the Philadelphia Convention must have returned home thinking they'd given the country a congressional form of government, in which Congress would generally pick the president. They believed that governing meant legislating—enacting laws that the president would enforce as Congress's faithful agent. Like Montesquieu, they thought the executive power would mostly be confined to war, and defensive war at that. In the eighteenth century there was no vast regulatory state to administer, and the very smallness of the government made the executive largely a creature of Congress.

The Framers didn't anticipate that presidents would come to enjoy George III's royal prerogative, the kingly discretion to adopt rules by personal decree. The rise of democracy and a popular election of the president first made the executive branch coequal to the legislature, and then allowed it to emerge as the modern presidency—commanding, decisive, and possessing all the authority of the only person elected by the nation at large. It is remarkable how little the fetters designed by the Framers have constrained the executive branch, and how readily it has mimicked the monarchy they found so objectionable.

For example, the presidency has acquired something like a royal power of patronage. There are no peerages or knighthoods to hand out, but there are more than enough honorific awards and offices, such as the ambassadorships given to campaign bundlers. Over four thousand federal workers hold their jobs as political appointees, virtually all of whom lose their jobs when a different party wins the White House. While Senate confirmation is required for cabinet members, ambassadors, and other officials, there is a convention that a president is entitled to pick whomever he wants,[15] and it is very rare that the Senate refuses to confirm a nominee, even when the president is of a different party. (In today's hyperpartisan politics, however, one is bound to wonder whether the tradition of deference to the president is apt to continue.)

It's easy to see why the executive branch dominates American federal politics. First, the president is not just the chief executive but also the head of state, the symbol of the country, the person who gives his name to the period in which he presides. If there is a national tragedy, it requires a healing speech from the president. If there is an especially meritorious citizen, he deserves a presidential medal.

Second, the president has a natural advantage over Congress, for he more plausibly represents all Americans than does a congressman elected in a particular district or state, or a Speaker of the House from someplace in Ohio or Wisconsin you never heard of. While Congress is a cacophony of confused, little voices, the president is a trumpet speaking over them all with a single message. In a contest between the president and a hydra-headed Congress, the advantage always lies with the president. That's something Jean-Jacques Rousseau understood. As the number of legislators increases, said Rousseau, the influence of each one weakens until they become ineffectual as a group, and a strong executive will emerge to fill the void. That's why he believed that larger states, requiring more legislators, are less free than smaller ones.[16] Perhaps the United States is simply too darned big.

Third, presidents also have better incentives than congressmen. Since he is elected by the entire country, the president has little incentive to favor only one part of it, in contrast with members of Congress, who can be expected to promote pork-barrel projects for their own region. The president's private incentives may thus supply what virtue might otherwise have provided, as Gibbon understood when he praised the efficient policies of Septimus Severus.

> The true interest of an absolute monarch generally coincides with that of his people . . . and were he totally devoid of virtue, prudence might supply its place. . . . Severus considered the Roman empire as his property, and had no sooner secured the possession, then he bestowed his care on the cultivation and improvement of so valuable an acquisition.[17]

Fourth, when Congress is gridlocked by partisan or regional divisions, the president can act in the name of the whole country. "If Congress won't act, I will," Obama told us. A president may complain about legislative gridlock while secretly regarding it as his friend, since it gives him an excuse to rule by decree. If the constitution of separated powers was designed to prevent the accumulation of power in a single person, as Madison argued it would, it's been a complete failure. On the contrary, it has served to increase executive powers.

Lastly, the devices with which Congress was supposed to monitor the president have proved ineffective. Presidents control the flow of information from the agencies of government, and when challenged they can assert a doctrine of executive privilege to deny oversight powers to Congress. Then when congressional committees hold hearings to get to the bottom of a scandal, they're condemned for indulging in partisan fishing expeditions. The president can sit on scandals like the partisan abuses by the IRS until they become old news and fade away.[18]

Modern presidents are relatively immunized from accountability in comparison with prime ministers who must face a daily grilling by the opposition in Parliament. The level of scrutiny is far higher than in a presidential regime, where the president's public statements tend to be tightly scripted and controlled. A parliament can also send a prime minister packing with a simple vote of no confidence.

The Framers would be surprised to learn that the impeachment power they gave to Congress is now virtually a dead letter, thanks to a procedural amendment so obscure they may not even have noticed it. Through most of the convention it had been contemplated that the Senate could remove the president by a simple majority vote after an impeachment in the House of Representatives. Then the Committee on Unfinished Parts changed the threshold to a two-thirds vote in the Senate, and the amendment was never debated by the delegates in the two remaining weeks of the convention. There was much to digest in the committee's report, and the delegates were anxious to go home, so very possibly the change to the impeachment rule simply went unnoticed. But it would be enormously consequential. Members of Congress tend to protect a president of their own party, and only once has it happened that the president was of one party while a majority of the House and two-thirds of the Senate were in the hands of the other party (if one counts Andrew Johnson as a Democrat). Had the simple-majority standard been retained, the presidency would have been much weakened. Bill Clinton might have been removed from office for obstruction of justice, as the Senate vote was 50-50. That would have placed Vice President Al Gore in the embarrassing position of casting the tie-breaking vote—and wouldn't that have been fun to watch?

Theoretically, a presidential government offers an advantage over a parliamentary one in that it might be easier to turf out a corrupt president who was elected by voters across the country than a prime minister who was elected only in one riding.[19] In addition, the separation of powers gives voters the opportunity to hold politicians in different branches of government to account independently. If a congressman proves to be corrupt while the president does not, we can re-elect the latter and ditch the former.[20]

Each system has its advantages, but which is more effective against corruption is an empirical question. As we have seen, Transparency International provides a widely respected index of corruption in governments around the world, and Appendix A uses that data to present evidence of more corruption in presidential as compared with parliamentary governments. Modern presidents enjoy more real power than prime ministers, almost absolute power; and such power almost corrupts absolutely, to paraphrase Lord Acton.

A Grim Logic

When two wrestlers step into the ring, we expect only one to walk out victorious. That's not supposed to happen between the branches of government under the separation of powers, but it does. A strong presidential form of government has largely replaced one of shared power with coequal executive and legislative branches.

An equipoise of power, balanced from here to eternity, is as unnatural as Oliver Wendell Holmes Sr.'s "logical" one-hoss shay in "The Deacon's Masterpiece." Written in 1858, with the country and the Constitution collapsing around him, Holmes's doggerel likened the separation of powers to a deacon's small carriage or chaise ("shay").

Now in building of chaises, I tell you what,
There is always somewhere a weakest spot,—
In hub, tire, fellow, in spring or thill,
In panel, or crossbar, or floor, or sill.

If a shay breaks down, it's because one part goes first.

> And that's the reason, beyond a doubt
> A shay breaks down, but doesn't wear out.

The trick, then, is to make every piece as strong as every other part. And that's what the deacon did, with a shay "that was built in such a logical way, it lasted one hundred years to the day." But then, exactly one hundred years later, every part wore out at the same time, and the new deacon found himself sitting on a pile of sawdust.

> You see, of course, if you're not a dunce,
> How it went to pieces all at once,—
> All at once and nothing first,—
> Just as bubbles do when they burst.
> End of the wonderful one-hoss shay
> Logic is logic. That's all I say.

Your carriage may seem to be rolling along in perfect balance, but it won't keep doing so forever. So much for logical plans for government.

While the separation of powers might have seemed logical to the Framers, it was natural that power would tend over time to become concentrated in one branch. That's what has happened in Britain and other parliamentary countries, where the House of Commons became everything, the monarch and the House of Lords nothing. It's also what has happened in presidential regimes, where power typically accumulates in a president who dominates the legislature. In America, this brought us Obama's "I have a pen and a phone" approach to governance. Conservatives might wish for a return to an older constitution of balanced powers, but is that inconsistent with power's grim logic?

But then America has always been exceptional, and the election of a president known to enjoy deal-making encourages one to hope that we'll avoid the fate of other presidential countries. In the end, nothing is inevitable. When Goethe met Napoleon in 1808, the emperor told the poet that the idea of destiny belonged in the dark ages. "There is no destiny," said Napoleon, "only politics."[21]

PART THREE

FEDERALISM

There is no torture like the torture of law.
—Francis Bacon

Federalism and Corruption

FEDERALISM WAS NOT PART of the Framers' original vision for a virtuous republic, as we have seen. It was only the small-state delegates who insisted on retaining the separate identities and governments of their states. Delegates from the larger states of Virginia and Pennsylvania wanted power centralized in the federal government, which they hoped would curb the misbehavior of corrupt state governments. When the large state delegates realized that their plans had been frustrated by the Connecticut Compromise, in which all the states would have equal representation in the Senate, several of them argued for a walkout from the convention.

Those who wanted a walkout very likely included Madison, who had a talent for sowing discord at the convention. He strove to prove himself the smartest person in the room, dug in his heels when criticized, and left Philadelphia with all his pet ideas rejected. One of these was the federal veto power, under which the national government could have disallowed state laws. The delegates voted it down again and again,[1] and even Madison's nationalist allies found it politic to chuck the idea.[2] But Madison had a point, for he recognized the costliness of an excessive delegation of powers to the states.

That was certainly a problem when America was governed under the Articles of Confederation, which had created a "firm league of friendship" among sovereign, free and independent states, with the thinnest of central governments. Congress could not levy taxes directly on the people, but only ask the states to honor requisitions of funds. If the states refused or were tardy in complying with a requisition, Congress could not compel them to pay up.

States had devalued their own currencies and had run up massive deficits. They had treated creditors shabbily, so it was difficult to raise funds for investment projects and the country was in a depression.

States had welched on their obligation to fund the national government during the Revolutionary War, failing to respond to the requisitions by Congress, and had refused to honor Loyalist claims for debts owed to them under the Treaty of Paris (1783). They had also begun to poach on each other by erecting barriers to interstate commerce, as New York did with tariffs on goods shipped between New Jersey and Connecticut. It all added up to states exploiting each other, failing in their responsibilities to each other and to the national government, and this was a form of corruption.

This is why Madison thought a federal veto over state laws was "absolutely necessary to a perfect system."

> Experience has evinced a constant tendency in the States to encroach on the federal authority; to violate national Treaties, to infringe the rights & interests of each other. . . . A negative was the mildest expedient that could be devised for preventing these mischiefs.[3]

What Madison wanted was nothing less than the disallowance power that the British Board of Trade had employed to strike down colonial laws before the revolution. In particular, the British objected to the insolvency laws that many of the American colonies had enacted, which permitted debtors to wipe out their debts as they can today in a federal Chapter 7 bankruptcy discharge. An insolvency state could then use the prospect of a debt discharge to lure residents away from states that lacked an insolvency law. The insolvency state would get the benefit of a new resident, while the cost of the discharge would be borne by creditors in the exit state, and that's a form of interstate exploitation.[4]

Madison was right to believe that an excessively decentralized government could result in one state burdening another. But he was wrong to suppose that solving this problem required giving a disallowance power to the federal government, and he lost that point. Nevertheless, the delegates didn't want to leave things as they were. What they wanted, and got, was federalism split down the middle. Truly national objects, such as the war power and a federal tax power, were consigned to the national government so as to avoid free riding, and the commerce power was taken from the states so as to avoid interstate tariff barriers.[5] All of this was worked out by a five-member Committee of Detail (from which Madison was excluded), and the committee's report elicited little by way of debate.

Bigness and Badness

What had eluded Madison when he aimed to establish a federal veto power was a foundational principle of public choice economics: the geographic scope of an issue should determine the level of government to which it is assigned in a federal system.[6] If the matter is confined to the borders of a single state, such as local police powers, then the state should be seized of the issue and not the federal government. If it extends beyond the borders of a single state or is national in scope, such as the postal service and national defense, it should be the responsibility of the federal government. James Wilson, who was a member of the Committee of Detail, expressed the idea succinctly at the Pennsylvania ratifying convention: "The states should resign to the national government that part, and that part only, of their political liberty, which, placed in that government, will produce more good to the whole, than if it remained in the several states."[7]

The list of powers assigned to Congress under the Constitution was intended not to deprive states of the ability to determine policy within their own borders, but to curb interstate exploitation by limiting the power of the states to legislate over national or interstate matters. Only Congress could maintain an army and navy, pass immigration laws, or regulate commerce with foreign countries.[8] Subsequently, the Supreme Court held that the national commerce power, by inference, barred explicit interstate trade barriers of the kind the states had imposed upon each other under the Articles of Confederation.[9] What was not delegated by the Constitution to the federal government was left to the states or to the people under the Tenth Amendment.

Madison's national veto would have represented an improvement over the decentralized government established by the Articles of

Confederation, but the division of power between the federal government and the states was better still. Had the states been nothing and the federal government everything, we'd have seen more corruption. The corrupt official who might have been voted out of office in a state or local election could more easily remain in place if appointed by a distant national government with little knowledge of local affairs.

There's a second reason why we'd expect to see more corruption when all power vests in the national government. As noted earlier, when the costs of wasteful laws are dispersed across the whole country, they're hard to recognize and harder still to oppose. As for the interest groups that sponsor those laws, the payoff is so much greater when the scope is countrywide. Setting sugar prices across the United States is going to bring the industry vastly more money than setting the price for Rhode Island alone.

Edward Gibbon identified another cost of bigness in *The Decline and Fall of the Roman Empire*, where he observed that the sheer size of the empire magnified the harm that a bad emperor could do. Not all the Caesars were bad rulers, he said, for "if a man were called to fix the period in the history of the world, during which the condition of the human race was most happy and prosperous," it would be Rome during the reign of the Antonines, from Nerva in 96 AD to the death of Marcus Aurelius eighty-four years later.[10] Trade flourished, the empire was at peace and its enemies were subdued. It required luck to have a succession of good emperors, however, and for all his virtues Marcus permitted his vicious son Commodus (familiar to those who have seen the movie *Gladiator*) to succeed him. And from bad emperors there was little escape, for as Gibbon noted, "The empire of the Romans filled the world, and when that empire fell into the hands of a single person, the world became a safe and dreary prison for his enemies."[11]

The various European countries of Gibbon's own time offered an instructive contrast. If a tyrant arose in one country, the objects of his displeasure could find refuge in another, as Voltaire had done by moving around among France, England, and Switzerland. One ruler would be restrained by the example of his more liberal neighbors, and

Gibbon saw this as "productive of the most beneficial consequences to the liberty of mankind."

Exit rights promote honest and good government, as Frederick Jackson Turner recognized in his Frontier Thesis. In nineteenth-century America, states competed for residents by liberalizing their laws, and eastern states that were losing people to the West through migration had to liberalize in order to keep up.[12] If newer states extended the franchise to all white male voters, Virginia was compelled to follow suit. Similarly, the impetus to gender equality came from the frontier. When Wyoming (the "Equality State") discovered it had too few women, it offered them the right to vote in order to tempt the New England schoolmarm to move west. Jurisdictional competition of this kind promoted freedom and democracy, since people tended to leave illiberal and antidemocratic states for the freer air of the West. The competition among states also serves to keep them honest, as people will want to flee from corrupt states to more honest ones.[13] It's harder to escape corruption and oppressive laws when they come from the central government.

Small-is-beautiful arguments would have seemed pointless in 1789, when the states were so powerful and the fledgling federal government so puny. At that point, the federal government consisted only of the Departments of State, Treasury, and War, plus the attorney general. The Post Office was permanently established in 1794, and for most of the next century it would be the chief source of political patronage. Federal spending was miniscule by modern standards. In the republic's early years, the federal government spent only about $30 per person annually (in 2000 dollars). By 1910, this sum had grown only to $129.[14] But then came the rise of the regulatory state, beginning with Woodrow Wilson and especially with Franklin Roosevelt and Lyndon Johnson. Today, the federal government spends $11,000 per person.[15]

Constitutional changes also contributed to the growing power of the federal government. The Seventeenth Amendment, ratified in 1913, took power from the states by requiring that all senators be popularly elected, and no longer appointed by state legislatures. The Supreme Court also transferred power to Washington by holding that any private economic activity could be seen as falling under the rubric of interstate commerce and thereby under the purview of the federal government. In *Wickard v. Filburn* (1942),[16] the Court upheld a fine imposed on a farmer who grew more grain than he was permitted under federal law, when all he wanted to do with the excess grain was feed it to his own animals. The feed stayed on his farm, but the Court nevertheless held that it affected interstate commerce because the farmer would otherwise have been obliged to go to the market for the feed, which might have come from out of state. Further, Washington has assumed the ability to influence state policies through the federal "spending power," under which Congress is permitted to provide for the general welfare of the United States.[17] By conditioning federal moneys on compliance with the earmarks attached to the grant, Washington is able to shape state spending on education, roads, health care and a host of purely local matters.[18]

In sum, power has come to be centralized in Washington, and we shouldn't be surprised if this concentration of power has brought more corruption. We've made it harder to escape from unjust and corrupt laws by moving from one place to another, and we've given interest groups a greater incentive to promote wasteful countrywide laws.

Smallness and Badness

While the expansion of the federal government's power helps explain American corruption, there is one particular area where a transfer of power from the states to the federal government would reduce corruption. Today, state courts are permitted to decide on cases in which the plaintiffs and defendants are from different states, or even from different countries, and the potential for favoritism toward in-state parties is great. An object lesson in how state courts tarnish our reputation for integrity is provided by a 1995 Mississippi decision on a contract dispute between two competitors in the funeral insurance industry. One was a Mississippi company, the other Canadian, but the dynamics of the case were not unlike those where one party is from a different state within the United States.

The defendant was the Loewen Group from Canada, the second largest funeral home company in North America, owned by Ray Loewen. In 1991, Loewen had entered into an agreement with Jerry O'Keefe, who operated a small company on the Gulf Coast of Mississippi, giving O'Keefe the exclusive right to sell funeral insurance in his area. Subsequently, however, Loewen sold funeral insurance through another Mississippi company, in an apparent breach of O'Keefe's exclusive license, and O'Keefe sued Loewen. If Loewen was at fault, the damage to O'Keefe might have amounted to $1 million, or stretching things, perhaps $8 million. But the jury awarded him $100 million in compensatory damages, including $75 million as compensation for emotional distress, which is almost never awarded in contract disputes. O'Keefe had told of stress and sleepless nights, but there was no expert evidence of distress, no physical sign of unusual anxiety, and no indication that O'Keefe had sought medical or psychiatric treatment. On top of the compensatory damages, the jury tossed in $400 million for punitive damages, bringing the total up to $500 million.

The damages ballooned up because of the outrageous conduct of O'Keefe's lawyer, which the judge, James E. Graves, shamefully did nothing to police. According to a judicial panel that reviewed the case under the auspices of the North American Free Trade Agreement (NAFTA), Judge Graves failed in his duty to take control of the trial, instead permitting O'Keefe's lawyer to make irrelevant, persistent and highly prejudicial appeals to xenophobic, racial and class prejudices.[19] O'Keefe was portrayed as "a fighter for his country" against the Japanese, and the Loewen Group as a ruthless foreign predator that had come to town like gangbusters, backed by Asian money, which—who knows?—might have come from Japanese banks.

The NAFTA panel included a member of the British House of Lords and a former chief judge of the Australian High Court, who were evidently surprised at what must have seemed like a Third World kangaroo court. O'Keefe was "one of your own," his lawyer told the jury. Ray Loewen wasn't. He didn't spend time in Mississippi. "He's not here today. Do you think that every person should be responsible and should step up to the plate and face their own actions? Let me see a show of hands if you feel that everybody in America should have the responsibility to do that."

As a character witness for his clients, the plaintiff's lawyer brought in Mike Espy, the former secretary of agriculture, who spoke of his experience protecting Americans from predatory Canadian wheat farmers who exported low-priced wheat into the American market and then, having beaten the competition and secured a market, jacked up the price. The lawsuit, the jury was told, was really all about defending America against foreigners. O'Keefe had fought for his country, "and [Loewen is] going to put him down for being American." As jury members, "your service on this case is higher than any honor that a citizen of this country can have, short of going to war and dying for your country."

The "Blame Canada" tactic belonged in a *South Park* comedy, but it seems to have worked. Just in case it didn't, O'Keefe's lawyer also appealed to racial and class biases before a predominantly African American jury, inviting them to stick it to the man. In summation, O'Keefe's lawyer told the jury:

> You know your job as jurors gives you a lot of power. You have the power to bring major corporations to their knees when they are wrong. . . . Ray [Loewen] comes down here, he's got his yacht up there, he can go to cocktail parties and all that, but do you know how he's financing that? By 80 and 90 year old people who go to get to a funeral, who go to pay their life savings . . . , and it doesn't mean anything to him. Now, they've got to be stopped. . . . Do it, stop them so in years to come anybody should mention your service for some 50 odd days on this trial, you can say "Yes, I was there," and you can talk proud about it. . . . You've got to put your foot down, and you may never get this chance again. And you're not just helping the people of Mississippi but you're helping poor people, grieving families everywhere. I urge you to put your foot down. Don't let them get away with it.

Loewen moved to appeal the damages award, but was met with a Mississippi procedural rule that would have first required the company to post a "supersedeas" bond of $625 million with the court. Loewen couldn't afford to do this and appealed the bond requirement, which courts could waive "for good cause." But the trial judge and the Mississippi Supreme Court refused to lower the amount. With its back to the wall, Loewen was forced to settle the claim for $130 million.

American companies aren't very happy when Russian courts play the same tricks on them. That's what we've come to expect from the Russians, but then we'd like to think we're better than that and will want our courts to treat foreign businesses fairly. No one wants to do business with a legal kleptocracy, and that's why the NAFTA treaty permits aggrieved Canadian firms to seek redress against biased American judicial decisions, and vice versa. The treaty forbids discrimination against foreign investors, and guarantees them fair and equitable treatment, and that's what Loewen didn't get from Judge Graves and the wayward Mississippi courts.

The NAFTA tribunal concluded that Judge Graves was guilty of a gross failure to conduct the trial in a fair manner. His judgment was improper and discreditable, and it could not be squared with the minimal requirements of international law. "By any standard of measurement, the trial . . . was a disgrace," said the court. Nevertheless, the NAFTA tribunal washed its hands of the matter on technical grounds. Before the United States could be found in breach of its treaty duties, Loewen had to show that it had exhausted all its remedies under American law, and this it had not done since it had failed to seek relief in U.S. federal courts.

The litigation took the Loewen Group into bankruptcy reorganization, and Ray Loewen resigned as CEO and sold his shares in the company. Mike Espy, who had testified as a character witness for O'Keefe, had to stand trial for accepting illegal gifts when he was the secretary of agriculture. He was acquitted, but Tyson Foods pleaded guilty to a charge of making illegal gifts to him at a time when the company was under investigation by the Department of Agriculture. The one person who did well, apart from O'Keefe and his lawyers, was the judge, James Graves, whom Obama appointed to the Fifth Circuit Court of Appeals.

Judge Graves ruled unfairly, though he didn't take a bribe. The NAFTA panel thought him incompetent at best, but there was a suggestion of a deeper problem, a systemic bias against foreign litigants. It's not that Graves hated Canadians, but that he was a willing participant in a corrupt system of justice whose purpose was to shift resources from out-of-state to in-state parties. It's the kind of minoritarian misbehavior we saw in Chapter 8, with Judge Graves cast as a Robert Byrd in judicial robes.

— 10 —

The Mississippi Story

MISSISSIPPI COURTS have a long history of favoring locals and sticking it to people from out of state. Think of it as judicial pollution. When an industrial operation releases sludge into a river, it's going to have a pretty ugly and unhealthy river next door. That's going to impose a cost on the business, but in doing its cost-benefit analysis it won't take account of the people downstream who will now be living with a polluted river. That's why they'll be given a right to take the polluter to court. Pollution becomes a federal matter when one state's pollution finds its way into the backyards of downstream people in other states. The upstream polluting state won't take adequate care to protect people in the other state who don't vote or pay taxes in the upstream state. Similarly, judges in state courts may be only too happy to favor in-state interests and leave out-of-staters with a big bill to pay. Mississippi shows us how it's done.

Mississippi Burning

When Judge Graves decided *O'Keefe v. Loewen* in 1995, Mississippi was the poorest state in the union, and southern Mississippi, where O'Keefe carried on business, was one of the poorest parts of the state. The case was litigated in Hinds County, where the per capita income is $20,600, less than half that of the United States as a whole. The district isn't the poster child for judicial integrity. One of its circuit court judges, Bobby DeLaughter, was recently released from a federal prison to which he had been sentenced for obstruction of justice for his role in a judicial bribery scandal.

Hinds County isn't very far—less than a hundred miles—from Neshoba County, another monument to Mississippi's judicial localism and the disposition of its state courts to favor local residents over out-of-state parties. It was in Neshoba County that Deputy Sheriff Cecil Price engineered the murders of three civil rights workers in 1964. The murders shocked the nation and spurred the passage of the Civil Rights Act eleven days later, followed by the Voting Rights Act the next year. Yet state authorities did not bring criminal charges against the murderers until forty years later.

On June 21, 1964, Price arrested James Chaney, Andy Goodman and Michael Schwerner on speeding charges and locked them up in the county jail in Philadelphia, Mississippi. Goodman and Schwerner, both white, were civil rights workers from New York; Chaney was black and from Mississippi. Price released the three from jail that evening, but not before organizing a lynch party to capture and kill them before they left the county. President Johnson and Attorney General Robert Kennedy, under the 1948 Lindberg Kidnapping Law, ordered a massive search for the missing civil rights workers, with hundreds of FBI agents and sailors detailed for the task. The bodies were recovered several weeks later, but only after searchers uncovered the remains of eight other missing African Americans. Goodman and Schwerner had each been shot in the heart. Chaney had been savagely beaten and shot three times.

With Mississippi authorities refusing to press murder charges, the federal government took action. Federal criminal law at the time did not provide a remedy for murder, but in December the Department of Justice charged nineteen men with conspiring to deprive the three victims of their civil rights under a Reconstruction-era statute.

A local Mississippi judge subpoenaed the FBI agents investigating the crime to reveal their sources, but the acting attorney general, Nicholas Katzenbach, refused to allow it, thinking the Mississippi court system so corrupt and tainted with racism that the information would be turned over to the murderers and their lawyers.[1] The case went to the Supreme Court, where Thurgood Marshall, the solicitor general, and John Doar, assistant attorney general, successfully argued that the murderers could be prosecuted under federal law.[2]

The case was sent back to be heard by a federal judge in Mississippi. William Cox was no one's idea of a liberal on racial issues, but he agreed to Doar's motion that the jury be drawn statewide since a local Philadelphia jury would never convict the defendants. At the trial in October 1967, Doar explained to the jury why the case was being argued in federal court:

> I am here because your National Government is concerned about your local law enforcement. . . . When local law enforcement officials become involved as participants in violent crime and use their position, power and authority to accomplish this, there is very little to be hoped for, except with assistance from the Federal Government.[3]

In what Doar subsequently described as a turning point in the trial, defense counsel asked a government witness whether Schwerner had tried to get "young male negroes" to sign a pledge to rape a white woman once a week. That provoked a reaction from Judge Cox: "I'm not going to allow a farce to be made of this trial. I don't understand such a question and I don't approve." The judge took the matter very seriously, the jury learned, and it returned with guilty verdicts against seven defendants. Cox sentenced two of them to ten years in prison, the maximum sentence under the statute. Cecil Price got six years.

Remarkably, none of the accused was prosecuted under the Mississippi Criminal Code until 2005, after the voting rights campaign for which the three had died finally bore fruit and a different kind of electorate had cast its ballots. But Mississippi's refusal to pursue the murders in the 1960s wasn't so surprising at the time, and the murderers knew it. That would explain the demeanor of Price and Sheriff Lawrence Rainey at their arraignment in federal court, where they were photographed slouching in their chairs, smirking and joking, stuffing Red Man chewing tobacco into their mouths, the very picture of relaxed self-assurance. The feds couldn't try them for murder, and the locals back in Philadelphia would never turn against them. It was a place where out-of-town reporters were met with sullen contempt and were lucky to emerge with nothing worse than a beating. And it's not as if Goodman and Schwerner hadn't been warned. In an editorial published ten weeks before the murders, Philadelphia's newspaper, the *Neshoba Democrat*, opined that "outsiders who come in here and try to stir up trouble should be dealt with in a manner they won't forget."[4] In his "I Have a Dream" speech, Martin Luther King identified the Magnolia State as the most racist part of the Union, "a state sweltering with the heat of injustice, sweltering with the heat of oppression."

The story of American resistance to segregation is one of individual heroism and courage, but also a story of federal prosecutors such as John Doar and a handful of brave federal judges in the South. These included the "Fifth Circuit Four": the appellate judges Elbert P. Tuttle of Georgia, John Minor Wisdom from New Orleans, John R. Brown of Texas and Richard Rives from Alabama, as well as federal district court trial judges such as Frank Johnson from Montgomery, Alabama and Adrian Duplantier from Lafayette, Louisiana. Through their efforts, and the changes brought about through federal legislation, the civil rights revolution has been so successful that the Supreme Court in 2013 overturned a portion of the 1965 Voting Rights Act on the grounds that it is now unnecessary.[5] The act had banned nine southern states from tinkering with their voting requirements without first getting approval from the U.S. Department of Justice, while northern states were not so fettered. In 1965 it made sense to single out southern states in this way, but the factual basis for doing so is now absent. In 1965, only 6.7 percent of black adults in Mississippi were registered to vote, compared with 69.9 percent of whites. But by 2004, blacks were more likely to be registered than whites, 76.1 to 72.3 percent, as they no longer faced the old discriminatory barriers.

Mississippi Cashes In

Racial attitudes in Mississippi have changed dramatically since the 1960s, but the state's clublike judicial politics have not. This was a phenomenon across the South, though it had its roots in Mississippi, first growing from segregationist soil and eventually shedding the racial agenda for a mercenary one.

In July 1954, two weeks after the Supreme Court's *Brown v. Board of Education* decision, Mississippi conservatives met in Indianola to found the White Citizens Council, an upscale version of the Ku Klux Klan, dedicated to massive resistance against integration. White Citizens Councils soon spread across the South, and the chapter in Philadelphia, Mississippi was formed shortly thereafter. Like the Klan, they would oppose demands for justice by African Americans and "outside agitators" like Goodman and Schwerner who had come from the North to help blacks register to vote.

Mississippi's politicians reflected the views of their constituents—the white ones, anyway. From 1943 to 1978, Mississippi's senior U.S. senator was an ardent segregationist, James ("Big Jim") Eastland. Born eighteen miles down the road from Indianola, Eastland served on the White Citizens Council's board of advisers, and when the three civil rights workers were first reported missing, he told President Johnson that he didn't think they were really dead. "I believe it's a publicity stunt. . . . I don't think there's a damn thing to it." Half an hour later, Eastland called back to report that Governor Paul Johnson Jr. expected the three to turn up. In between the two calls, however, the FBI director, J. Edgar Hoover, had informed the president that Schwerner's burnt-out car had been found. "Okay, now here's the problem, Jim," the president said to Eastland. "Hoover called me one minute ago . . . ." But Eastland persisted: "There's no violence, no friction of any kind."[6] Later, on the floor of the U.S. Senate, Eastland would denounce Martin Luther King as a communist.

Eastland was a Democrat, but the Mississippi Democratic Party was only notionally aligned to the national party. In the 1964 election, the state would deliver 87 percent of its votes to the Republican presidential candidate, Barry Goldwater, who had voted against the 1964 Civil Rights Bill on constitutional grounds. Local politicians soon began the slow process of switching their affiliation to the party of Abraham Lincoln, but Eastland remained a Democrat throughout his career in order to keep his seniority on the Senate Judiciary Committee, which he chaired from 1956 to 1978. He was also the chief figure in the state's political machine, which survives to this day, twenty years after his death. His organization was spread throughout the state, from legislators and judges down to local county officials, but was invisible to outside observers and prying northern reporters. As Curtis Wilkie described it,

> Eastland's men gathered over coffee at local cafés to consider the merits of various candidates rather than holding regular meetings at political clubhouses. But ultimately they took their cues from Eastland, and following the Sphinx-like characteristics of the senator, who rarely made public speeches, they preferred to carry out their work in private.[7]

The machine evolved with the times, of course. The voting rights revolution transformed Mississippi politics and changed its language. Eastland was not slow to adapt. "When [the blacks] get the vote," he said, "I won't be talking this way anymore."[8] Like other southern politicians, including George Wallace and Strom Thurmond, he soon began to court black voters as assiduously as white ones. But the establishment remained in place, even under different party labels, and Senator Trent Lott, a Republican, became a senior leader of the old Eastland machine.

In the beginning, the machine was founded upon a bedrock of shared racial prejudices, but it swiftly became a self-serving financial industry.[9] In southern Mississippi, for example, P. L. Blake ("Mr. Fixer") traded on his friendship with Eastland to obtain federal government financing for an agricultural empire. Born in a tarpaper shack, Blake dug himself out of poverty through his prowess on the football field (Ole Miss, and then the Saskatchewan Roughriders) and his political alliance with Eastland. The very model of crony capitalism, Blake's company received $17 million from the federal Commodity Credit Corporation to store surplus government-owned corn. He tended to overreach, however, and that brought him federal criminal charges for offering $500,000 in bribes to obtain a $20 million loan from a Mississippi bank. Happily, Blake had good legal advice from a Mississippi lawyer named Dickie Scruggs, to whom he had been introduced by Trent Lott's chief aide. Scruggs was Lott's brother-in-law, and with Scruggs's help Blake got his charge reduced to a misdemeanor and avoided jail time.

Nothing is more natural than the instinct to repay a favor, and the Blake/Scruggs connection proved valuable for both men. By 1988, Scruggs had become a leading plaintiff's lawyer, and his friend Michael Moore, the Mississippi attorney general, appointed him "special assistant attorney general" to sue asbestos manufacturers on behalf of the state. In return, Scruggs would be reimbursed for expenses and receive a 25 percent contingency fee for anything he collected from the defendants. The moneys were deposited into a trust account over which Scruggs had control and from which he could transfer funds to his private operating account. Steven Patterson, the state's auditor general and no friend of Michael Moore, thought the whole thing smelled fishy, especially since Scruggs had contributed to Moore's campaign fund. The threat of an indictment loomed over Scruggs, but then Blake asked him to visit. "You helped me a lot, now I'm going to help you," Blake told him. How he would do so became clear a few minutes later when Patterson arrived. "This is chicken-shit stuff," Blake scolded Patterson. "I want you to back off." Not only did Patterson back off, but he wrote a letter to Louisiana officials urging them to hire Scruggs to represent that state against the asbestos industry.[10] In Wilkie's gripping account of the scandal, "Scruggs suddenly felt as though he had become a 'made man,' like a character anointed by the Mafia."[11]

Friendship is a two-way street, and Scruggs began to loan Blake $15,000 a month, then $25,000, on unsecured promissory notes. The payments were small potatoes to Scruggs, who had become immensely wealthy through the settlements his firm received from corporate defendants. From tobacco litigation alone his firm took in $900 million (of which $50 million was to go to Blake for unspecified services). And so Scruggs's single-engine plane was traded for a Learjet, the sailboat for a 120-foot yacht, the Mercedes for a Bentley. *Newsweek* magazine caught up with him at the premiere of *The Insider*, a big-budget Hollywood film that celebrated his take-down of the tobacco industry.

> Richard Furlow Scruggs, "Dickie" to his friends, may be the most influential man in America that you've never heard of. The 53-year-old former Navy fighter pilot is a master at marshaling the forces of fellow attorneys against industries that he believes betray the public's trust. Using a web of high-powered political connections and a keen sense for what plays on Wall Street, Scruggs embodies the class-action lawsuit gone thermonuclear, a new weapon hovering over corporate America.[12]

What Scruggs had done was to make mass tort litigation a big business. He would persuade a local judge to consolidate a mass of cases, trying general liability first and then in a second stage quantifying the damages to be paid each plaintiff. After the defendant was found liable at the first stage, the pressure to settle was enormous, and few cases went to trial. "The idea," said Scruggs, was "to raise the stakes so high that neither the plaintiffs nor the defendants can afford to lose. And when the stakes get that high, then you generally resolve the cases—you settle."[13]

Scruggs had another thing going for him: a pro-plaintiff bench composed of Mississippi judges like James Graves who were only too happy to stick it to deep-pocketed out-of-state corporate defendants. Some judges seemed especially eager to welcome the cases that Scruggs brought them. They sat in what Scruggs called "magic jurisdictions," and he was remarkably candid about their role in his state's culture of corruption.

> The trial lawyers have established relationships with the judges that are elected; they're State Court judges; they're populists. They've got large populations of voters who are in on the deal, they're getting their piece in many cases. And so, it's a political force in their jurisdiction, and it's almost impossible to get a fair trial if you're a defendant in some of these places. . . . The cases are not won in the courtroom. They're won on the back roads long before the case goes to trial. Any lawyer fresh out of law school can walk in there and win the case, so it doesn't matter what the evidence or the law is.[14]

All was going swimmingly for Scruggs until the unexpected happened: He encountered an honest state court judge. Scruggs was being sued by another lawyer over the split they were to receive on a settlement with State Farm over Katrina-related damages. Scruggs wanted the dispute sent to arbitration, so the judge who was charged with the case, Henry Lackey, was visited by a Scruggs associate. The Scruggs firm was not being treated fairly, the associate said. He just wanted fairness. And maybe, down the road, after he retired, the judge might want to join the firm "of counsel." Lackey sensed that he was being bribed, so he went to his fellow judges for advice. Don't go to state prosecutors, he was told. Scruggs is simply too powerful for them to take on. So Lackey turned to the U.S. Attorney's Office. Telephone taps were authorized and the judge was wired. The next time the Scruggs associate visited him, the conversation got down and dirty. The associate offered Lackey a $40,000 bribe, and then walked from the judge's chambers thinking he'd done a good day's work. But when he drove away, he was met by FBI agents who told him, "Your life as you know it is over." Given the chance to cooperate in exchange for a deal on sentencing, the associate agreed to be wired and meet with Scruggs. The judge needs another $10,000, he told Scruggs, who answered, "I'll take care of it." That was enough for the feds, who charged him with bribery.

As the crime was a federal one, the matter ended up before a U.S. district judge, Neal Biggers. A soft-spoken man with the love for William Faulkner that comes naturally to residents of Oxford, Mississippi, Judge Biggers is also a student of history who enthuses over the lectures he heard from Gordon Wood about the republican virtues of the founders and their fear of corruption. At sentencing in June 2008, he told Scruggs (who had pleaded guilty) that he had committed one of the most reprehensible crimes a lawyer could commit. The court system had made Scruggs a rich man, and yet he had attempted to corrupt it. Judge Biggers suggested that this was not the first time Scruggs had done it, considering how easily he entered into the scheme. Then he sent Scruggs away for five years. He also sentenced the associate who had ratted him out, as well as Patterson (the former state auditor general) and Scruggs's lawyer son. At trial, the son had expressed his respect for the legal profession. That's fine, said the judge. "Of course, the legal profession that you say you love so much, you will not be a part of it for the rest of your life."[15]

In *The Leopard*, Giuseppe di Lampedusa wrote that "everything must change so that everything remains the same." Much had changed in Mississippi between the trial of the Neshoba County murderers in 1967 and the trial of Dickie Scruggs forty years later, but some things remained the same. The state's justice system still favored local residents against out-of-state parties, and redress was still to be found only in federal courts.

— 11 —

Designing a Virtuous Justice System

SALVATION IS NOT OF THIS WORLD, and you'll find biased judges in every country. What's needed is a judicial system that makes it harder for them to display their bias or incompetence. And that is what the Framers sought when they created the federal judiciary. Before 1787 there had been state courts in each of the thirteen former colonies, but now there would be a federal government, and federal courts would be needed to resolve issues that arose under federal law.

The Genius of the Framers' Constitution

In designing the federal judiciary, the Framers needed to address three basic questions. First, how should judges be chosen? Second, how might a corrupt judge be removed? Third, when should a party sue in a state court and when in one of the new federal courts? On each of these questions, a central concern was avoiding corruption.

There are only two ways to choose judges: by election or by appointment. Given their distaste for democracy, the Framers didn't want federal judges to be elected. They didn't even want presidents to be popularly elected. Back then, state court judges were all appointed, either by the governor or by the state legislature. Similarly, the only option that the delegates considered for the federal bench was an appointment by the president or by Congress.

As a strong nationalist, James Wilson wanted the president to appoint judges, since this would strengthen his office and draw power to the federal government. Were Congress to do the appointing, there would be "intrigue, partiality, and concealment."[1] The other delegates shared Wilson's concern about corruption, but feared that an executive appointment would make the president too powerful. In the end, the delegates split the difference, giving the president the power to nominate, but subject to the advice and consent of the Senate under Article II, § 2, cl. 2. (The subject prompted Benjamin Franklin to recall a jest: If local lawyers were given the appointment power, they would always pick the best man so they could share his practice after he became a judge.)[2]

In case a judge proved to be unfit, a formal procedure was needed for his removal, as it could not be left to the whims of the president. The bill of particulars in the Declaration of Independence charged that George III had made "Judges dependent on his Will alone, for the tenure of their offices, and the amount and payment of their salaries." That's inconsistent with the rule of law, and to prevent this kind of corruption the Framers' Constitution gave federal judges lifetime tenure "during good Behavior."[3] That isn't the same thing as lifetime tenure *tout court*, but it ensures that a federal judge, once appointed, will remain on the bench unless he is gaga or corrupt. Over the course of the last 225 years, only eight judges have been impeached and removed from office, although more have resigned under threat of impeachment.

The third issue in establishing the federal judiciary was the question of jurisdiction, or where to sue. In a compound republic, with federal and state governments, there are two ways of dividing up lawsuits. The first is a federal takeover, which is the Canadian solution; and the second is the mixed regime of the United States, with a shared jurisdiction between the two levels of government.

In 1867, the Canadians thought the United States was too decentralized, for the Civil War had seemed to demonstrate the danger of an excessive grant of power to the states.[4] So they adopted a unified judicial system in which the federal government would appoint all but the most junior provincial court judges. Provinces could adopt their own statutes, but for the common law regions of the country there would be a single system of judge-made law, held in place by appeals to the Canadian Supreme Court.

Canada's version of federalism has several advantages. For firms that do business across the country, it makes planning easier: with uniform rules, nobody has to worry about weird judge-made law in Saskatchewan. More importantly, a national court system eliminates the fear of corrupt local judges who permit out-of-state visitors to be terrorized, or who wink at baseless claims against nonresident firms. In Canada you wouldn't find a Dickie Scruggs making tort law a judicially sanctioned form of theft, or a Judge Graves letting it happen.

The Canadian solution of a national judiciary wasn't going to be an option for Americans, however. At the Philadelphia Convention, Pierce Butler of South Carolina protested against federalizing the courts. "The people will not bear such innovations," he warned. "The States will revolt at such encroachments."[5] A year later, at the North Carolina ratifying convention, Richard Spaight recalled that no one at Philadelphia had wanted state courts to be supplanted by federal courts.[6] After all, the state courts were well established, and in most states they had been around for more than a century. There were sixteen lawyers and four judges at the convention, and they didn't want to see a radical change in the new country's judicial system.

This meant that the country would need competing judicial systems, state and federal. It wouldn't do to let state courts decide on purely federal matters, such as how to interpret the country's treaties. Otherwise, there might be a checkerboard of treaty obligations across the United States, and foreign countries would never trust us. We would also need a uniform legal system for the general laws of the federal government, such as its criminal, customs and patent laws. Accordingly, Article III, § 2 provides that wholly federal issues are to be litigated in federal courts.

> The [federal] judicial power shall extend to all cases, in law and equity, arising under this Constitution, the laws of the United States, and treaties made, or which shall be made, under their authority;—to all cases affecting ambassadors, other public ministers and consuls;—to all cases of admiralty and maritime jurisdiction.

So far, so good, but the Framers had a second concern about the possibility of corruption if state courts were to rule on interstate matters. A rule of natural justice is that no man is allowed to be a judge in his own cause.[7] Extended to states, the principle explains the rest of Article III, § 2.

> The [federal] judicial Power shall extend to . . . to Controversies between two or more States;—between a State and Citizens of another State,—between Citizens of different States,—between Citizens of the same State claiming Lands under Grants of different States, and between a State, or the Citizens thereof, and foreign States, Citizens or Subjects.

Purely private disputes "between Citizens of different states" would be removed to federal courts, a principle that came to be called *diversity* jurisdiction.

This proposal emerged from the Committee of Detail six weeks before the convention's end,[8] and it raised little debate. Roger Sherman, who was otherwise a champion of states' rights, didn't see a problem with enlarging the scope of federal jurisdiction in this way. At a time when travel was so difficult, he expected that ninety-nine times out of a hundred the parties would be in the same state and therefore state courts would have exclusive jurisdiction. But for the one-in-a-hundred case where the parties were in different states, the problem of judicial bias and corruption required a system of federal courts "to preserve justice and harmony among the states."[9] This was one of those times when the nationalists agreed with the defender of states' rights. At the Virginia ratifying convention, Madison argued that "it may very [well] happen that a strong prejudice may arise, in some states, against the citizens of others, who may have claims against them."[10] In *Federalist* 81, Hamilton noted that cases where "the state tribunals cannot be supposed to be impartial" would be decided in federal court.

By dividing things up in this way, the Framers offered Americans the best of both worlds. Purely federal matters would belong in federal courts, and we wouldn't have Texas treaties that conflict with New York treaties. And since diversity cases would belong in federal courts, we'd also be saved from state courts sticking it to out-of-state defendants. At the same time, letting state courts decide on purely in-state disputes would give states the incentive to adopt the best set of laws. States would compete with each other in their legal regimes, just as they had competed for migrants by liberalizing their policies according to the Frontier Thesis of Frederick Jackson Turner. There would be experimentation with different tort and contract laws in what Justice Louis Brandeis called the "laboratory" of the states,[11] and then each state could look at the others to see what works and what doesn't.

When states compete in this way, there's a "race to the top," won by the state with the best set of laws. We've seen this in corporate law, where Delaware won the race and became the "home of corporations."[12] It also seems to happen in contract law, with bargainers choosing to opt out of California law in favor of more efficient New York law.[13] On the other hand, jurisdictional competition can also be a race to the bottom. Mississippi's legal rules may be wasteful, but other states might seek to copy them in order to stick it to their out-of-state defendants. Neither of these races, to the top or to the bottom, can happen in federal countries with a unified legal system, such as Canada.

The genius of the Framers' solution was to give America the prospect of a race to the top while preventing a race to the bottom, and the key was sending interstate cases to federal courts. A federal judge, appointed by Congress and given lifetime tenure, would have little or no incentive to favor an in-state party at the expense of one from outside. Letting defendants remove an interstate dispute to a federal court would serve the ends of justice and efficiency.

A problem remained for the Framers, however. While state courts had long been established and were located in many small towns throughout the country, federal courts were few and far between in the early republic. For a plaintiff in Alexandria, Virginia, who was suing a defendant just across the Potomac in Maryland, the nearest federal court would have been in Richmond, ninety miles away, so it would make more sense for both parties to allow the suit in a local state court, either in Virginia or in Maryland. The alternative was ludicrous, as George Mason complained at the Virginia ratifying convention. Suppose he was being dragged to federal court by a plaintiff alleging a small unpaid bill. "What! Carry me a thousand miles from home—from my family and business—to where, perhaps, it will be impossible for me to prove that I paid it? Perhaps I have a respectable witness who saw me pay the money; but I must carry him one thousand miles to prove it, or be compelled to pay it again."[14]

Many of the Framers were elected to the country's first Congress, and they knew that Mason had a point, so they sought to address his concerns in the Judiciary Act of 1789. First, they gave defendants the option of letting diversity cases be decided in state courts. That way, they could have small-ticket disputes litigated in a local state court, but transfer big-ticket cases to federal courts if they feared that state court judges would be biased. There would be two parallel legal systems, state and federal, but there wouldn't be an impermeable barrier between them.[15] Giving defendants an unrestricted right to transfer cases to federal court could be unfair to plaintiffs if the latter would have to travel a long distance to the court, and the plaintiff in such a case might abandon the suit even if it was meritorious. This explains why the 1789 Judiciary Act restricted federal diversity jurisdiction to lawsuits exceeding $500 ($14,000 in today's dollars).[16] For that kind of money, it was presumed that the plaintiff would be prepared to travel.

Genius Frustrated

The same concerns about the costs of an extensive federal court system plausibly explain why, in *Strawbridge v. Curtiss* (1806),[17] Chief Justice Marshall took a narrow view of diversity jurisdiction. A Massachusetts plaintiff had sued several other Massachusetts defendants and a lone Vermont defendant in federal court. On a literal interpretation of Article III and the 1789 Judiciary Act, this would have seemed entirely proper. As long as *one* defendant is out-of-state, the case would belong in federal court, and that's called *minimal diversity*. Marshall, however, thought the Judiciary Act required *complete diversity*, in which *every* defendant is out-of-state. In *Strawbridge*, some of the defendants were in the plaintiff's state of Massachusetts, and Marshall held that the case should have been heard in a Massachusetts state court.

The decision has been seen as an occasion when Homer nodded. It was only six sentences long and was delivered without the benefit of oral arguments. It was also a decision that Marshall later regretted. Nine years after his death, a subsequent Supreme Court cast doubt on *Strawbridge* and added that Marshall himself thought it wrongly decided.[18] The decision narrowed the scope of federal authority, but that's not what a strong federalist such as Marshall would have wanted. He was likely influenced by the same prudential concerns that underlay the 1789 Judiciary Act. When most of the parties lived in Massachusetts, that state's courts should have carriage of the case.[19]

When *Strawbridge* was decided, no one worried that a complete diversity requirement would work a hardship. That was too far up the road. Subsequently, however, complete diversity became a tool of oppression in the hands of a Dickie Scruggs. A trial lawyer could game the system and ensure that complete diversity was lacking by suing a sham in-state defendant along with the deep-pockets out-of-state defendant. The in-state defendant might be a small-pockets local business, but it would permit the plaintiff to stay out of federal court and litigate before a biased state judge.

A small-town Mississippi drugstore owner, Hilda Bankston, told the Senate Judiciary Committee in 2002 about how this abuse had led to her being sued hundreds of times. The real targets were out-of-state drug manufacturers, but the lawsuits were brought in Mississippi, in one of Dickie Scruggs's "magic jurisdictions," and Bankston was joined as a defendant in order to keep the lawsuits out of federal court. Her store had filled prescriptions for FDA-approved drugs, and that was enough for the trial lawyers. The lawsuits greatly troubled Hilda and her husband, who suffered a fatal heart attack three weeks after the first time they were sued. She had to spend an untold number of hours responding to requests for documents, and had to hire part-time workers to mind the store when she was dragged into court. Even after she sold the drugstore, she was sued again and again.[20]

Other states had followed the lead of Mississippi in adopting unjust rules that penalized out-of-state parties, knowing that the plaintiff's lawyer could bar the door to the federal court by adding a local business as a defendant. In sparking a race to the bottom, Marshall's complete diversity requirement had frustrated the genius of the Framers' Constitution. Moreover, the prudential reasons that might once have justified a complete diversity requirement have now disappeared. There are many more federal courthouses today, and travel is much easier. George Mason's fear that a plaintiff might game the system by bringing an action in a hard-to-reach federal court no longer seems worrisome.

The stakes have also changed, utterly. The country is immeasurably wealthier, the payoff from a successful lawsuit is far greater, and the substantive and procedural rules of civil liability are vastly different and much more favorable to plaintiffs today. In Marshall's day, tort law was largely confined to intentional wrongdoing. People weren't held liable for being negligent or for failing to provide a lengthy warning label on goods. Product liability law, in which non-negligent manufacturers might be sued by someone who did not purchase the goods from them directly, was unknown. There were no class actions, in which trial lawyers bring claims on behalf of the thousands or millions of unnamed users of a product. There were no contingency fees, in which lawyers could take a case on spec with no money down and then share in the recovery. There was nothing like modern rules of discovery, by which an unmeritorious plaintiff might ask a defendant to bear millions of dollars in costs to produce the requested documents, and then propose a settlement offer for less than that amount. Crucially, there was nothing like the modern rule of damages, under which the Loewen Group was threatened with bankruptcy by an absurd $75 million award for emotional distress and $400 million in punitive damages.

Debates about American civil justice mostly occur without reference to other countries, but we are the world's outlier in this regard. In a scholarly analysis of American legalism, Robert Kagan reviewed more than thirty-four detailed cross-country studies of litigation in specific policy areas, such as hazardous waste cleanups and exposure to harmful chemicals. All but two studies found substantially higher litigation rates in the United States.[21]

One reason for this is the highly pro-plaintiff rules of civil procedure in America. Elsewhere, for example, the initial pleadings must provide a summary statement of the facts supporting the claim, a requirement that excludes unmeritorious lawsuits. That's not required here, so lawsuits can be a form of legal blackmail. Silicon Valley firms are often sued when there's been an unexpected change in stock price, on the theory that the company must have known about it and therefore is liable for failing to disclose the information. There might be no evidence to back up the charge, nor any suggestion of wrongdoing, but trial lawyers still sue in order to prod the defendant to settle rather than bear the enormous costs of producing documents on a motion for discovery.

We seem especially to fly off the rails in the high-profile, big-money disputes of the kind that made Dickie Scruggs rich.[22] Other common law countries rarely award damages for emotional distress, and physical injury awards are also much lower elsewhere. For example, the Canadian Supreme Court in 1978 limited recovery for personal injuries to $100,000 (indexed for inflation). American courts, by contrast, have done just the opposite. When state legislatures have enacted liability caps for personal injuries, state courts have struck them down as unconstitutional.[23] What is banned by Canadian courts—the possibility of enormous liability awards—is often mandated by American ones.

We're one of the world's richest countries, but that doesn't mean we've gotten everything right, and there are some things we might usefully do without—murders, corruption and just possibly some of our lawyers. There is such a thing as too few lawyers, but there's also such a thing as too many lawyers. (In Northwest Washington, D.C., they seem to approach 100 percent of the adult population.) There's a *juste milieu*, represented by an upside-down U-shaped curve called the Magee curve, invented by Stephen Magee. The curve plots GDP growth on the vertical axis against number of lawyers per thousand population on the horizontal axis. At the top of the curve, things are copacetic, but moving to the right by adding more lawyers represents a cost to the economy. That's intuitive, but what is controversial is just where the apex of the curve might be, and Magee puts it significantly to the left of the American level of 3.65 lawyers per 1,000 people. We'd be worse off economically with no lawyers, but we'd be even better off if we had 33 percent fewer lawyers, says Magee, and he calculates that the excess of lawyers costs the American economy more than $1 trillion in GDP.[24]

That's speculative and open to dispute, since there are other variables at play. For instance, Japan relies more on social disapproval to police behavior than exuberant, individualistic America ever could. We might therefore have more need of lawyers than Japan does. And if one-third of our lawyers retired tomorrow, their places would simply be taken by new lawyers, since the problem is not so much the number of lawyers itself as the legal system that appears to make it profitable for so many to practice law. Of course, the value of lawyers can't be measured solely in terms of GDP. Things such as the protection of civil liberties obviously matter as well. But somehow, other countries—England, France, Canada—manage to be more or less civilized even if they lack America's prodigious number of lawyers.

— 12 —

The Silver Bullet

LET'S ASSUME THAT we might be better off with a less plaintiff-friendly set of civil justice rules. That doesn't get us very far if we can't agree on what needs fixing. Cases that may appear to be egregious examples of a litigation-mad culture might look different on closer analysis. A classic example is the "McDonald's Coffee" case from twenty-five years ago.

In 1992, a seventy-nine-year-old woman ordered a cup of coffee at a McDonald's drive-through in Albuquerque. She placed the coffee between her legs. It spilled, burning her severely. She sued McDonald's, and a jury awarded her $160,000 for her injury and $2.7 million in punitive damages. Outrageous, right? Well, not so fast. For one thing, she wasn't driving when the coffee spilled. She was holding the cup between her knees and had removed the lid to add cream and sugar when it tipped over. The coffee caused third-degree burns, requiring skin grafts. She offered to settle for $90,000, but McDonald's never offered more than $800. The jury was told that McDonald's served coffee at 180 or 190 degrees; that a liquid at this temperature would cause third-degree burns; and that this fact was well known to McDonald's. Also, the trial judge reduced the final award to $640,000.

So a case that became a poster child for a broken legal system doesn't seem quite so outrageous after all. We may disagree on the merits of this or another court decision, but reasonable people can still agree on the need to restore the Framers' vision of a judicial system that promotes a race to the top among states, while discouraging a race to the bottom.

The Way Back

The first principle for restoring integrity to our judicial system is that states should be permitted to compete with each other in the judge-made rules they offer in-state parties, but prevented from imposing unfair costs on out-of-state defendants. To do this, only one simple reform is needed: Whenever an in-state plaintiff sues an out-of-state defendant for a nontrivial amount, the latter should be given the option of removing the case to federal court. In other words, we should return to the pre-*Strawbridge* world of minimal diversity, where a plaintiff's lawyer can't bar the door to the federal courthouse by strategically joining an in-state party as a defendant.

To make this happen, all that is necessary is a legislative end run around *Strawbridge*'s complete diversity requirement. And that would work because, in *Strawbridge*, Chief Justice Marshall was interpreting the 1789 Judiciary Act and not the Constitution. If Congress thinks that minimal diversity makes more sense, it's free to adopt that standard, which is precisely what Congress tried to do in the 2005 Class Action Fairness Act (CAFA).[1] In two respects, however, CAFA failed to reflect the Framers' vision of a corruption-free justice system. First, it spoke only to class or mass actions brought on behalf of a group of plaintiffs, and not to cases such as *Loewen* in which a single in-state plaintiff sues an out-of-state defendant and then invokes the complete diversity requirement. Second, CAFA was burdened with technical requirements that the plaintiff's bar soon learned to exploit. For example, it had a 100-plaintiff threshold, so a plaintiff's lawyer suing on behalf of 990 clients might simply bring ten actions on behalf of 99 clients each.[2] What is needed to restore the Framers' vision, then, is a reinforced CAFA that would permit any out-of-state defendant to transfer a case to federal court so long as it meets minimal monetary standards. Just such an amendment is proposed in Appendix B, as the Fairness in Interstate Litigation Act (FILA).[3]

FILA would serve two purposes. First, it would address the problem of judicial bias when state courts treat out-of-state parties unfairly. Second, it would result in an improved legal system for purely in-state disputes. There isn't a Chinese Wall between the two kinds of cases, and the wasteful rules applied against out-of-state defendants would also creep over to cases where the defendant is in-state. Recall that in *Loewen* the court granted an enormous recovery for emotional distress on a breach of contract in the absence of any real evidence of bruised feelings. That's silly, and few states permit such a recovery, with or without a note from one's psychiatrist. But that's the law of Mississippi, for both out-of-state and in-state defendants. Mississippi might have little interest in such a rule except for the possibility of sticking it to out-of-state parties. But in-state defendants are then stuck with it, too. By eliminating the incentive to adopt wasteful rules to ding out-of-state defendants, FILA would correct this secondary abuse.

FILA would be a remedy for the abuse of punitive damages in state courts. Punitive damages are awards that exceed whatever is necessary to compensate the plaintiff for his loss, with the idea that a merely compensatory award might not deter a defendant from doing the same thing again. In other countries, punitive damages are seldom awarded, and in this country the Supreme Court has held that a punitive award of ten times the compensatory award is presumptively excessive.[4] That doesn't much help defendants when the compensatory award itself is inflated, as it was in *Loewen*. And while one might have expected conservatives on the bench to see the need to limit punitive damages, Justices Scalia and Thomas dissented. Justice Scalia said he didn't know what "excessive" meant when used to describe a punitive award, and he had a point. What the Court's measure of ten times the compensatory award had going for it was being a round number, and not much else. What Scalia missed, however, was how state courts have an incentive to stick it to out-of-state defendants through outrageous punitive damages awards. He prided himself on fidelity to the Framers' Constitution, but with a better understanding of their debates he might have recognized in cases like *Loewen* the very kind of corruption they loathed.

It's a problem of federalism, since enormous punitive awards are nearly always against out-of-state defendants. Were Congress to adopt FILA, we'd likely not have to worry about excessive punitive damages, because out-of-state defendants could seek a fair hearing before an unbiased federal court. FILA would produce a race to the top without the costs of a race to the bottom, and that's why it's a silver bullet.

FILA would also have the happy effect of putting an end to judicial forum shopping, the practice that turned Madison County, Illinois, into the national center for asbestos litigation. The courts in this semirural county near St. Louis have been inventive in extending liability to companies that never produced asbestos. After its health risks became known, people stopped using asbestos and firms stopped producing it. Most of them went into bankruptcy. Trial lawyers then succeeded in persuading Madison juries to assess liability against firms that had premises in which asbestos could be found. While the industry is dead, the litigation lives on, and the number of asbestos personal injury claims has increased over time.[5] No more than 10 percent of the claims have any connection with Madison County,[6] but its courts see themselves as courts of general jurisdiction for the entire country. They have welcomed forum shopping and have dispensed with the need for a specific nexus between the county and the parties to the suit. With FILA, out-of-state defendants dunned in such courts could remove the cases to federal courts.[7]

At its heart, the problem is not a matter of incompetent judges, runaway juries or unscrupulous lawyers. Solve the federalism problem, and everything else is self-correcting. And the federalism problem can be solved by adhering to three simple principles, well understood by the Framers. First, litigation among purely in-state parties should be handled solely by state courts. Second, litigation against an out-of-state defendant should be presumptively removable to a federal court, at the option of the defendant, above a certain monetary threshold. Third, state courts should have exclusive jurisdiction for small-dollar cases, even when a defendant is out-of-state. All of this can be done with FILA's silver bullet.

State Judicial Elections

Since all judges at the federal level are appointed rather than elected, FILA should appeal to anyone who objects to judicial elections. In thirty-nine states, judges either are chosen or can be removed through competitive elections. In twelve of these states, judges are elected in partisan elections, while in others, they run without a party label. In some states, judges are appointed by a "merit" panel and thereafter run for retention.[8]

We're the only country with elected judges, and partisan judicial elections have been thought especially troubling. The American Bar Association and the National Center for State Courts have both come out against them, and former Supreme Court justice Sandra Day O'Connor frequently inveighs against them. There's some evidence to back up their concerns. Alex Tabarrok and Eric Helland report that awards against out-of-state defendants were 69 percent higher in states with partisan elections than in states with appointed judges, which on average worked out to an additional $268,000 per case in states with elected judges.[9] Why this should be the case is easy to understand. Because they depend on their supporters for campaign contributions, elected judges can be expected to be attentive to their needs, and Richard Neely, a former chief justice of the West Virginia Court of Appeals, explained just what this meant for him:

> As long as I am allowed to redistribute wealth from out-of-state companies to in-state plaintiffs, I shall continue to do so. Not only is my sleep enhanced when I give someone else's money away, but so is my job security, because the in-state plaintiffs, their families and their friends will re-elect me. It should be obvious that the in-state local plaintiff, his witnesses, and his friends, can all vote for the judge, while the out-of-state defendant can't even be relied upon to send a campaign donation.[10]

There are, however, things to be said in favor of judicial elections, even partisan ones. Party-line voting for judges might seem a little déclassé, but it does tell voters something about judicial candidates. Brand-name advertising offers the same kind of informational benefit in judicial elections as it does in consumer markets, and it's more faithful to the constitutional value of free speech than a ban on party affiliation in an election. Moreover, judicial elections don't seem to result in a lower quality of judges if one looks at citation counts, which scholars use a proxy for intellectual ability. For judges, that means the number of times their opinions have been cited by other judges. Individual opinions by appointed judges are more frequently cited on average than those by elected judges, but elected judges themselves are cited more because they write more opinions, and judges elected in partisan elections are cited most of all. Another measure of the quality of a judge is his independence. We would want our judges to be free of political bias and to judge each case on its merits, and there is not much difference between the two kinds of judges on measures of independence, such as the willingness to write opinions in which one disagrees with ostensible political allies.[11]

It's therefore not clear that judicial elections are bad per se. They let voters express their preferences about their system of justice directly, not just through the mediation of elected representatives, and even some conservatives have thought this a good thing. For example, Senator Ted Cruz (R-TX), in signaling his unhappiness with recent U.S. Supreme Court decisions, proposed that federal judges be subject to recall elections. Conservatives might also remember how a chief justice of the California Supreme Court was sacked by voters in 1986 for her opposition to the death penalty.

What is bad, and corrupting too, is a judicial system in which elected judges can stick it to out-of-state defendants, as Judge Neely boasted of doing. That wouldn't happen if the defendants were given the option to remove their cases to federal court. Enact FILA with its silver bullet, and we wouldn't worry about judicial elections. The most worrisome kind of cases would be decided by federal judges appointed by Congress. State judicial elections would be much less expensive when the stakes are lower and when state courts are no longer the venue for oppressive awards against out-of-state defendants.

A Judicial Aristocracy

Federal judges constitute the closest thing to America's natural aristocracy. Compared with state judges, they are far more likely to have attended a top university and law school, and the difference is readily observed at judicial conferences. At federal circuit conferences, you'll hear leading scholars speak about broad questions of legal policy, history, and judicial philosophy. At conferences of state judges, you're more likely to hear a practitioner drone on about recent changes to the Code of Civil Procedure before an audience that fulfills its continuing education requirements while reading *USA Today*.

It's not that highly intelligent judges can't be found on the state bench, particularly in larger states where the appellate courts are strong. Indeed, there are brilliant state court judges in every state. Some have remained on the state bench because of politics: for Republican judges in Republican states, that's as high as one can get during a Democratic administration, and the same is true for Democrats during a Republican administration. Many an able state court judge has missed his chance by being aged out of consideration when a president aims to stack the federal bench with younger appointees.

There is no higher ambition for a lawyer who seeks a judicial appointment than the federal bench, at either the trial or the appellate level. Once appointed, a federal judge is more apt to hold himself apart from his community, especially from members of the bar with cases in his court. By contrast, state court judges are more closely integrated into their local communities. They'll join the Elks, the Masons or the Rotarians, and that can invite improper overtures. When Dickie Scruggs bribed a judge, the approach was made through an intermediary, a lawyer who was a close friend of Judge Lackey. The two had a father-and-son kind of relationship, and would meet in Lackey's chambers to chat. "Earwigging," it was called. One wasn't supposed to talk with a judge about cases he had before him, but the subject was all too easy to slip into. It's difficult to imagine anything like that happening in the chambers of a federal judge, apart from the rare out-and-out rogue.

In secular America, the federal bench is a national priesthood, conscious of its high calling and dedicated to the rule of law. Under the Constitution, it is the third branch of government, coequal to the presidency and Congress, and the final arbiter of what the other two branches may do. In every country there must be one final sovereign power. In Britain it is the King-in-Parliament, in the laws adopted by the House of Commons and approved by the monarch. In America, sovereignty resides ultimately in the Supreme Court, as the highest federal court of the land. The Supreme Court is also what the queen is for Britons, the final guarantor of democratic government. If Congress and the president attempt to rule undemocratically, the last bulwark against tyranny is the federal bench.

Federal judges have an esprit de corps seldom seen in the United States outside of the military or the priesthood. It is rooted in a sense of their constitutional responsibilities and in the shared experience of being attacked for defending the rule of law. When pilloried by a politician—as Judge Frank Johnson was by Governor George Wallace of Alabama—they'll feel constrained to keep silent rather than speak in their own defense. Harsh criticism isn't the only threat, either. Recently, Judge Kevin Duffy of the Southern District of New York was granted

24/7 protection by U.S. marshals after the CIA intercepted a phone call from an Islamic jihadist threatening his life. Duffy had sentenced Ramzi Yousef for his part in the first World Trade Center bombing in 1993, and the jihadist vowed to "get both Duffy and his wife."[12]

Martin Luther King understood that the civil rights revolution would not have succeeded but for the federal bench's sense of integrity, courage, and high calling. Without knowing its members, he knew he could rely on them to enforce the law, even in the Alabama of the 1950s. When Rosa Parks was arrested in 1955 for refusing to move to the back of a Montgomery bus, King organized a boycott of the city's bus service. His house was firebombed, and a state court judge sentenced him to two weeks in jail for his part in the boycott. Parks herself was sentenced by a state judge to fifty-six days of hard labor. That sentence was stayed when lawyers brought an action before the local federal judge, Frank Johnson, for an order declaring Mississippi's segregation code illegal.

Johnson came from a region of famous contrarians, the "Free Republic" of Winston County in the hill country of northern Alabama, which had had few slaveholders and had voted to secede from Alabama after the state voted to secede from the Union. During the Second World War, Johnson signed up for a combat unit, even though as a lawyer he might have joined the Judge Advocate General's Corps. He received a Bronze Star in Normandy and was twice wounded as Patton's Third Army moved across France. After the war he returned to his practice in Mississippi, and in 1952 he served as president of Veterans for Eisenhower in Alabama. That in turn led Eisenhower in 1955 to nominate Johnson to serve on a federal district court.

When Johnson received the motion to declare Alabama's segregation code illegal, he wrote the same day to the chief judge of the Fifth Circuit Court of Appeals, requesting that the matter be heard before a three-judge panel, a step that would permit an immediate appeal to the Supreme Court. This was a most unusual request from a new district court judge, but Johnson was nevertheless able to persuade the chief judge that the matter was so momentous as to warrant special treatment. Richard Rives from the Fifth Circuit was assigned to the case, along with a conservative federal judge.

The question was by no means an easy one. In *Brown v. Board of Education*, the Supreme Court had asked that school desegregation proceed with all deliberate speed, but less than two years had passed since then, and white southerners were conducting a massive campaign of resistance. Moreover, *Brown* was a case about public schools, while the Rosa Parks case was about public transportation. *Brown* had overruled the 1896 Supreme Court decision in *Plessy v. Ferguson*[13] insofar as it was inconsistent with *Brown*, but *Plessy* had upheld segregated seating in public transportation, which was precisely the issue before the three-judge panel. Did *Brown* overturn *Plessy* and all forms of state segregation, and not just in public education? As the junior judge on the panel, Johnson voted first. "As far as I'm concerned," he said, "state-imposed segregation violates the Constitution." The third judge shook his head, but then Rives looked at Johnson and said, "You know, I feel the same way as you."[14] And that was that. The decision was affirmed by the Supreme Court,[15] but the legal revolution that extended *Brown* to set aside every vestige of Jim Crow laws had begun in the federal court of Montgomery, Alabama.

Anyone who recalls how a perverted legal system discriminated against minorities during the civil rights era, and how it nurtured people like Dickie Scruggs in "magic jurisdictions," should logically support FILA. Given the sorry record of state courts with out-of-state defendants, those who oppose the transfer of cases to federal courts are on the wrong side of corruption.

PART FOUR

MONEY

There are two things that matter in politics.
The first is money. I can't remember the other.

—Mark Hanna

— 13 —

Bribes

ALEXANDER HAMILTON called the judiciary the "least danger-ous branch" in *The Federalist Papers*, and Montesquieu thought of it as "invisible and null" when properly separated from the other branches.[1] But when abused, the power of judging can become "so terrible among men," since it touches the particular individual more closely than the other branches. Montesquieu offered a remarkable definition of political liberty as the "tranquility of spirit which comes from the opinion each one has of his security,"[2] and that tranquility is never more disturbed than when a corrupt judge takes a bribe.

The Ordeal of Francis Bacon

Writer, philosopher, statesman and judge, Francis Bacon was the ornament of his age. His *Essays*, published in 1597, established him as his country's greatest prose stylist, and some even think him the secret author of Shakespeare's plays. For that alone we'd remember him, but he is also credited as the founder of the scientific method, with his *Advancement of Learning* and *Novum Organum*. Then there is Francis Bacon, MP, the politician, author of the 1609 report on the Virginia Colony and one of America's early founders. Finally, there is Bacon the judge, Lord Chancellor of England, Baron Verulam and Viscount St. Albans. All that were great and good loved and honored him, wrote John Aubrey. For his sixtieth birthday, in January 1621, his friend Ben Jonson wrote a poem in which he asked, "How comes it all things so about thee smile?" And yet four months later, Bacon was utterly disgraced and sent to the Tower of London.

The charge was bribery, and the trial was held in Parliament. Ba-con's prosecutor, Sir Robert Phillips, began humbly, as befitting the accused. "The Petition against whom it is alleged," he began, "is no less than the Lord Chancellor, a man so endued with all the Parts, both of Nature and Art, as that I will say no more of him; being not able to say enough."[3] But people with cases before Bacon had given him "presents," often quite valuable. Bacon might not have solicited them himself, but his favorites and followers did so on his behalf, and Bacon had pocketed the money.

Bacon would plead that this was the way of the world, that people in power commonly made themselves wealthy this way, that everyone had winked at it. Indeed, Bacon could point to a custom whereby powerful men accepted gifts as New Year's presents from those who sought favor. Many of Bacon's accusers had themselves taken questionable gifts from suppliants; and Sir Robert Cecil, chief minister to Queen Elizabeth, had received a secret pension from the king of Spain, his country's principal enemy.[4]

It was only the most exceptional of judges, such as Sir Thomas More, who could defend themselves with clean hands. When More refused to accede to the 1535 Act of Supremacy, by which Britain broke with the Catholic Church, every legal device was employed to persuade him to abandon his religion, including a trumped-up charge of bribery. Before the King's Council, a losing litigant complained that More had accepted a "great gilt cup" from the winning party's wife, whereupon More's enemy, the Earl of Wiltshire (Anne Boleyn's father), said, "Did I not tell you, my Lords, that you should find this matter true?" Yes, said More. I took the cup, and ordered my butler to fill it with wine, and drank to her, and then returned the cup as a present to her husband.[5] So More had done—but then More was a saint, and no one ever thought that of Bacon.

"Thus you see *Corruption* laid to the Charge of a Judge too, a great Judge," concluded Bacon's prosecutor, "nay to the Great Keeper of the King's Conscience."

Bacon was not without friends, however, and they began to defend him. The witnesses were suspect, they had entrapped Bacon, they had contradicted themselves, their testimony lacked corroboration. They were also discontented suitors, for if they had meant to buy favor they had failed, since Bacon had ruled against them.

And then Bacon's chief enemy, Sir Edward Coke, showed his hand. For his furious and vituperative prosecutions of the Earl of Essex and Sir Walter Raleigh, the British historian G. M. Trevelyan called Coke "one of the most disagreeable figures in our history,"[6] but he was a leading member of the House of Commons, its great defender against the king, and thus the enemy of king's men such as Bacon. The prosecution of Francis Bacon was an opening salvo in the long battle between king and Parliament that led to the English Civil War, the establishment of Oliver Cromwell's Commonwealth, the execution of Charles I, and eventually the restoration of the Stuart dynasty under Charles II.

For Coke, it had also become personal. Five years before, on Bacon's advice, James I had sacked him as chief justice of the King's Bench for defending the common law and opposing king-made justice. Coke was the greatest common lawyer of his day, and now he would bring his knowledge of judicial precedents to impeach Bacon. There was never a need for corroborating witnesses at common law, said Coke. "For in such Works, it is Marvel there are any Witnesses." Later, in his *Institutes of the Laws of England*, Coke borrowed from Deuteronomy in his pronouncement that "bribery has so great force as to blind the eyes of the wise judge, and to change the words of the just."[7]

Bacon had hoped that the king would shut down the prosecution, but Stuart monarchs seldom kept faith with their followers. James I wrote to the House of Commons saying he was sorry about the accusation of bribery, "for it has always been his care to have placed the best; but no Man can prevent such Accidents." Some think James abandoned Bacon to protect his favorite, the Duke of Buckingham, but in any event the message was clear to everyone, Bacon included.

Bacon had been staying away from Parliament, where he sat as a member of the House of Lords. He wrote first to excuse his absence. "It is no feigning nor fainting" that keeps me away, wrote the elderly Lord Chancellor, "but sickness both of my Heart and of my Back . . . that persuades me that I am not far from Heaven." He pleaded for the right to challenge his accusers, but now came dozens more accusations of bribes paid to him. At this, Bacon threw in the towel. He had no other defense, he said, but that of Job. "I have not hid my Sin, as did Adam, nor concealed my fault in my bosom." He had read the new charges and confessed his guilt "without Fig-leaves."

That wasn't enough for his accusers. Bacon had admitted guilt in a general way, without responding to any of the particular charges. In answer, Bacon detailed how twenty-eight litigants had given him gifts worth more than £12,000 ($120 million in today's money). Some of these were loans, he said, some presents given before litigation, some after a trial and some in the middle. Some were given by people he ruled against. Some were given to him through the agency of his servants, and he confessed it a great fault that he had not had better servants.

Bacon's confession astounded the House of Lords. It was so broad and candid that they asked whether he indeed had meant it. To which Bacon answered, "My Lords, it is my Act, my Hand, my Heart; I beseech your Lordships to be merciful [as] to a broken reed." But Parliament was not so inclined. It asked that Bacon be stripped of his office, fined him the impossible sum of £40,000 ($390 million today), and imprisoned him in the Tower of London at the king's pleasure. James soon set him at liberty, and even granted him a pension, but Bacon remained in great want to the very last, living obscurely in his chambers at Gray's Inn, where "his lonely and desolate condition so wrought upon his melancholy Temper, that he pined away."

Corruption of the Heart

In America today there are about eight hundred Article III federal judges. Very few such judges have ever been removed from office, and then mostly for things like tax fraud and perjury. With one exception they didn't skim from the top, as Bacon did. The apparent exception was Alcee Hastings, who was removed by the Senate in 1989 for engaging in a conspiracy to solicit a $150,000 bribe in return for reducing the sentences of two mob-connected felons. That wasn't the end of him, however. Four years later he was elected to the U.S. House of Representatives from Florida. He's still in Congress, and the nonpartisan Citizens for Responsibility and Ethics in Washington reports that Hastings hired his girlfriend as a congressional aide and paid her $622,000 over a four-year period, from 2007 to 2010.[8]

Federal judicial ethics are evidently higher than congressional ethics. But then we knew that all along. A congressman needing money to finance his re-election campaign will solicit funds from donors, and we won't be surprised to find him supporting their interests. We don't expect politicians to be nonpartisan. Only judges—and baseball umpires. This was a principle that goes back to Magna Carta ("to no one will we sell . . . right or justice), and it was one that Bacon's accuser invoked. "For if the Fountain be muddy, what will the Streams be? If the Great Dispenser of the King's Conscience be corrupt, who can have any Courage to plead before him?"

A bribe corrupts the heart, said the author of Ecclesiastes.[9] For corruption of the heart, one need look no further than Judge Mark Ciavarella of Wilkes-Barre, Pennsylvania, and the "kids for cash" scandal that regularly put mildly misbehaving juveniles in lock-up. The story began with tougher drug laws that greatly increased the number of prisoners in Pennsylvania in the 1980s, putting a strain on the state budget. Then someone came up with the bright idea of offloading the jails to the private sector. Privatization was the new big idea, so instead of being guests of the state, the inmates would become guests of a for-profit prison. This was bound to save money, since private enterprise could be counted on to do things more efficiently—or at least more cheaply—than the state. What could go wrong?

One of the new for-profit facilities was PA Child Care, a juvenile detention hall and a division of Mid-Atlantic Youth Services, Corp. (whose motto is "inspiring brighter futures"). Like any seller of services, PA wanted more customers, but the supply of true offenders was limited. Then PA recognized that there was a much broader group of merely mischievous kids who might be inspired to a brighter future in its lock-ups. It's something like those billboards that lawyers put up: Just because you did it doesn't mean you're guilty. For PA, just because you didn't do it doesn't mean you're innocent. So PA bribed Judge Ciavarella to send children to its detention center for the crime of acting like kids.

It was a brilliant scheme, since juvenile court judges work under the radar, with the broadest possible discretion. The kids were sent to the police by teachers or parents who trusted the judge to get it right. Expecting that their child would get nothing more than a stern lecture, parents were easily persuaded to sign away their right to legal counsel. When the kids went before Judge Ciavarella, however, they were immediately pronounced guilty, shackled and led off to months of detention. Ciavarella had been elected on a platform of getting tough on juvenile crime, and the voters got more than they bargained for.

Hillary Transue, fourteen, had mocked her school's vice principal in her MySpace page. The teacher was a strict disciplinarian, so Hillary drew a picture of her with jackboots and a Nazi armband. She noted that all this was a joke, but the teacher, channeling her inner Nazi, filed a harassment complaint. The police told the girl's mother not to bother hiring a lawyer, but after a three-minute hearing Hillary was handcuffed and led away for ninety days. "What makes you think you can get away with this kind of crap?" yelled Ciavarella. "Adjudicated delinquent . . . You're gone!"[10]

Matt, thirteen, was troubled by his parents' bitter divorce. He accidentally knocked over a glass of beer in front of his mother's new boyfriend, who claimed that the boy had thrown a piece of steak at him. Matt was 4'3" and weighed 82 pounds. The boyfriend was 6'3" and weighed 210 pounds. Matt was patted down by the police for weapons, handcuffed and shackled. Because his mother had taken the boyfriend's side, Matt refused to speak to her, and that kept him in juvie longer. He spent seven weeks there, until his real father contacted a local newspaper. "I thought judges were supposed to help me," said Matt.[11] Now a young man, he battles depression and has been unable to attend college.

Ryan, eleven, was locked out of his house by his mother after a family squabble. Ryan called the police himself, but his mother told the officer that he was a behavior problem. She was persuaded to charge the boy with harassment after the policeman told her that there wouldn't be a fine. Nevertheless, she received a letter a few weeks later asking her to pay a fine of $488. This brought Ryan up before Judge Ciavarella. "Do you have $488?" the judge asked Ryan. When the boy shook his head, Ciavarella said, "Very good. He's remanded. He can stay there until he pays the fine." Ryan was handcuffed and placed in leg shackles. He was 4'2" and weighed 63 pounds.

The kids didn't come out of juvenile hall the better for it. They were taken from parents and friends and introduced to the company of drug dealers and violent offenders. When they got out of juvie, their records followed them. At school they were monitored by probation officers, and their old friends kept clear of them. Sometimes they had done nothing at all to deserve this.

Ed Kenzakoski was seventeen when his father planted a marijuana pipe in his truck. Ed had begun drinking, and his concerned father thought he could benefit from a good lecture by the police. Instead, the boy was shackled and led away to confinement. At nineteen, he was back in juvie again, sent there by Ciavarella after a fender-bender. When he got out this time, his personality had changed. Formerly just a mischievous lad, he was now filled with rage. He got into a fight and was sent to state prison. Returning home after his release, he fought with his father and then shot himself in the heart. He was twenty-three years old.[12]

When the "kids for cash" scandal came to light, federal prosecutors stepped in and charged Ciavarella with a breach of the right to honest services from an elected official, as well as wire fraud, conspiracy and obstruction of justice. In a plea agreement, the prosecutors agreed to a seven-year sentence for crimes that bore a maximum sentence of twenty-five years. On sentencing, however, the judge tossed the plea agreement and sentenced Ciavarella to twenty-eight years in prison. He had never acknowledged his moral failings, and there was one thing more. For judges, "integrity is their lot and proper virtue, the landmark, and he that removes it, corrupts the fountain. In this case the fountain from which the public drinks is confidence in the judicial system—a fountain which may be corrupted for a time well after this case."[13]

The Limits of Bribery Law

Sometimes the system works and corrects injustices. Sometimes less so. Judge Graves displayed a shocking disregard for the rule of law, and ended up on a prestigious federal appellate court. Then there's the sheer difficulty of proving that someone has taken a bribe, a burden of proof made more difficult by the Supreme Court in its recent unanimous decision absolving Virginia's former governor Bob McDonnell of bribery.[14]

Before his fall, McDonnell had been a rising star in national Republican politics. A handsome and charming conservative who in 2009 won the highest office in a state trending Democratic, McDonnell seemed to have a bright future—that is, until he met Jonnie Williams, the hustling CEO of a Virginia drug company, Star-Scientific. The company's signature product was Anatabloc, a tobacco-based dietary supplement, and Williams wanted the FDA to classify it as a pharmaceutical, which would have made it much more valuable. This would require expensive testing and clinical trials, and Star-Scientific couldn't afford it, so Williams wanted the governor to ask Virginia's public universities to do it for free.

The two men hadn't met before McDonnell was elected. Shortly after the inauguration, however, Williams took the new governor's wife to New York on a $20,000 shopping spree at Oscar de la Renta, Louis Vuitton and Bergdorf Goodman. That was for starters. Then came a $50,000 "loan" to McDonnell's company, a Rolex watch, a set of golf clubs, holidays and dinners—$175,000 in all over a two-year period. There was no question about the size of the gifts, but had the governor taken official action to repay the favors or agreed to do so? That's what is needed to prove a charge of bribery.[15]

McDonnell had been indefatigable in urging his subordinates to assist Williams and his company. What he hadn't done was *order* them to help the donor when they balked, and therefore, he argued at his trial in 2014, he wasn't guilty of bribery. All he had done, he said, was to give Williams the routine courtesies that all politicians provide for their constituents. He had set up meetings, called other public officials, hosted an event, and even popped an Anatabloc and announced that it was working well for him.

In the circuit court's finding, the governor had agreed to benefit Williams in return for all those gifts. Indeed, Williams must have thought he had an agreement. Otherwise, why would he have spent all that money? And shouldn't McDonnell have recognized that Williams thought he had a deal? One might have thought the two-year pattern of accepting gifts sufficed to establish the charge of bribery. Indeed, "it has been long established that the crime of bribery is complete upon the acceptance of a bribe regardless of whether or not improper action is thereafter taken."[16] That, after all, was enough to convict Francis Bacon.

The Supreme Court saw it differently. McDonnell's conduct might have been "distasteful," according to the decision written by Chief Justice Roberts for the unanimous Court, but it didn't add up to bribery.

With stronger evidence that the governor had agreed to benefit Williams, the case might have gone the other way. Of course, it's generally impossible to find an explicit agreement in bargains that are concluded with winks, except through the kind of FBI sting seen in the Abscam scandal, with wiretaps and secret recordings. For this reason, gifts to officials above a minimal ceiling are generally banned, as a prophylactic measure. The federal gratuity statute criminalizes gifts given to a public official "for or because of any official act," and federal regulations bar government employees from accepting gifts from people whose interests might be substantially affected by the employee's official duties.[17] Virginia had not adopted a gratuity law before the McDonnell scandal, but belatedly did so afterward, barring public officials from accepting gifts in excess of $100 from lobbyists. That will save the prosecutor from the burden of proving a corrupt agreement—unless the gift comes from a businessman like Jonnie Williams and not a lobbyist.

The presents that Williams gave the McDonnells were private gifts, like the moneys that Bacon and Ciavarella stuffed into their pockets. It's much harder to support a charge of bribery when the quid takes the form of a campaign contribution. No public good was served when Williams took Mrs. McDonnell shopping, but campaign contributions are used to educate voters about issues and promote democratic competition, and those are public goods.

There's less reason still to charge an official with bribery when the contribution was made to a charity or cause he supported. There have been few such cases, but the ones we've seen are troubling. One example is the conviction of Alabama's governor, Don Siegelman, for bribery in 2011, after he agreed to appoint a donor to a government board in exchange for a gift toward the governor's effort to establish a state lottery in support of public education.[18] There was nothing in it for Siegelman personally, and most elected officials have made similar promises. Nevertheless, the governor was sentenced to a seven-year jail term, on charges brought by what some observers regarded as a partisan Republican Justice Department.[19] If Siegelman was properly found guilty under current law, there's a case to be made for charging Hillary Clinton with bribery for the questionable dealings detailed in Chapter 1. But that, in turn, is an argument for a less expansive law of bribery.

Least of all would we want to criminalize the kind of legislative bargains among elected officials that greased the wheels when Obamacare was passed. The deals were distasteful, but no one stuffed money in his pockets as McDonnell did. The side payments to various states were simply a consequence of the Constitution's separation of powers. Deal-making was baked into the cake. Even when the official receives a direct personal benefit, the bargains are often entirely benign.

The designers of our constitutional system would have known about a major example of this kind of benign bargaining: the Declaration of Breda in 1660, through which Charles II wormed his way back to the British throne after nine years of exile. During his time in France, Germany, and the Low Countries, he had bargained with Anglicans, Presbyterians, Dissenters, indeed anyone who might restore him as king. When England appeared to be descending into anarchy on the fall of Cromwell's Protectorate, and General Monk brought his army from Scotland to restore order, Charles dealt with Monk as well. What Britain wanted after the turmoil of the Civil War and Cromwell's military dictatorship was the stability of a king who would make his peace with Parliament, and that is what the Declaration of Breda offered.

It was written from the Spanish Netherlands in the form of a letter to all of Charles's subjects, promising to take "a quiet and peaceable possession of . . . our right, with as little blood and damage to our people as is possible." Charles would not seek vengeance against the regicides who had his father executed, but would be content to let Parliament hang the worst offenders (having been assured that "some members of the Rump are content their Fellows should be hanged").[20] He also recognized the absolute authority of Parliament in matters of religion, and said he would defer to Parliament in the property disputes that arose during the Civil War and the Protectorate. In general, he would seek a "perfect union" with his subjects, "in a free Parliament, by which, upon the word of a King, we will be advised."

The declaration, artfully drafted by the Earl of Clarendon, could not have had a better effect. When Charles's envoy presented it to Parliament, both houses voted unanimously to restore the monarchy; and upon hearing of this, a delighted Sir Thomas Urquhart (author of *The Admirable Crichton*) is said to have laughed himself to death. The declaration studiously omitted to any definition of the royal prerogative or the powers that the king might exercise without seeking Parliament's approval, and it would take another two centuries to work that out. (In America, we still haven't done so for our presidents.) Nevertheless, the document was a milestone in British constitutional history, more important even than the 1689 Bill of Rights. It spared the country from another civil war, beginning a long tradition of peaceful and orderly transfers of power—with the notable exception of the Dutch invasion that installed William of Orange on the throne in 1688—and it established the constitutional structure that persists to this day.

The Declaration of Breda was the kind of bargain that Gouverneur Morris worried about if Congress were to have the power to appoint the president. Yet it instituted a form of shared governance between king and Parliament that the Framers would follow as their model for the separation of powers. And if that bargaining wasn't so bad, neither was the "Corrupt Bargain" that brought John Quincy Adams rather than Andrew Jackson to the White House in 1824, an agreement that arguably elected the better man.

Even poor Rod Blagojevich deserved a pass for some of the bargains he made. "Blago" was the governor of Illinois when Barack Obama was elected president in 2008, so he was given the responsibility of choosing someone to fill Obama's Senate seat for the remaining two years of the term. Blago thought he'd hit the jackpot. He knew that Obama and Valerie Jarrett were very close, so he signaled to Obama's team that he would appoint her so long as he was given something in return, and what he had in mind was a seat in Obama's cabinet. Blago was widely perceived as corrupt, however, and Obama refused to promise him anything. For Blago, that wasn't going to work. "They're not willing to give me anything except appreciation. F*** them!"[21]

Sadly for Blagojevich, everything he said was being recorded by the FBI, and in December 2008 he was indicted for a long list of offenses, one of which was his attempted sale of a Senate seat. He was impeached and removed from office, and after two trials he was sentenced to fourteen years in jail. On appeal, the Seventh Circuit reversed on one charge, concerning whether his offer to appoint Jarrett to the Senate in exchange for a cabinet seat was a criminal offense. It wasn't, the Court held. It was merely logrolling, and fundamentally different from selling an office for money. It was how the wheels were greased when legislators had to forge a compromise.

> A political logroll . . . is the swap of one official act for another. Representative A agrees with Representative B to vote for milk price supports, if B agrees to vote for tighter controls on air pollution. A President appoints C as an ambassador, which Senator D asked the President to do, in exchange for D's promise to vote to confirm E as a member of the National Labor Relations Board. Governance would hardly be possible without these accommodations, which allow each public official to achieve more of his principal objective while surrendering something about which he cares less, but the other politician cares more strongly.

That, the Court suggested, was how Earl Warren came to be appointed chief justice of the United States, in exchange for delivering the California delegation to Eisenhower at the 1952 Republican convention. And any theory of criminal law that made felons of Warren and Eisenhower just wasn't going to wash.

— 14 —

The Republic of Defection

WHEN THE SUPREME COURT announced its decision in *McDonnell v. United States*, ruling that the former governor of Virginia was not guilty of taking bribes when he accepted gifts from a businessman who wanted a favor done, some prominent conservatives rushed to applaud it. The *Wall Street Journal*'s editorial board called the decision a "much needed corrective" to "abusive" prosecutions and perhaps the "finest opinion" of Chief Justice Roberts.[1] That might seem a little over-the-top, considering that the case revolved around the Platonic Form of crony capitalism, which no one deplores more than American conservatives. For them, the pay-for-play networks of Washington, D.C. are a betrayal of the free-market capitalism that made our country the envy of the world. Curiously, however, it's the conservative who is most likely to resist legal barriers to crony capitalism, while it's the liberal who seeks to install such barriers with campaign finance reforms.

But there's a reason why stricter campaign finance limits won't work here the way they do in other countries. We're a low-trust society, where people break their promises and where laws are abused. This means that more restrictive campaign laws may end up being used as a partisan weapon, resulting in more corruption rather than less.

The Dismal Dialectic

To see the contrast between a high-trust country and a low-trust one, compare the Canadian and American responses to the recent Syrian refugee crisis. The first group of Syrian refugees arrived in Canada on December 15, 2015. Mostly families with small children, they were greeted at the Toronto airport by the prime minister. "You are home," he told them. "You are safe at home now." Days later, we saw refugee families welcomed at churches and mosques across the country. It was difficult to watch any of this without emotion.

The refugee program is hugely popular in Canada. In addition to 25,000 government-sponsored refugees, another 25,000 privately sponsored Syrian refugees are expected to arrive in the country. The sponsors are ordinary Canadians, one of whom was shown in a video taking a bewildered new arrival out in a canoe. Sponsorship duties cannot be assumed lightly, for sponsors must agree to provide the refugee with care, lodging, and settlement assistance for a year, and this assumes a financial commitment of $20,000.

The American response to the refugee crisis was puny by comparison. With ten times the population of Canada, the United States would have to admit 500,000 refugees to match Canada's commitment, and it has struggled to admit 4 percent of that number. Moreover, the United States bears a moral responsibility for the crisis, since its 2003 invasion of Iraq and the precipitous pullout of American forces in 2011 were the conditions that led to the creation of ISIS. America abandoned the refugees, like a child who walks away from a toy it has broken. And while 10 percent of the Syrian population is Christian and they are the most seriously threatened, only about 0.5 percent of those admitted as of September 2016 were of that religion.[2]

North of the border, all political parties supported the government's refugee program, while south of the border the issue sparked a bitter debate. Republicans believed that the administration wasn't capable of screening out terrorists, or that it would fail to do so for political reasons. The sense that the government couldn't be trusted became acute when the public learned that more vigilant screening might have prevented the jihad murders in San Bernardino in December 2015. The attorney general, Loretta Lynch, did nothing to allay conservative concerns when she expressed uncertainty that the mass shooting was a terrorist attack, and when she told a group of Muslim activists the next day that her greatest fear was the "incredibly disturbing rise of anti-Muslim rhetoric."[3] Several months later, in releasing the tapes of the Orlando nightclub mass murderer, she scrubbed his professions of allegiance to ISIS, until the public outcry forced her to reverse herself. Distrust of the administration may have been understandable, but the polarization that infects American politics prevented a cooperative response to the crisis. Instead, Republicans urged a complete halt to the Syrian refugee program, while Democrats called Republicans heartless bigots.

We shouldn't be surprised by this unedifying pathology of American politics, since we have a low trust-country in comparison with most of the industrialized world. A 2008 survey reported that only 49 percent of Americans felt a high level of trust in other people, far less than the Nordic countries (with Denmark at the top, at 89 percent), and substantially less than the OECD average of 59 percent.[4] Other reports suggest even lower levels of trust in America. In *Bowling Alone*, Robert Putnam reported that the percentage of people who thought that "most people can be trusted" fell from 55 in 1960 to 34 in 1998.[5] The decline has been especially dramatic when it comes to trust in the government. When asked in 2015, "How much of the time do you trust the government in Washington," only 19 percent of respondents said "just about always" or "most of the time." That is one of the lowest levels in the last fifty years,[6] and it's a report card on how voters feel about the federal government's competence and integrity.

The decline in trust harms us all. In high-trust countries, cooperation is repaid with cooperation. In low-trust countries, on the other hand, the cooperating party is thought a patsy, and a pattern of reciprocal defection emerges. We might hope for a synthesis between extreme positions, in which both sides let down their guard and search for what is just and right, and common to all. But that cannot happen when the level of distrust is so high, and we're left with a dismal dialectic that privileges those at the extreme corners of a debate and pitilessly tears asunder our self-image as a generous nation.

Crimes of Democracy

The dismal dialectic is starkly apparent in politically motivated prosecutions for violations of campaign finance laws. Take Dinesh D'Souza, for example. He's the author of a series of best-selling books that portray Obama as the leader of a criminal gang,[7] and if you're a Democrat he makes a big fat target. There's an enormous anti-Obama literature, but no one is so prolific or as biting as D'Souza. He is also the writer and producer of the second-highest-grossing documentary film, again a searing indictment of Obama. And he's a felon.

By law, campaign donors are limited to a $5,000 contribution to a political campaign. When a friend was running as a Republican for a New York Senate seat, D'Souza doubled this to $10,000 by adding a contribution from his wife. That wasn't the problem. What he did next was what made him a criminal. When the friend asked for more support, D'Souza made a further $10,000 contribution through the conduit of two other friends, after promising to reimburse them. Because this was a sham transaction, he was prosecuted for violating the monetary limits of American campaign finance law.

D'Souza had displayed an appalling lack of judgment, on more than one level. Had he wanted to contribute more than $5,000 to his friend's (quite unwinnable) campaign, there were other, legal ways of doing so. He might have given the money to the local Republican committee or to an independent expenditure committee. An independent expenditure is money spent on a political campaign, and it's "independent" if the person making the expenditure doesn't "coordinate" with the candidate or his campaign. Prior to 2010, such groups (called "527s," after a provision of the Internal Revenue Code) could sponsor ads that took a position on issues identified with a candidate so long as the ad didn't use "magic words" that expressly asked viewers to vote for or against a candidate. The difference between "issue ads" and express advocacy was largely artificial, however. For example, the "Swift Boat Veterans" ad against John Kerry in 2004 was an issue ad because it didn't say "Don't vote for Kerry," even though it conveyed the message that he was the lowest worm that God had suffered to crawl upon the face of earth. Since then, however, the courts have abandoned the distinction between issue ads and express advocacy, permitting 527s to use the formerly forbidden magic words.[8] So there were plenty of legal options for D'Souza to support his candidate. Instead, he used illegal means.

In his most recent book, D'Souza speculates that a vengeful Obama ordered his minions to find evidence of a crime, but searching through financial disclosure records wouldn't have revealed a fictitious transaction. Someone had to come forth and disclose the sham, which brings us to another way that D'Souza showed poor judgment: he chose to channel his contributions through his wife, his mistress, and his mistress's husband. With a personal life so messy, it doesn't take a Sherlock Holmes to narrow down who might have ratted him out.

That D'Souza was charged with an election law offense was not particularly shocking in itself. What *was* shocking was the government's decision to charge him as a criminal. Very few people are prosecuted criminally for exceeding the donation limits, and then only for much larger amounts and where there is evidence of quid pro quo corruption. D'Souza's sentence was eight months of confinement in a halfway house, five years of probation, a $30,000 fine and an order to submit to psychiatric evaluation. All this for a first offense, and for a matter that usually brings only an administrative fine.

Even if you're not convicted of a crime, there's a penalty to pay, as the Wisconsin Club for Growth found out. A conservative organization created under section 501(c)(4) of the Internal Revenue Code, it was permitted to keep its donor lists confidential provided it didn't coordinate with the candidates it supported. It's by no means unusual for politicians to speak at meetings of sympathetic 501(c)(4)'s, or to suggest that donors support them. But when senior aides to Governor Scott Walker spoke at Club for Growth meetings, Democratic prosecutors charged that the club and its members (the "Unnamed Movants" in the subsequent litigation) had unlawfully coordinated with Walker's re-election campaign.

Police wearing flak vests conducted paramilitary predawn raids on club members in October 2013, turning floodlights onto their homes and seizing their computers and phones as well as those of their families. They were not allowed to call their attorneys, and prosecutors subsequently demanded the club's confidential donor list. The breadth of the search was "amazing," said the Wisconsin Supreme Court.

> Millions of documents, both in digital and paper copy, were subpoenaed and/or seized. Deputies seized business papers, computer equipment, phones, and other devices, while their targets were restrained under police supervision and denied the ability to contact their attorneys. The special prosecutor obtained virtually every document possessed by the Unnamed Movants relating to every aspect of their lives, both personal and professional, over a five-year span. . . . Such documents were subpoenaed and/or seized without regard to content or relevance to the alleged violations . . . . As part of this dragnet, the special prosecutor also had seized wholly irrelevant information, such as retirement income statements, personal financial account information, personal letters, and family photos.[9]

It was right out of communist East Germany, and we wouldn't have known about it if the club's director, Eric O'Keefe, hadn't revealed it, thereby opening himself up to criminal prosecution for breaching a state gag law. O'Keefe has now been vindicated by the Wisconsin Supreme Court, which held that the activities of the Club for Growth were constitutionally protected speech. It was a bittersweet victory, however, for it came only after extensive and expensive legal proceedings in three levels of Wisconsin courts and two levels of federal courts. Meanwhile, the club's donor support dried up and the prosecution very effectively shut down its issue advocacy during the 2014 gubernatorial election. When you're charged with a breach of campaign finance laws, says O'Keefe, "the process is the punishment."

If we could agree on anything, it would be that people shouldn't be singled out for their political beliefs, as D'Souza apparently was, or subjected to predawn SWAT raids for the same reason, as happened to Wisconsin Club for Growth members. But for those things to stop, we'd have to be a less divided country . D'Souza's travails are a subject of mirth to his opponents, and the *New York Times* administered a rap on the knuckles to the Wisconsin Supreme Court and to Governor Walker for killing the law that permitted the proceedings against the Club for Growth.[10]

The U-Curve

Because of cases such as these, most conservatives reflexively oppose all efforts at campaign finance reform. In America's dismal dialectic, they recognize that more restrictive campaign finance laws can result in more corruption if administered in a partisan manner. It's true that many of the countries that rank higher than the United States on measures of economic freedom have either strict campaign finance laws or robust public financing and free television advertising, and they're also reported to be less corrupt.[11] But politically unfree countries also restrict campaign contributions. Try to fund an opposition party in Russia, for example.

Restrictions on campaign spending in America might therefore go either way. They might open up the political process, as liberal reformers assert; but they also might also limit freedom by protecting incumbent politicians from competition from political challengers, as conservatives counter.[12] Strict campaign laws can also result in more corruption if they are employed primarily against one party, and immunize a less-than-honest, dominant party from criticism. And if they are employed to silence dissent, the result is a weaker, not a stronger, democracy.[13] As they say in Third World countries, "For my friends, everything; for my enemies, the LAW."

FIGURE 2

More Anticorruption Laws, More Corruption?

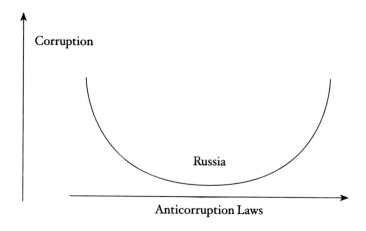

Think of it as a U-curve (Figure 2), with corruption represented on the vertical axis and the stringency of campaign finance laws on the horizontal. On the extreme left of the curve, there is no law of any kind and a great deal of corruption. More law would mean less corruption. But moving down the curve one comes to an inflection point, beyond which more law would mean more corruption, where truly innocent people are put in jail and political differences are criminalized. That's where Russia is, on the right-hand side of the curve. Some conservatives think America is there, too.

Election laws are highly technical, and the political party that enacts them can be expected to impose a disproportionate burden on the other party. There are different kinds of donors, and different kinds of finance regulations, and it's not beyond the skill of the draftsman to produce one-sided rules.[14] In particular, the politician who demands restrictions on campaign contributions, and tells us he does so to defund his political opponents, is the very last person to be trusted to come up with a set of fair and evenhanded standards.[15] Less trustworthy still are the breathless accounts of the dangers of Republican money in politics, in which left-wing donors are either ignored or given a pat on the head.[16] Even ostensibly neutral rules that give the regulator a degree of discretion can be employed in a partisan manner. That was the story of Lois Lerner and the IRS targeting of conservative Tea Party groups.

The Tea Party movement began in 2009 as a reaction to the Troubled Asset Relief Program (TARP) and drew strength from the highly partisan legislative agenda of the Obama administration later that year. Tea Party groups feared that their donors would be harassed, and therefore sought to register under section 501(c)(4) of the Internal Revenue Code, which permits anonymous donations. Democrats quickly realized that such groups could sway an election, as indeed happened in November 2010, and the administration began to vilify "dark money" from anonymous sources. The refrain was echoed by senior Democrats in the Senate and the House, in the letters they wrote to the IRS, with the result that partisan bureaucrats began to hold up applications for 501(c)(4) status from Tea Party groups.

One right-wing group whose application languished in this way was the King Street Patriots, formed in 2010 by Catherine Engelbrecht, a Texas businesswoman. The government had not investigated her or her business for the prior twenty years, but over the next three years they were subjected to more than fifteen inquiries by various federal agencies, including the IRS, OSHA, the FBI's Domestic Terrorism Unit, and the Bureau of Alcohol, Tobacco, and Firearms. The IRS asked her to provide every Facebook and Twitter entry she had posted and the names of her members or volunteers. The administration had seemingly unleashed its concentrated fury upon a small-time political opponent, suggesting a degree of corruption that reached down to four ostensibly apolitical agencies.

The campaign against the Tea Party groups kept many of them out of the next few congressional elections. They were given the choice of folding their tents, as many did, or disclosing their donors. In that case, liberal groups would be able to stigmatize them through the new social media tools, and other branches of the government could weigh in, as happened to Engelbrecht. Worse still was the threat of criminal prosecution. Shortly before the 2010 election, Lois Lerner, as head of the Exempt Organizations Unit of the IRS, transmitted more than a million pages of nonprofit tax returns to the FBI for possible prosecution, even though the IRS was required to keep this information from the bureau. The election crimes director at the Justice Department asked Lerner to help bring fraud prosecutions against the nonprofits, and the ranking Democrat on the House Oversight Committee, Elijah Cummings, told Engelbrecht that she was engaged in a criminal conspiracy. It all added up to what Kimberley Strassel calls the "intimidation game," the ways in which a corrupt government uses all the resources of the regulatory state to suppress political dissent.[17]

In corrupt countries, no distinction is made between law and politics, and political enemies are fair game for everything the government can throw at them. That it will seek to prosecute and harass its opponents is to be expected. The question, however, is what happens afterward. Will the government get away with it; will it escape censure? In America it didn't—at first. When news of the IRS scandal broke, major newspapers such as the *New York Times* and the *Washington Post* were quick to condemn what seemed like the politicization of a major government agency. Lois Lerner would resign in disgrace, and subsequently plead the Fifth Amendment in congressional hearings. But thereafter the government stonewalled congressional efforts to uncover what had happened. The IRS reported that Lerner's emails had been lost, delayed informing Congress of this, and then resisted judicial efforts to produce missing documents.

Meanwhile, the Democrats had taken the offensive. The onus was on the Tea Party to prove harassment, they argued. "Where is your proof?" demanded Rep. Gerry Connelly (D-VA), who saw nothing more than "innuendo, drawing conclusions, and paranoia." The scandal had come to light because an audit by the IRS inspector general, J. Russell George, was about to be made public, and George quickly found himself in the crosshairs of Democratic congressmen. Inspectors general are charged with serving as nonpartisan congressional monitors of executive agencies, but George was now accused of having a secret Republican agenda.[18] In time, Obama told us there was "not even a smidgen of corruption" behind the affair and blamed Fox News for promoting it.[19] The *New York Times* walked back its criticism of the IRS,[20] and the scandal faded away for everyone except conservatives.

Unlike prime ministers in parliamentary countries, a president can employ the separation of powers to shield the executive branch from inquiry until damaging news is forgotten. This allowed the Obama administration to cover its tracks in what looked like an effort to criminalize political differences. In addition, three features of the American criminal justice system make corrupt prosecutions more likely here than in comparable countries.

First, state prosecutors are mostly elected in partisan contests, while prosecutors in other countries are unelected civil servants, with much less incentive to favor one party over another. American prosecutors are often highly political animals, and not a few of them have a taste for the kind of publicity that a high-profile case might generate, particularly if they see their position as a stepping-stone to higher office. Further, American prosecutors are often elected at the local level, which means they tend to represent the political views that predominate in their community. That was the case when a prosecutor in liberal Madison decided to pursue the Wisconsin Club for Growth.[21] Rick Perry, former governor of Texas, can tell a similar story about a district attorney from liberal Austin. When the Democratic DA of Travis County was caught driving drunk, with blood alcohol three times the legal limit, Perry asked for her resignation, and when she refused he vetoed funding for her public integrity unit. That brought him an indictment for coercion and abuse of office, two felony counts carrying up to 109 years in prison. All this happened as Perry was considering a bid for the 2016 Republican nomination for president, and it's one of the reasons why he dropped out of the race.[22]

A second reason for corrupt prosecutions in America is that the sanctions for prosecutorial misbehavior are weak, so prosecutors often pursue their defendants with the intensity of Inspector Javert.[23] "It's a result-oriented process today, fairness be damned," reports a former U.S. district attorney.[24] According to Judge Alex Kozinski of the Ninth Circuit Court, violations of the prosecution's duty to turn over exculpatory evidence "have reached epidemic proportions."[25] In Canada and England, crown attorneys may be sued for malicious prosecution if they lacked a reasonable and proper cause for the prosecution and were motivated by an improper purpose, but prosecutors in America enjoy an absolute immunity from personal liability.[26]

Third, criminal procedure rules are heavily tilted toward the prosecution compared with other common law countries, and that helps explain the difference in conviction rates. In America, federal prosecutors secure guilty pleas from 96 percent of the defendants, and they also win convictions against three-quarters of the remaining 4 percent. In Canada, one-third of the criminal defendants either are acquitted or emerge victorious after crown attorneys decide to abandon the prosecution.[27]

In America, those who argue that we'd see less corruption with stiffer campaign finance laws seem to assume that such laws would never be abused as a political weapon, that corruptible politicians who do the bidding of their donors would be models of integrity when it comes to election laws. Nothing could be more naïve. Campaign finance reformers may burn with honest zeal, but they seem to think they're living in Nirvana—or New Zealand. Campaign finance laws might work well in less corrupt countries, but in America, First Amendment guarantees of free speech and free assembly are very possibly the best we can do.

There's something that Madison forgot when he borrowed the idea of a separation of powers from the "celebrated Montesquieu," thinking it might somehow limit corruption. What he forgot is that Montesquieu was a sociologist more than a theorist, and knew that each culture requires its own form of laws and government. Before it is anything else, American law, including its campaign finance laws, must be American, and suitable for a country with less than sterling levels of trust and public integrity.

— 15 —

Policing Crony Capitalism: What Doesn't Work

THE GIFTS THAT GO straight into an official's pockets are intrinsically suspect when the official subsequently favors the giver. If that's the most troubling kind of lapse, the least worrisome is logrolling, the trading of concessions in a bill, as happened in the bargaining over Obamacare. It's the intermediate kind of case that defies easy answers, the contribution of money to the official's political campaign, followed by favored treatment for the donor. For the politician who spends many of his waking hours trying to raise campaign cash, there will be every reason to offer donors what Justice Kennedy blessed as "ingratiation and access,"[1] and this goes some way to explaining crony capitalism in America.

We might complain of the distorting effect of money in politics, but if campaign contributions were entirely banned, we'd doubtless see more corruption. Incumbents would then enjoy a virtually insurmountable advantage, and corrupt officials would be all but impossible to dislodge. But if we wouldn't ban campaign contributions, we can still regulate them, within the First Amendment confines established by the Supreme Court, and that's what Congress sought to do in the Federal Election Campaign Act of 1971, as amended by the Watergate Congress in 1974.[2]

Building on prior law, the act restricted campaign financing in three ways: disclosure requirements, contribution limits and expenditure caps.

- *Disclosure requirements:* Donors were made to disclose their identities and the amount of their contributions.
- *Contribution limits:* Donors were limited in how much they could give.
- *Expenditure limits:* Candidates and parties were limited in how much they could spend.

None of these did the trick. Disclosure requirements can mostly be avoided with a wee bit of effort. Contribution limits have effectively been abolished by judicial and regulatory decisions, at least for donors with a lawyer at their side. Expenditure limits were struck down in 1976 by the Supreme Court in the seminal case of *Buckley v. Valeo*, which was brought by Senator James Buckley, a conservative Republican, and Eugene McCarthy, a liberal Democrat, to contest the 1974 law.[3]

To the extent our campaign finance laws have any teeth, they've managed to be both vague and highly technical, and that's a trap for the unwary. Given the possibility of politically motivated prosecutions for violation of the laws, they might cause more corruption than they cure, and a strong case can be made that we'd be better off without any of them.

Disclosure Requirements

Disclosure requirements were upheld in *Buckley v. Valeo*, and in 2010 the Supreme Court, in *Citizens United v. FEC*, held that donors to political action committees could also be required to identify themselves.[4] That might not sound terribly burdensome as a remedy for the much-decried "dark money" of anonymous contributions. But it is a real burden, for two reasons.

First, disclosure requirements can amount to a substantial restriction on First Amendment free-speech rights when they are triggered by too low a threshold. I saw this myself when I organized a support group for a political candidate. It was mostly a matter of networking among friends, until we had 160 people on board. That was costless, and creating a website took less than $40. But then we needed a publicist to get the message out, and some of us wondered whether we might also sponsor content on the web. The problem was that we'd have been required to form a political action committee if we raised or spent more than $1,000, and reading through the Federal Election Commission's helpful 124-page brochure we discovered that doing so would require a segregated bank account, a taxpayer ID number and a treasurer who would assume personal liability if he didn't file complete and accurate quarterly reports on time. All this was simply too much to contemplate. The $1,000 limit isn't going to be a problem for groups that plan six- or seven-figure efforts, but it put a stop to our plans for a relatively modest outreach campaign.

The message sent out by these rules is that politics is too important to be done by ordinary citizens and is best left to the professionals. When a small local group wants to get active, it's all too easy for powerful opponents or IRS officials to accuse them of breaking election law. To compound the problem, grassroots groups that do emerge are labeled "AstroTurf" organizations, allegedly directed by wealthy donors. As the former Federal Election Commission chairman Bradley Smith observes, "We are hacking at the most basic levels where people learn democracy, and then we wonder why Congress is so dysfunctional."[5]

The second reason why donors should be permitted to remain anonymous is the threat of legal, economic or social sanctions if they back an unpopular cause. There is always a temptation to suppress opposing voices, as Oliver Wendell Holmes Jr. noted in his dissent in *Abrams v. United States*.

> Persecution for the expression of opinion seems to me perfectly logical. If you have no doubt of your premises . . . and want a certain result with all your heart you naturally [want to] sweep away all opposition. . . . But when men have realized that time has upset many fighting faiths, they may come to believe . . . that the ultimate good desired is better reached by free trade in ideas—that the best test of truth is the power of the thought to get itself accepted in the competition of the market, and that truth is the only ground upon which their wishes safely can be carried out.[6]

If Americans ever agreed with Holmes, fewer would seem to do so today, since our sense of fair play has been withered by bitter partisanship.

This makes it easier for a government to evade responsibility when it pursues political enemies, as we saw in the IRS targeting scandal. If we've lost the sense of what in justice is owed to people with whom we disagree, we'll not object when the government persecutes a common foe. With the innumerable and obscure public welfare offenses created by the modern regulatory state, moreover, it's not difficult to find a stick to beat up political opponents. The growth of executive power and the shrinking of congressional oversight enable a president to call out political enemies and let loose his regulatory minions upon them. That's something Nixon did, with his "enemies list," and conservatives argue that Obama outdid Nixon in that respect.

As devastating as legal attacks can be, the economic and social sanctions for supporting a controversial cause might be even more intimidating, thanks to new media resources. Movies filmed in the *Buckley v. Valeo* era, such as *All the President's Men*, have become an unintended source of humor, as we watch a Bob Woodward dig up out-of-town telephone books to search for contact information. Today, with only a few clicks, we can find out who has made a campaign contribution, to whom and where they live. Our private space has shrunk, and our public face is visible anywhere in the world; and this has made it easier to target political foes. We're at the mercy of people with an ideological animus a thousand miles away who can brand a person as the enemy of all decent people and then pursue a vendetta through his customers or employer.[7] It's all done in the name of purity, but it's really about intimidation.

In the past, boycotts were highly localized affairs aimed at the neighborhood store. Today, a national boycott can be organized within days, as happened to Chick-fil-A when its chief operating officer was found to have opposed same-sex marriage.[8] The same thing happened when the National Organization for Marriage supported the Proposition 8 ban on same-sex marriage, and its donor list with home addresses was made searchable by the *Los Angeles Times*. What

followed was a blacklist and the forced resignation of one of the donors, Brendan Eich, the Mozilla CEO.[9] Those who support same-sex
marriage may think such punishments are well deserved, but if so
one might question their commitment to free speech.

The rise and fall of the *Journal of American Greatness* (JAG) un-
derscores just how things have changed. Launched by a group of
Straussian Trump supporters (really!) in early 2016, JAG mounted
an intellectual defense of American nationalism and realism in foreign affairs, of "Trumpism" if not of Donald Trump. On its website, it
identified its contributors as follows.

> *Who are you?*
>
> You mean in the Samuel Huntington sense? We are American
> patriots aghast at the stupidity and corruption of American poli-
> tics, particularly in the Republican Party, and above all in what pass-
> es for the "conservative" intellectual movement.
>
> *No, literally—who are you guys?*
>
> None of your damned business.
>
> *Why won't you tell us?*
>
> Because the times are so corrupt that simply stating certain
> truths is enough to make one unemployable for life.
>
> *That's a bit dramatic, isn't it?*
>
> Ask Brendan Eich.

After only six months on the web, JAG went dark, and one reason
was the fear that its writers might be identified and fired from their
jobs. They wrote under pseudonyms, but still believed they might
be outed, or "doxed." That's when an Internet researcher identifies
an anonymous blogger through public records or other social media
sites, and then metes out a dose of online vigilante justice.

Stendhal called small-town social sanctions "the most irritating
form of despotism,"[10] and to escape them many of us sought the anonymity and freer air of big-city life. But now Marshall McLuhan's
global village has caught up with us, in the virtual world in which we
increasingly live. And while the village Robespierre might sometimes

forget, the Internet never does. A stray comment taken out of context, a joke even, lives on forever, as fresh today as on the day it was uttered thirty years ago, a hammer in the hands of an ideological enemy.

That's why campaign donors should be allowed to remain anonymous. Under the Internal Revenue Code, there are three ways they can do so, and notwithstanding the outcry against "dark money," each should be preserved.

• 501(c)(3)'s—First, donors can remain anonymous through a tax-deductible gift to a tax-exempt charity registered under section 501(c)(3) of the tax code. The (c)(3) might be a hospital or a university, but it might also be a think tank that shapes the political debate by educating the public on issues of the day, such as health care or foreign policy.

Think tanks are not permitted to solicit votes for or against a candidate, but their educational mission can include "issue ads" on television or social media. Where the ads mention a particular candidate and in substance amount to political campaigning, *Citizens United* ruled that the donors might be required to identify themselves.[11] In other cases, however, the donors are permitted to remain anonymous, just as James Madison, Alexander Hamilton and John Jay did when they published *The Federalist Papers* under the pseudonym of "Publius."

The donors must disclose the gifts on their individual tax returns, and the (c)(3) is also required to disclose large gifts to the IRS, but in both cases the IRS is required to keep donor names confidential. That won't help if the (c)(3) chooses to disclose its donors, and in any event the IRS has been known to release donor names.[12] So too have state authorities, in states that require (c)(3)'s to register with them. Like the IRS, the states have pledged to maintain donor confidentiality, but the names of conservative donors to 501(c)(3)'s have nevertheless been released in California, inadvertently it is said.

Even where a state requires donor disclosure, savvy donors might work their way around this rule by routing their support through a donor-advised fund ("DAF"), such as Donors Trust in Alexandria, Virginia. The DAF can contribute to a 501(c)(3), and while the decision to do so formally rests with it alone, it will seek the donor's advice and presumably seldom depart from it. Had Brendan Eich asked the DAF to support the National Organization for Marriage's 501(c)(3) Education Fund, neither the IRS nor the State of California would have been able to link him to it, and he would have kept his job. He would have told the IRS about his gift to the DAF, and the DAF would have told the State of California about its support for the National Organization for Marriage, but no one could have linked Eich to the same-sex-marriage debate.

• **501(c)(6)'s**—Second, donors may keep their support secret by routing it through a group organized under section 501(c)(6) of the tax code, such as the U.S. Chamber of Commerce. That won't work unless the donor and the (c)(6) see eye to eye on issues, but if they do the donor can enjoy the same anonymity as it would with a DAF. The Chamber may campaign for or against a political candidate provided that this isn't its primary activity, and can also spend an unlimited amount on lobbying. To the extent that the Chamber uses the moneys for political ends or for lobbying, its donors lose their tax deduction but may nevertheless remain anonymous.

• **501(c)(4)'s**—Third, donors who aren't looking for a tax deduction can hide their identities through gifts made under section 501(c)(4) of the tax code to social welfare organizations such as the Wisconsin Club for Growth. Like the charitable institutions organized under section 501(c)(3), a (c)(4) is permitted to keep its donor lists confidential.[13] But there's a trade-off. On the one hand, unlike a (c)(3), a (c)(4) is permitted to advocate for or against a political candidate. On the other hand, the (c)(4) donor pays for this permission by losing the tax deduction that (c)(3) donors have.

To qualify under the tax code, a (c)(4) must operate "primarily to further the common good and general welfare," and that's a matter of controversy among those who don't see much common good or general welfare in what the Club for Growth is up to. By convention, the requirement has come to mean that the (c)(4) can't spend more than 50 percent of its moneys on political advocacy. For a highly partisan (c)(4), that can look like a tax on anonymity. In return for keeping its donor lists confidential, the organization can spend half its moneys on the political causes in which it's really interested, provided it spends the other 50 percent on hospitals and colleges it doesn't really care about. Mind you, some of that other money can go to ideologically aligned (c)(3) think tanks, and a partisan (c)(4) might even think it worthwhile to win a bit of goodwill through a gift for cancer research. Even apart from that, the 50 percent rule needn't be much of a barrier. A (c)(4) that spends half on politics and donates the other 50 percent to a second, like-minded (c)(4) can ensure that 75 percent of its support goes to politics, and this becomes 87.5 percent if a third (c)(4) is employed.

In addition, the (c)(4) cannot coordinate its activities with the candidate it supports. This requirement, which was the excuse for the police raid on the Wisconsin Club for Growth members, was premised on the belief that political parties, being required to disclose their donors, would otherwise set up shell (c)(4)'s to solicit funds from anonymous donors. That's increasingly not how politics works today, however. A (c)(4) doesn't need a political party's input or advice. Knowing how to respond to a negative ad is seldom rocket science, and it's not even clear that the party is better informed than the (c)(4). The reality is that social welfare organizations don't take direction from political parties but instead employ their own advisers to determine how moneys should best be spent.

The best-known (c)(4), Americans for Prosperity, organized around Charles and David Koch and the donor base they have assembled, bids to eclipse the Republican Party itself. It employs 1,200 full-time staffers, three times as many as the Republican National Committee, and announced plans to spend nearly $800 million on 2016 congressional races. It carries out its own searches for like-minded political candidates, performs opposition research, plans legislative agendas and conducts microdata analyses of likely voters, all at a more advanced level than the Republican Party does. It doesn't need the RNC to tell it what to do, and reasonably thinks itself more sophisticated than Party regulars.[14] The flow of information is often from the (c)(4) to the party, rather than the other way.

It's a similar story with the Center for American Progress (CAP), a $45 million (c)(3), and its "sister advocacy organization," a (c)(4) called the Center for American Progress Action Fund. Created by John Podesta in 2003, CAP quickly became the country's leading progressive think tank. Podesta had been Bill Clinton's chief of staff in the White House, and he left CAP to serve as Hillary Clinton's campaign chairman. While doing so, he continued to serve on the CAP board and looked to it as an idea factory and potential war room for a Hillary Clinton White House. Neera Tanden, a veteran Democratic operative who succeeded Podesta as the CAP president, emailed top Hillary advisers with a suggestion about an issue the campaign should pursue, and boasted that CAP Action, the (c)(4) organization, "can get that story started." When the Clinton Foundation scandal broke in 2015, Tanden asked Podesta, "Let me know if there's anything I or we [thru c4] can do to help."[15] That's coordination if anything is, but CAP Action has escaped prosecution, which is an argument for permitting all (c)(4)'s to coordinate with political parties. Where we've seen hackles raised about coordination, it's been mostly an excuse for a hypocritical and partisan attack on political enemies.

The various channels for anonymous support usefully serve the donor who reasonably seeks anonymity, and who has a lawyer at his side. But they're hemmed with vague technical requirements that have been used for one-sided charges against ideological foes, and they've exposed the legally unsophisticated and politically incorrect donor to the wrath of a new media mob. We'd be better off if we simply permitted all campaign contributions to be anonymous.

Contribution Limits

While it struck down spending caps, the Supreme Court in *Buckley v. Valeo* upheld contribution limits. Campaign spending gives voters more information, and that's not corruption. Voters are free to believe or not believe what they're given. But with contributions, there's a donor-official nexus, and that makes it different. Like bribes, campaign contributions can result in a quid pro quo and influence official decisions.

That's going to require a judgment call about what the right contribution level might be. If the limit is set too low, it deprives political parties of needed funds and serves to protect corrupt incumbents from challengers. It might also drive cash-starved politicians to raise money from corrupt donors through illegal means. That's why, in the abstract, contribution limits might either reduce or increase corruption levels.[16] In the United States, however, contribution limits have essentially been nullified after *Buckley*. First, donors found a way to amass large amounts of money by bundling contributions from groups of friends, with each individual donor adhering to a $5,000 limit. More recently, in 2015, a semi-truck was driven through the limits imposed on presidential campaign contributions. Instead of being restricted to $30,800, an individual is now permitted to contribute up to $366,100 per year to a presidential candidate and party organizations working to elect the candidate. That works out to just under $1.5 million for a couple over a two-year period.[17]

Second, donors can contribute unlimited amounts of money to independent expenditure Super PACs that call for the election or defeat of a particular candidate but do not coordinate with a political party. Political action committees have been around for a long time. Some are sponsored by interest groups, such as PorkPAC for the National Pork Producers Council, or SNACK PAC for the Snack Food Association. Then there are corporate-connected PACs organized by business firms, which pay overhead expenses and accept individual contributions from executives, employees, or shareholders. Donors to such PACs must adhere to election contribution limits, but in *Buckley v. Valeo* the Supreme Court ruled that no limits could be placed on donations to PACs that do not coordinate with the candidate and simply produce issue ads that speak to policies of the day, without explicitly urging viewers to vote for or against a candidate.

Then, in *Citizens United*, the Court held that PACs could also run ads that ask viewers to vote for or against a candidate.

TABLE 2

2016 Contribution Limits

	An individual may give	Corporations may give
To himself, as a candidate	No limit	—
To each candidate	$2,700 per election	0
To a corporate-connected separate segregated fund (PAC) or a nonconnected PAC	$5,000 per year	Administrative expenses for corporate-connected PACs
To the national party committee	$33,400 per year	$33,400 per year
To each state, district, or local party committee	$10,000 per year	$10,000 per year
Total permissible giving to presidential candidates and party organizations working to elect the candidate	$366,100 per year	$366,100 per year
Total permissible giving to independent expenditure groups (Super PACs)	No limit	No limit

Citizens United, a private corporation, produced a movie that was ostensibly an issue ad but in essence was express advocacy, "a feature-length negative advertisement that urges viewers to vote against Senator Clinton for President."[18] In striking down contribution limits for the company, the Court implicitly gave us today's Super PACs, and lest any doubt remain, the District of Columbia Court of Appeals held *en banc* in *SpeechNOW v. FEC* that Congress could never limit contributions to independent expenditure groups.[19] As they are independent, the possibility of pay-for-play corruption is much weaker than in cases where the donor deals directly with the candidate.[20]

Citizens United has been roundly condemned for holding that corporations can contribute to independent expenditure groups. Memorably, Obama lectured the Supreme Court about the error of their ways in the 2011 State of the Union Address. The ruling has not resulted in a corporate takeover of American elections, however. Corporate support didn't increase afterward, and has been dwarfed by individual donations. Much of the corporate support, in fact, comes from individuals who employ shell corporations in an effort to maintain anonymity.[21]

What we *have* seen is an explosive growth in spending by Super PACs. In the 2012 election they were still relatively novel and were outraised ten to one by the official party campaigns. By 2014, Super PAC fundraising had increased threefold, to $700 million, which was nearly half the total amount that the two parties spent, according to the Open Secrets blog of the Center for Responsive Politics. In 2016 the sum was $1.1 billion, approaching the $1.5 billion of official party spending in the presidential election.[22]

The rise of Super PACs has transformed American politics, though not in a way anyone expected. What has happened is what in the business world is called disintermediation, where the middleman is cut out—as where one books a flight or a hotel room directly, with the aid of an online resource like Kayak, instead of going through a travel agent. Similarly, instead of relying on a political party to choose candidates or finance campaigns, one can donate to a Super PAC that is more reliably aligned with one's political preferences. As this happens, the parties become weaker, with fewer donors.[23] That's why Republicans and Democrats agreed to increase the maximum amount that an individual could give to a party or a presidential candidate by more than tenfold, in order to meet the challenge from insurgent Super PACs.

The spectacular growth of Super PAC spending has outraged campaign reformers, who complain that it permits big-bucks conservative donors to buy elections. There isn't much evidence of that happening, however, since the top givers are as likely to support

Democrats as Republicans. In 2016, Super PACs for Hillary Clinton outspent Trump Super PACs by three to one.[24]

Contribution limits have therefore been an abject failure, as there are too many ways to get around the restrictions. If one side of the henhouse is fenced up, the other three are left open. And while the rules are easily avoided by political sophisticates, they have served to criminalize political speech by naïfs such as Dinesh D'Souza, and have given us more corruption in the form of partisan prosecutions. And that's a reason to do away with them.

Spending Caps

Beginning with *Buckley v. Valeo*, the Supreme Court struck down legislative limits on campaign expenditures while upholding limits on campaign contributions. Some people find the distinction troubling, since contributions and expenditures are obviously linked, like a faucet to a garden hose. Turn off the faucet and nothing comes out of the nozzle. Why the distinction, then?

First, limiting expenditures affects free-speech rights more directly than limiting contributions. With spending limits, a popular insurgent voice like Bernie Sanders, funded by small-dollar donors, might be entirely silenced while an establishment candidate is insulated from attack. Spending limits would also protect incumbents, who have the advantage of name recognition and a ready network of supporters. It's the outside challenger who needs to spend money to get his name out there.[25]

Second, contribution limits more clearly focus on the possibility of corruption, which the Court thought was the only justification for regulating political campaigns. In the eyes of the Court, what constitutes corruption is the undue influence a campaign donor may have over an official. That problem won't occur when a candidate such as Donald Trump decides how much of his own money to spend on his campaign, but it might arise when someone else contributes to a campaign, because this creates the cash nexus between donors and elected officials from which pay-for-play favors may follow.

Buckley's critics have feared that there would be too much money in politics if campaign expenditures weren't capped.[26] But what is the right amount of expenditures? Those who say that today's campaign spending is excessive ask us to compare it with spending levels of the past. On one estimate, $540 million (in 2012 dollars) was spent on the 1976 election, compared with $7 billion on the 2012 election.[27] That's a 1,300 percent increase, which does seem huge. It's substantially more than the threefold increase in the size of government over the period, and more than the 250 percent increase in personal disposable income.[28] But even if we're putting more money into politics now than we did forty years ago, who's to say that we had the optimal level back then? We spend three times as much on video games as we do on campaign spending, and no one is trying to pry our controllers away from us. How much more foolish would it be to try to limit the information that voters receive about their government. One study of the spending increase from 1978 to 2000 reported that campaign spending tracked personal income and the degree to which electoral races were competitive.[29] What appeared to fuel the increase was a greater interest in the political process, and that's more a sign of virtue than of corruption.

This is not to dispute the claim that money matters in winning elections. Even in the topsy-turvy 2016 presidential primaries, more spending was significantly correlated with more votes, for candidates of both parties. In a linear regression using data provided by Inside.gov, an additional $0.67 spent on a campaign produced one more vote.[30] Yet the election also showed that there's a limit to the value of money, as we saw in Jeb Bush's spectacular flameout when he spent $150 million on the primaries without winning a single state.[31] Similarly, Lee Drutman reports that outside spending (including Super PAC spending) didn't do much for congressional candidates in 2012. It may have increased the vote share, but there was no evidence that it made the difference in electing anyone.[32]

Whether or not money really matters in elections, the Supreme Court has effectively banned legislative limits on campaign spending, which it held to trench impermissibly on First Amendment rights. As for campaign disclosure requirements and contribution limits, they've become traps for the unwary. To the extent that the Federal Election Campaign Act took aim at public corruption, it's been a gun that shoots blanks. That's not an argument for surrender, but rather an invitation to examine other ways in which to address America's problem with crony capitalism.

— 16 —

Three Reforms

CAMPAIGN FINANCE RESTRICTIONS inevitably put fetters on First Amendment rights of free speech and assembly, and those rights are so close to the core of our constitutionally protected liberties that the Supreme Court has held that only the threat of corruption or the appearance of corruption can justify impeding them. Yet the campaign finance restrictions we saw in the last chapter have done little or nothing to diminish corruption or its appearance, and instead have bred a cynicism about whether anything can be done to arrest the slide into crony capitalism. Moreover, what solutions have been proffered are often prompted by partisan motives, and might lead to *more* public corruption.

This doesn't mean that nothing can be done, and in this chapter I look at three useful reforms that would pass constitutional muster. First, we might require that all political contributions be made under a seal of anonymity, in order to keep officials in the dark about the sources of support. Second, targeted contribution laws might restrict gifts from a narrow set of donors from whom pay-for-play is most likely to be encountered. Finally, certain donors might be barred from accepting a position in government, and congressmen and their staffers might be prohibited from working as lobbyists after they leave government.

Mandated Anonymity

In a previous life, I was the executive director of my law school's judicial education program, the George Mason Law & Economics Center. We offered courses for judges on price theory, American history, political theory, literature and philosophy, and our instructors included such people as the economist (and Nobel laureate) Jim Buchanan, the historian Joe Ellis, the philosopher John Searle, and the literary critic Roger Shattuck. We told instructors to stay away from political topics, and we posted reading lists on our website. No one had a serious problem with the content of the programs. What people objected to, primarily, was our policy of keeping our donor list confidential.

I resisted releasing the names. The donors were simply your usual suspects: a bunch of blue-chip firms and some conservative foundations. Corporate support was only 10 percent of the budget, and I argued that revealing their names would create problems where none had existed before. The canons of judicial ethics recommend that donations to state judicial election campaigns be anonymous so that a judge can't be accused of showing favoritism to a named donor, and the same principle applied to our judicial education program. But after three bills were introduced in the U.S. Senate to shut down our program, a backroom accommodation was worked out in which we would publish our donor list in return for some peace and quiet—which we got, since our corporate support was shown to be small potatoes.

As we saw in the last chapter, political donors can remain anonymous if they contribute to a 501(c)(4) organization. That raises storms of protest from the left about the scourge of dark money in politics. But there's bound to be less corruption attached to the money when the gift is anonymous. If the donor's identity is truly hidden, the left hand won't know what the right hand has given, and pay-for-play concerns won't arise.

There's a second way in which public disclosure might result in more rather than less corruption. The theory behind disclosure requirements is that shining a flashlight on the contribution will deter both the donor and the official from striking a corrupt bargain, but it might instead have the opposite effect. By identifying corrupt officials to the world, disclosure tells us who can be bribed; and by identifying their donors, it tells other corrupt officials who might want to buy influence from them. For example, donors might not know whom to support when they back an energy bill. Knowing that a congressman from a nonenergy state regularly receives support from Exxon might then be very useful. Further, knowing that a congressman receives Exxon support and subsequently votes against Exxon interests will tell donors whom not to support. They'll know who can be bought, and who can't be trusted to stay bought.[1]

Suppose, therefore, that we made anonymity the rule and not the exception. That's what two Yale law professors, Bruce Ackerman and Ian Ayres, have suggested in *Voting with Dollars*, arguing that anonymity would eliminate the possibility of quid pro quo corruption.[2] Imagine how far Jonnie Williams would have gotten with Bob McDonnell if the gifts to his wife had taken the form of an anonymous gift card from Chanel.

Anonymity would have the further benefit of shielding the donors from boycotts and other forms of public pressure. This principle was upheld under the Fourteenth Amendment when the Supreme Court struck down a 1956 Alabama law that required the NAACP to turn over its membership lists to the state.[3] Alabama had simply wanted to harass NAACP members, in violation of the right of association. Today, when conservative donors are personally vilified by the president, or fired by their employers for their political beliefs, a rule of anonymity in political donations would protect the same association rights.[4]

Mandated anonymity is the rule when we vote, and a good case can be made that it should be likewise for political donations. Anonymity would sacrifice the informational value associated with knowing the donor's identity, but in most cases that doesn't amount to much. Knowing that an ad praising the coal industry was paid for by members of the coal industry, or that one opposing school choice was placed by a teachers' union, won't greatly increase the sum of our knowledge.[5] Its isn't that voters don't pay attention to donor disclosure at all. Some people, for example, will give less credence to a political ad if they learn it was produced by a controversial donor such as the Koch-backed Americans for Prosperity.[6] Charles and David Koch have been vilified by Obama and by major media outlets, and the mud has stuck, turning them into Enemies of the People.[7] Donor disclosure may stir up partisan emotions, but often it doesn't make us much wiser. Without disclosure, we could still reasonably assume that an ad attacking Obamacare has come from a right-wing donor, and which one in particular wouldn't matter much.

Those who charge that anonymity is a way of hiding nefarious secrets may actually be providing reasons to keep the protection of anonymity. In 2016, for example, after twenty-two conservative think tanks had expressed their concerns about measures to combat global warming, nine Democratic senators responded with a letter painting the groups as part of a shadowy "web of climate denial" and asking them to disclose their donors. "Because your organizations do not regularly disclose where your donations come from," they wrote, "we cannot know for sure how deep and wide the web of denial truly is."[8] The letter was posted online, and the senators could depend on the Internet to echo the charge of "climate denial" and impose its social sanctions. But disclosure requirements were meant to promote democracy, not muffle it. When they've become a viewpoint-based restriction on free speech, including core political speech, that's a good reason to get rid of them.

In *Buckley v. Valeo*, the Supreme Court suggested that donors would not be required to disclose their identities if there was a reasonable probability that it would "subject them to threats, harassment, or reprisals from either Government officials or private parties."[9] That's where we are today, and since a rule of mandated anonymity would serve the further purpose of reining in corruption, the Supreme Court would likely uphold it.

Mandated anonymity wouldn't remove money from politics. Elected officials would still need financial support, and would bid for it through the policies they promote. If contributions dried up after they announced their support for policy X, they'd be tempted to back *not-X*. Mandated anonymity would dampen pay-for-play, however. The politician who wants to maximize his war chest might be led to vote for or against a broad policy, such as free trade, but with anonymous support he wouldn't get the signal to push for the narrow and targeted provision in a thousand-page bill that benefits one company only. That means we'd see less big-donor money in politics, while small-donor and ideological money would become more influential.

Would a rule of mandated anonymity be effective, though? What's to stop a donor from telling the candidate about his contribution? Private messages of this kind might be criminalized, but they'd mostly escape detection. Worse still, making a federal offense out of a wink and a nudge opens up the possibility of partisan prosecutions.

A better solution would be to muffle the contribution by making it difficult to verify that the donor is telling the truth. For example, the fund into which the contribution is made might be required to pay it out in dribs and drabs, making it hard to link the contribution to the donor. At that point, the donor's claim might be dismissed as "cheap talk." But then what's to stop the donor or his lobbyist from sending the official the cancelled check or other evidence of payment, with his name on it? In response, Ackerman and Ayres argue that giving the donor a ten-day cooling-off period, during which the gift could be withdrawn, would take care of this. The official would see the check but wouldn't know if the donor was going to exercise his withdrawal rights. This proposal assumes a degree of deceit and craftiness that most people lack, however. In addition, a donor who provides support on a regular basis might be able to pierce the veil of anonymity through a series of repeated gifts, none of which he withdraws.

Finally, it would be virtually impossible, as a political matter, to adopt a rule mandating anonymity. Those who object to dark money in politics would reject it out of hand, while politicians who have invested capital in blackening the names of particular donors would have even greater reason to oppose it. The proposal has been studiously ignored by congressmen on both sides, and politically it's a nonstarter.

Suspect Donors

The Supreme Court has upheld general contribution limits. Taking this a step further, contributions from a particular class of donors might be entirely banned. Federal courts have so held for the dodgiest of donors, and it's not very difficult to see how a ban might be extended to other suspect donors.

One kind of suspect donors is *government contractors*, who were prohibited from contributing to political campaigns by an amendment to the Hatch Act of 1939.[10] The original act limited the political activities of federal officers and employees, in part to ensure that the government could hire the best-qualified people, and has been upheld by the Supreme Court.[11] In 1940 the ban was extended to government contractors, since they so closely resemble federal employees,[12] and this extension was recently upheld by a unanimous *en banc* District of Columbia Court of Appeals in *Wagner v. FEC*.[13] The court held that concern about pay-for-play corruption justified prohibiting all donations from contractors, rather than just placing a ceiling on them: "A contribution made while negotiating or performing a contract looks like a quid pro quo, whether or not it truly is."[14]

What the court had in mind was the possibility of the kind of rent-seeking we saw in Chapter 2, where the donor seeks a favor from the official. Without the ban, the court noted, officials might also engage in *rent extraction* by demanding a contribution in return for a favor or the threat of a government sanction.[15] A congressman's threat advantage against a government contractor is even greater than that against civil servants, who at least have job protection.

A second example of suspect donors is *municipal bond dealers*, given the great possibilities for rent extraction in the highly lucrative municipal bond market. Bond dealers complained that the state and local officials from whom they sought business had shaken them down for political contributions. Fed up with being dunned for money, they proposed a rule change to bar contributions to city and state officials, and the Securities and Exchange Commission adopted this as Rule G-37. On appeal, it was upheld by the District of Columbia Circuit Court in *Blount v. SEC* (1995).[16] Judge Stephen Williams noted that Rule G-37 did not prevent the brokers and dealers from engaging in other forms of political support.

Might a similar ban on other kinds of donors be justified in the "full-blown modern interest-group state" where Judge Williams found himself?[17] A good place to start would be America's *lobbyists*. In 2012, direct lobbying expenses amounted to $3.3 billion, about twice that of 2000, according to the Open Secrets blog of the Center for Responsive Politics. That's more than the $1.2 billion that both major candidates spent in the 2012 presidential election, and it even exceeds the $2.6 billion in total spending by the parties and outside groups on the presidential campaign. Of the $3.3 billion, only about 3 percent came from ideological donors like the NAACP, or labor unions such as the American Federation of Teachers. The rest came from corporate America. If a sugar cartel succeeds in maintaining its subsidies, we shouldn't be surprised.

With the expansion of the regulatory state and the rise of crony capitalism, business firms learned that they needed a lobbying presence in Washington. In the early 1990s, Microsoft's Bill Gates thought he could live in splendid isolation from the world of politics. The firm had only a one-man lobbying shop, located above a suburban Washington shopping mall. The firm's business rivals—notably Netscape, Sun Microsystems and Oracle—spent heavily on lobbying, however, and spread the word that Microsoft, with its Windows operating system, had become a monopolistic threat to the high-tech industry and to democracy itself. With the benefit of hindsight, the concern seems foolish today, but after a media campaign sponsored by the lobbyists, the press began to vilify Microsoft. Gates was a "rich spoiled brat," warned Maureen Dowd, and Microsoft was an "egomaniacal, dangerous giant that has cut off the air supply of competitors in a bid to control cyberspace."[18] In spring 1998, the Justice Department and twenty states filed an antitrust suit against Microsoft, and at trial Gates's display of arrogance was rewarded with an order that the company be split in two. This was reversed on appeal, but along the way Microsoft discovered the need to beef up its own lobbying. The firm hired Republican bigshot Haley Barbour, former congressman Vin Weber and a pair of former White House counsels, Boyden Gray and Lloyd Cutler; and they embarked on their own media campaign to defend Microsoft.[19] Today, Microsoft has one of the biggest government-relations offices in Washington, having discovered that every business in a crony nation is in partnership with the federal government, and woe to those who forget it.

Along the way, something had happened to the way in which big business regarded government. It could no longer be ignored, as Microsoft had tried to do in far-off Washington State. Firms now had to be pro-active, to anticipate threats of government intervention. And they would have every incentive to do so. For example, firms that lobby have a significantly lower probability of being detected for fraud.[20] And it's not just a question of keeping the regulatory wolves at bay. Instead, government relations departments have become profit centers, as the firms and their lobbyists exploit the new business opportunities provided by an expansive federal government. As we saw in chapter 2, firms that lobby lower their tax rate, and one study reported that for every dollar a firm spent on targeted tax loopholes, the payoff was between six dollars and twenty dollars.[21] *The Economist* reported in 2011 on a study finding that American firms that employed lobbyists had outperformed the S&P 500 by 11 percent a year since 2002.[22]

If lobbying increases a firm's value, there's not much evidence that corporate political contributions do so. While business firms are barred from making a direct grant to a campaign, they can do so indirectly by sponsoring a connected PAC to which their executives, employees or shareholders may contribute, and to which the firm pays overhead expenses. Prior to the 2002 Bipartisan Campaign Reform Act (McCain-Feingold), firms were also permitted to contribute "soft money" toward party-building activities, such as get-out-the-vote drives. And today they can support independent expenditure groups, particularly Super PACs after *Citizens United*. But the jury is out on whether this will increase a company's value. Michael Cooper and his colleagues reported a positive and significant relation between political contributions and future profitability among politically active firms.[23] But in a study that compared political donors to the much larger group of firms that stayed out of politics, the former performed worse than the latter.[24]

To complicate things, there's the difficulty of identifying just how interest group donors might use their leverage. The failure to give support can speak as powerfully as any contribution, since interest groups can employ their clout through threats of nonsupport, or of giving support to an opposing candidate or position.[25] An example of the sound of silence occurred during the backdoor negotiations over the Affordable Care Act (Obamacare). The Obama administration didn't want a replay of what happened when the Clinton administration tried to pass a health-care overhaul in 1993, and the pharmaceutical and health insurance industries sponsored a highly effective television ad campaign against the plan, with "Harry and Louise" throwing up their hands in exasperation over its complicated provisions. So before launching its own health-care legislation, the Obama administration threatened the pharmaceutical industry with higher taxes if it opposed the bill, but agreed to drop its support for letting Americans buy cheaper foreign prescription drugs if the industry kept quiet this time. The threats worked. In fact, the industry sponsored a new set of "Harry and Louise" ads, with the same actors explaining why this time they liked health-care reform. "A little more cooperation, a little less politics," said Louise to Harry.[26]

What the pharmaceutical industry experienced in the Obamacare negotiations looks something like a shakedown. And that may be one explanation for why businesses keep making political contributions even if they aren't getting much for their money. If a company has been dunned for contributions by threats from misbehaving officials, it should welcome restrictions on political spending, just as municipal bond dealers welcomed a rule restricting their own political contributions. Indeed, many firms were happy when corporate contributions were banned by the Tillman Act in 1907. The act resulted from a public backlash against the way Mark Hanna had demanded contributions from large corporations to the McKinley campaign, and from a general sense that big money was corrupting politics. When the Tillman Act was passed, one business leader said that he greeted it "with very much the same emotions with which a serf would his liberation from a tyrannous autocrat."[27] Similarly, corporate America welcomed McCain-Feingold's ban on soft-money corporate contributions, and the market reacted to news of the law with a yawn.[28]

Corporate political donations are therefore small potatoes compared with lobbying expenses. According to Lee Drutman, firms that make major lobbying expenditures (more than $1 million a year) spend fourteen times as much on lobbying as on their PACs. For firms that spend less than $50,000 in lobbying, the ratio is 40:1.[29] And the reason isn't hard to see. Corporate political donations don't appear to benefit the firm, but lobbying is an eminently sensible business expense. And unlike political contributions, which are diffuse, lobbyists will seek targeted regulatory relief, tax breaks, subsidies and earmarks. An object lesson on how small lobbying dollars can produce enormous gains was provided by the effort to pass the American Jobs Creation Act of 2004. The act gave American firms a one-time opportunity to repatriate earnings of foreign subsidiaries at a low 15 percent tax rate. A study found that ninety-three firms lobbied for the bill, at a cost of $283 million. That's not chump change, but what they received was $62.5 billion in tax savings, or a 220:1 return on investment.[30]

Counting up total dollars spent on a lobbying campaign doesn't necessarily tell us much, when what matters is marginal and not total dollars. We would expect the rational client to ask his lobbyist to spend resources up to the point where one more dollar of expenses equals the marginal benefit of an increased probability of a sought-for rule being adopted. When it's an uphill battle, when the rule in question is highly salient but deeply unpopular with the public, it can be rational for those who propose the rule to spend a lot and those who oppose it to spend little. There's also a great deal of status quo inertia when something novel is proposed, so one side can always be expected to spend more than the other.[31]

Studies that focus on counting dollars spent also fail to reflect the myriad ways in which lobbyists can weigh in to prevent issues from coming to the table. Keeping an unwanted rule from emerging out of committee can be as valuable as adopting a wanted rule, and often much easier too. Then there are all the regulatory refinements that are never contested, as well as the details of a thousand-page bill. In any event, it's hard to argue with the business judgment of corporate managers that money spent on lobbying is money well spent.

But if lobbying significantly shapes government policies, that's obviously not to say that it should be banned. First, the "grassroots lobbying" of nonprofits and citizen groups should not be hampered, and indeed cannot be fettered under any plausible interpretation of First Amendment rights, if only corruption or the appearance of corruption can justify restrictions on campaign activity. Grassroots lobbying is issue advocacy directed to the general public, typically asking citizens to voice their opinions to public officials about such high-salience issues as abortion and same-sex marriage. If the issue ad is successful, it's not going to line the pockets of a private party. While there is a gray area between the two kinds of lobbying, grassroots lobbying ordinarily has little in common with the paid, professional lobbying that seeks a regulatory furbelow for the benefit of a business client. Thus the Supreme Court properly held in *FEC v. Wisconsin Right to Life, Inc.* that an incorporated nonprofit that had accepted corporate contributions could not be prevented from spending resources on an issue ad.[32]

Another reason not to ban lobbying is that even professional lobbyists provide useful information to clients and to congressional staffers about the legislation and regulations being considered. Congressional staffers can't keep up with all the legislation that crosses their desks, and for new congressmen the learning curve is very steep. They'll rely on lobbyists to inform them about the unintended consequences of proposed legislation and keep them abreast of new initiatives, studies, and legislation. A trade bill might seem attractive in the abstract but will look far less appealing when a congressman learns it would mean major job losses in his district.[33] There is nothing wrong with any of this, and talking to legislators is constitutionally protected speech under the First Amendment's right to petition the government for a redress of grievances. However, that doesn't prevent Congress from regulating lobbying activities.

Lobbyists are required to disclose their activities, but that hasn't much hampered them. The 1995 Lobbying Disclosure Act required lobbyists to reveal their contacts with legislators, what issues they were lobbying, and how much they and their firms spent on it.[34] If that was meant to chill lobbyists, it's been singularly ineffective. Disclosure standards are lax, and lobbyists need not reveal the earmarks they are seeking or even the particular congressman they have contacted. The law did nothing to stem the flow of football tickets, expensive dinners and paid travel sent from lobbyists to congressmen and staffers. For example, Jack Abramoff arranged a $70,000 golf outing at St. Andrews in Scotland for the House majority leader, Tom DeLay, and his entourage. After this came to light, Congress banned most gift-giving practices with the 2007 Honest Leadership and Open Government Act (HLOGA).[35] That was a start, but more can be done along the lines proposed by an American Bar Association committee chaired by Harvard law professor Charles Fried.[36]

The First Amendment right to petition the government is a right to inform Congress of a grievance and to propose solutions. It's not a right to couple the request for legislative action with a payoff to the congressman. That's too much like a quid pro quo, and for this reason the ABA committee recommended that HLOGA's ban on gifts be extended to campaign contributions. The need to tighten contribution limits is especially pressing today, given the increased amounts that people can now give to candidates. With an individual limit of

$366,100, ten lobbyists could donate a total of $15 million to a presidential candidate or party organization over a four-year campaign cycle. They'll be spending their clients' money to do so, and this amounts to an implicit repeal of the Tillman Act's ban on corporate support.

Lobbyists should also be prohibited from "bundling," in which they persuade a group of people to write checks for a candidate and then hand over all the checks to the candidate committee. The prohibition should include organizing fundraising events, soliciting contributions, and serving on fundraising committees for a candidate. Beyond this, the ban might be extended to financial gifts in kind that go beyond the provision of advice to clients or information to officials, such as polling, mass communication efforts and coalition building.[37]

Federal circuit courts are divided on whether state bans on lobbyist contributions are constitutionally permissible.[38] There is reason to expect that the proposed federal ban would be upheld, however. It would simply be an extension of existing restrictions for government contractors and municipal bond dealers. It would also be a reasonable response to the extraordinary influence that lobbyists enjoy over our Congress in an era of crony capitalism, and wholly consistent with the Supreme Court's oft-stated concern about corruption and the appearance of corruption.[39] Finally, the much-deplored *Citizens United* decision has made it easier to argue for restrictions on campaign contributions from suspect donors. By widening the gate for contributions to independent organizations, the decision justifies a narrowing of the gate for contributions that are tainted by the possibility of pay-for-play. If lobbyists couldn't contribute to candidates and parties, they could simply channel their support into more innocent avenues.[40]

Chinese Walls

Apart from lobbyists, a good many Americans bundle support for presidential candidates, and many of them have their eyes on a political appointment. That's how our former ambassador to Hungary, Colleen Bell, got her job. She's a soap opera producer who was one of Obama's top campaign bundlers, raising more than $1 million for him together with her husband. The problem is that Hungary isn't exactly Ruritania. It's a NATO ally that is trending away from the West in the direction of Russia, and Bell's want of foreign policy chops led to this embarrassing exchange with Senator John McCain (R-AZ) at her nomination hearing.

> SEN. McCAIN: So what would you be doing differently from your predecessor, who obviously had very rocky relations with the present government?
>
> Ms. BELL: If confirmed, I look forward to working with the broad range of society . . . [Pause]
>
> SEN. McCAIN: My question was, what would you do differently?
>
> Ms. BELL: Senator, in terms of what I would do differently from my predecessor, Kounalakis . . . [Pause]
>
> SEN. McCAIN: That's the question.
>
> Ms. BELL: Well, what I would like to do when—if confirmed, I would like to work towards engaging civil society in a deeper . . . in a deeper ... [Pause]
>
> SEN. McCAIN: Obviously, you don't want to answer my question.

McCain was so unfair! Had he watched Ambassador Bell's *The Bold and the Beautiful*, he would have realized that those are perfectly good answers.

Then there was our ambassador to Argentina, Noah Mamet, a political consultant who raised $3.2 million for Obama in 2012. When he took some flak for admitting that he didn't speak Spanish and had never been to Argentina, the comedian Jon Stewart saw a virtue in his inexperience. Perhaps we should have a rule against nominees visiting a country before being appointed ambassador, he said, so we don't "ruin the surprise."

Of course, Obama didn't begin the practice of repaying political favors by appointing incompetent cronies to represent our country abroad. It's been a long, bipartisan tradition, but it's a slap in the face to career U.S. foreign service officers. In other countries, a distinguished civil servant might aspire to represent his country as its ambassador in one of the world's glittering capitals. In America, however, we appoint bundlers to serve as ambassadors in London, Paris, and Rome. As for our career diplomats, let them go to Libya.

Political cronyism of this kind is an insult to the countries to which we send the bundlers. Hungary's ambassador to the United States was an economist who had worked for the International Monetary Fund for twenty-seven years, but we sent a message to the Hungarians that they're less important to us than someone who can raise a spot of cash for a political campaign. No wonder they don't seem to like us. Ambassador Bell took up her appointment on January 21, 2015, and a month later Hungary signed an economic cooperation agreement with Russia. Mind you, Ambassador Bell had only just begun her work of engaging civil society.

Ambassadors are the official face of America to other countries. When they get the nod, the host country's media will tell its citizens just how they got their job, and for many it's an education on how we order things differently in America. Our ambassadorial appointments advertise to the world our tolerance for political corruption.

We wouldn't want to ban all offers of government positions to political donors, as we would lose too many able (and generous) public servants. On the other hand, there comes a point where the most avid of donors and bundlers begin to appear self-serving. Who they are is well known, as they are searchable on the web from Federal Election Commission records. Many are lobbyists, who would be banned from contributing under the proposed ABA rule, while others are simply ideological partisans who have no desire for a government position and who wouldn't be bothered by a ban on political appointments. But then there are people like Colleen Bell, and since bundling is notoriously the easiest way for an incompetent to get an ambassadorship, a prohibition on accepting a government position for a period of time after the donation wouldn't deprive us of many able public servants.

A Chinese Wall between bundlers and officials would likely pass constitutional muster, if the corruption concerns expressed in the *Wagner* and *Blount* decisions are found compelling. For similar reasons, courts would likely uphold a wall against migration in the other direction, from the executive branch to lobbying jobs, as Donald Trump has proposed, and this barrier should be extended to Congress. On leaving elective office, many congressmen and senior staffers become lobbyists and cash in on the contacts they have made. The Center for Responsive Politics reported in 2011 that at least 285 out of an estimated 1,000 former members of Congress were registered as lobbyists, and another 85 provided "strategic advice" for clients.[41]

"Revolving door" laws bar those people from lobbying their former colleagues for a period of time,[42] but the "cooling-off" periods of a year or two are entirely too short. When the most recent period expired in 2015, about 30 percent of the former congressmen and staffers had already begun work in corporate government-relations departments or as registered lobbyists.[43] Even without such a position, a newly retired politician might call up a former colleague in Congress and say, "I can't talk to you but you'll be getting a call tomorrow from someone in my office." In the cynical view of former congressman Jim Cooper, Congress has become a "farm league" for a lucrative K Street job as a lobbyist.[44] The gifts to the McDonnells were chump change by comparison with an ex-politician's potential earnings.

The hope for future employment with a lobbying firm corrupts Congress and legislative staff in the same way that the suggestion of a job at the Scruggs law firm was meant to corrupt Judge Lackey (Chapter 10). More than a campaign contribution, the promise of an enormous personal reward will incline a congressman to favor whatever the lobbyist might be seeking. It's also the kind of regulatory capture we saw in Chapter 2, but this time with a financial explanation for why the rule-maker permits himself to be captured.

It would doubtless be impossible to persuade congressmen to shut the revolving door with K Street that might lead them to millions of dollars upon retirement. There's a way around this problem, though, and that is to exempt any currently sitting congressman from the restrictions. In addition to permitting them to cash in after retirement, this would further benefit them as long as they wish to remain in Congress by making the office less attractive to prospective challengers. This reform measure would thus amount to an incumbent protection device for a time, but the long-term benefit would be worth that price.

— 17 —

The Heavenly City of the Enlightened Reformer

V ENAL THOUGH HE WAS, Francis Bacon believed that wisdom came from experience, and as the moderns had more accumulated experience to draw upon than the ancients, it stood to reason that the moderns would be wiser than those who came before. The ancients lived in the youth of the world, and it is we, the moderns, who are the true ancients, the adults in the room.[1]

If that's how we stand in relation to the past, what of the future? With more experience still, surely a Heavenly City awaits us. "O coming posterity," beseeched Robespierre, "hasten to bring forth our prosperity and happiness!"[2] That was how the Enlightenment philosophes spoke. "They denied that miracles ever happened," observed Carl Becker, "but believed in the perfectibility of the human race."[3]

There was an American Enlightenment, but apart from solitary figures such as Thomas Jefferson it was a sober affair that owed much more to Protestant divines than to the philosophes. They had Rousseau, we had Jonathan Edwards and John Witherspoon, for whom Rousseau's idealized vision of uncorrupted human nature would have seemed a dangerous snare; and it was Edwards and Witherspoon whose dark view of fallen mankind was represented at the 1787 Constitutional Convention. At Philadelphia they sought to write a constitution that would minimize the threat of corruption, but they had no illusions that the voters could be relied on to elect honest officials. They believed that voter preferences should be filtered by an intermediate set of politicians who could better judge the character of higher officials, and that the separation of powers would create a double filtration in which wasteful and self-interested bargains could not survive.

That didn't work out as expected, and there are two kinds of remedies that we might now try: seek to weaken corrupt influences, or aim to empower noncorrupt ones. The first strategy was that of the Framers and the Supreme Court, and it's what we would do by singling out bundlers and lobbyists for restrictions, as suggested in the previous chapter. The second sort of remedy proposes a return to a Golden Age of republican virtue through public financing of electoral campaigns, or through election vouchers given to voters for spending as they wish on campaign speech.[4]

Public financing has been tried and has proved a failure. Presidential candidates who accept spending limits can receive public funds for the general campaign, and from the time the program was adopted in 1974 until 2008 each of the two major party candidates agreed to do so. In 2008, however, Obama backed out of the public funding option, and in subsequent elections neither of the two major candidates has bought into it. The problem is that the expenditure limits are too low ($96 million for the general campaign). With a more generous public financing scheme, Obama might not have been so quick to bail. On the other hand, it's unlikely that public moneys could ever keep pace with private funding since the Supreme Court has held that spending limits for private funds are unconstitutional. In 2016, Hillary Clinton raised $1.2 billion, more than twelve times the limit for public funds.

The Supreme Court has steadfastly refused to countenance spending limits, and in 2011 it struck down an Arizona law that looked like a clever attempt to ban private campaign money by indirect means.[5] The statute matched private with public money, dollar for dollar. If a candidate opted for public funding, he would receive one public dollar for every private dollar that his opponent spent or that independent groups spent on the opponent's behalf. Had the statute been upheld, the incentive to offer private support to a candidate would disappear, since one more dollar to him would result in one more dollar for his opponent. To add insult to injury, the support for the opponent would come out of tax dollars, including the private donor's taxes.

Election vouchers are no more promising. In November 2015, Seattle adopted a "Democracy Voucher Program," giving each voter four $25 vouchers to contribute as he wishes to municipal political campaigns. Applied nationally, the tab for an election voucher system might come to $20 billion. And it wouldn't ring in an era of direct democracy, because intermediate groups would arise to collect the vouchers and direct them to their preferred candidates. Obama called them "community organizers," and Lee Drutman calls them "policy entrepreneurs," people who can recognize the hidden issues that would command majoritarian support and who are savvy enough to assemble a coalition and effectively oppose entrenched interests.[6] We already have such groups, in movement organizations such as Media Matters and the Koch brothers' Super PACs, so a voucher system might not make much difference.

The main argument for voucher programs is the claim that private funding distorts democratic government by giving more weight to the preferences of wealthy donors. This might be seen as a form of corruption, if our representatives are regarded as the agents of the electorate charged with mirroring a Rousseauian popular will.[7] In that case, any failure to carry out the wishes of a majority is a breach of faith. Democratic distortion is an overbroad definition of corruption, however. It would stigmatize the Burkean representative who puts what he regards as the good of the country above the wasteful self-interests of his constituents. Madison too understood that the voters might themselves be corrupt, and the very point of the filtration theory was to temper their wishes. The voters of West Virginia were evidently happy when Senator Robert Byrd sent copious amounts of federal money their way, but had he been a little less assiduous in doing so, had he cared more about the national interest and less about his constituents, we would have thought better of him.

Instead of defining corruption in terms of democratic distortion, we should think of it as a matter of self-dealing, an improper quid pro quo between the official and a donor. And that is the only sense in which the Supreme Court has understood corruption. In *Buckley v. Valeo*, the Court explicitly rejected an antidistortion rationale for campaign spending limits, holding that "the concept that government may restrict the speech of some elements of our society in order to enhance the relative voice of others is wholly foreign to the First Amendment."[8] This reasoning was followed in *Citizens United*,[9] which has been condemned as a betrayal of the Framers' intent.[10] But it's not. Distortion is what most of them wanted, in the sense of filtering voters' desires, since they were so suspicious of democracy.

A stronger objection to voucher schemes is that they couldn't begin to match the leverage that special interests enjoy. A voucher given to an indifferent voter will simply be tossed, and one given to the careless or busy voter might be lost in the shuffle of paper. Some vouchers will be bartered away, even if that's made illegal, since a $100 voucher might be worth only pennies to its recipient but could fetch dollars from someone who values it more. Voucher schemes could also be expected to increase private spending on elections, in an effort to influence how voucher dollars are spent. And however generous a voucher system might be, it could always be outbid at the margin by special interest money, applied interstitially between the cracks in the laws and regulations that escape public scrutiny. Even grand reforms can be reduced to rubble in the dead of night by a clever lobbyist and his servile officials.

But the most telling objection to the idea that a voucher scheme might somehow make us less corrupt is the 2016 election, where Hillary Clinton attracted 65 million votes in spite of her corrupt practices. In the end she was defeated, and doubtless some Democrats stayed home because they were repelled by the Clinton Cash machine. Nevertheless, she received almost three million more votes than her opponent, and one takeaway from the election is that one can't assume that popular elections will police corrupt candidates.

What then is to be done? In a giddy moment, we might imagine a revolution in our political culture, with voters rejecting corrupt officials. Or we might fondly pin our hopes on another constitutional convention under the Constitution's Article V, with thirty-eight of the states somehow agreeing on a remedy for crony capitalism. Neither outcome is within the realm of possibility, and in any event the chimera of a perfect Republic of Virtue, such as Robespierre imagined, should be abandoned as hopelessly naïve. What Baudelaire said of laughter might equally be said of corruption: it reveals a fall from grace, and is thus profoundly human.[11] Rather than rely upon people's intrinsic goodness, we should look more modestly for feasible ways to guard against particular kinds of corruption where we find them. That's what the Framers did in aiming to design an anticorruption covenant, and the best we can do is keep tinkering with the machinery of government they gave us.

The Determinants of Public Corruption

I N   WHAT   FOLLOWS, I employ regression analysis to estimate how a country's rank on measures of public corruption is affected by different explanatory factors. Regression analysis is a statistical technique used to estimate the relationship between a dependent variable (the corruption ranking, in this case) and one or more explanatory (or independent) variables. Regression analysis cannot prove that one thing causes something else, but it can show how one set of numbers is statistically correlated with another set of numbers.

In regression analysis, a dependent variable y is estimated from one or several explanatory variables, though a *regression equation* in the following form:

$$y = \alpha + \beta x$$

where α is a constant and β is the fixed number or *coefficient*, which is multiplied by an explanatory variable x. Where there is only one explanatory variable, we have what is known as *simple regression*; if there is more than one, we have *multiple regression*. In multiple regression, one can examine how the dependent variable is affected by one explanatory variable, shorn of the effects of the other explanatory variables.

Several different estimation techniques may be used in regression analysis, and the canonical one employed for the data set below is the Ordinary Least Squares (OLS) procedure, which minimizes the squared value of the distances between the estimate of y and the observed value.

The Variables

Table A.3 estimates a country's 2011 levels of corruption, employing the variables listed in Table A.1. For the dependent variable, I employ Transparency International's Corruption Perceptions Index as a measure of political corruption.

The explanatory variable of greatest interest, Presidential, is described in Table A.2. The variable takes the value of 1 if it is presidential and 0 if parliamentary. I list 82 countries as presidential and 47 as parliamentary. Not every country with a president counts as presidential, but only those whose president is the head of government as well as head of state. This excludes countries such as Germany that have a merely ceremonial president. I generally relied on the categorization provided by Arthur S. Banks, User's Manual, Cross-National Time-Series Data Archive 2011, except that I consider Macedonia, Poland, and Switzerland to be parliamentary. I also list as presidential those "semi-presidential" regimes in which the legislative chamber can dismiss the presidential cabinet. Nondemocratic countries are excluded from the data set.

Richer countries are less likely to be corrupt, since a wealthy middle and upper class will demand clean government.[1] For a measure of a country's wealth, I employ the logged value of its per capital gross domestic product. One might expect to see less corruption in countries with a British inheritance, and more in Latin American countries. The longer a country has been independent, the less corrupt it is likely to be. Governments that have recently transitioned from colonialism often struggle to become democratic, while countries that have recently emerged from dictatorship, as in the states of the former Soviet Union, are often dominated by their former nondemocratic leaders. With a longer history as a democratic country, a state develops "democratic capital," which tends to minimize corruption.[2] Finally, a Population explanatory variable tests Madison's "extended republic" hypothesis that larger states are better managed than smaller ones.

Results

The regressions in column 3 of Table A.3 report an adjusted R-squared of approximately 70 percent. That is, they explain about two-thirds of the relationship between the variables, with one-third unexplained. In estimating corruption, there is (unsurprisingly) more going on than the explanatory variables I employ. There are cultural differences among different countries that remain unaccounted for

TABLE A.1

Variables and Sources

Dependent Variable	Corrupt TI	Transparency International Corruption Perceptions Index 2011
		Source: http://cpi.transparency.org/cpi2011/
Explanatory Variables	Presidential	Equals 1 if a presidential regime; 0 if a parliamentary regime
		Sources: F. H. Buckley; Cross-National Time-Series Data Archive, Databanks International, at http://www.cntsdata.com/
	Wealth	Log of Gross Domestic Product per capita
		Sources: World Bank; United Nations, at http://unstats.un.org/unsd/snaama/dnllist.asp
	British	Equals 1 if the country is Britain or was once a British colony; 0 otherwise
	Latin	Equals 1 if the country is a Spanish or Portuguese-speaking country in South or Central America; 0 otherwise
	Age	Number of years the country has been independent/210 (on the assumption that the oldest country achieved independence in 1800)
		Source: Democracy Cross–National Codebook, compiled by Pippa Norris, at http://www.hks.harvard.edu/fs/pnorris/Data/Democracy%20CrossNational%20Data/Democracy%20Crossnational%20Codebook%20March%202009.pdf
	Population	1 if country's population exceeds 100,000,000; 0 otherwise
		Source: Cross-National Time-Series Data Archive

TABLE A.2

Presidential and Parliamentary Governments

Presidential	Albania, Algeria, Angola, Argentina, Armenia, Azerbaijan, Belarus, Benin, Bolivia, Botswana, Brazil, Burma, Burundi, Cameroon, Central African Republic, Chad, Chile, Columbia, Congo (Brazzaville), Congo-DR, Costa Rica, Croatia, Djibouti, Dominican Republic, Ecuador, Egypt, El Salvador, Equatorial Guinea, Eritrea, France, Gabon, Gambia, Georgia, Ghana, Guatemala, Guinea, Guinea-Bissau, Guyana, Haiti, Honduras, Indonesia, Ivory Coast, Kazakhstan, Kenya, Kyrgyzstan, Liberia, Lithuania, Madagascar, Malawi, Maldives, Mali, Mexico, Mozambique, Nicaragua, Niger, Nigeria, Pakistan, Panama, Paraguay, Peru, Philippines, Romania, Russia, Rwanda, Senegal, Somalia, South Africa, South Korea, Sri Lanka, Sudan, Suriname, Taiwan, Tajikistan, Tanzania, Togo, Tunisia, Turkmenistan, Uganda, Ukraine, United States, Uruguay, Uzbekistan, Venezuela, Zaire, Zambia, Zimbabwe
Parliamentary	Antigua, Australia, Austria, Bahamas, Bangladesh, Barbados, Belgium, Belize, Bulgaria, Burma, Canada, Czech Republic, Denmark, Dominica, Finland, Germany, Greece, Grenada, Hungary, Iceland, India, Ireland, Italy, Jamaica, Japan, Latvia, Luxembourg, Macedonia, Moldova, Netherlands, New Zealand, Norway, Poland, Portugal, Singapore, Slovak Republic, Slovenia, Spain, Sweden, Switzerland, Thailand, Trinidad, Turkey, United Kingdom

Sources: Arthur S. Banks, User's Manual, Cross-National Time-Series Data Archive 2011; F. H. Buckley (Macedonia, Poland, Switzerland).

and help explain the willingness to tolerate levels of corruption and departures from the rule of law.

We'd also like to know the extent to which the β coefficient associated with each explanatory variable assists in explaining corruption. To that end, the model reports on the coefficient's *p-value*, which is the probability that there is, in reality, no relationship between x and y, and that the observed correlation is due to chance, i.e., the probability that the coefficient is zero. The smaller the p-value, the better

TABLE A.3

Determinants of Transparency International's Corruption Perceptions Index 2011

	1	2	3
Presidential	-3.14***	-1.54*** (.35)	-1.42*** (.37)
Wealth	—	-1.90*** (.24)	1.51*** (.26)
British	—	—	.48 (.30)
Latin	—	—	-1.38** (.45)
Age	—	—	2.26*** (.51)
Population	—	—	-.68 (.44)
Constant	6.19*** (.27)	-1.83 (1.05)	-18.62 (6.09)
Number of observations	123	117	114
Adjusted R²	0.42	0.65	0.70

the fit, and by convention anything less than .05 is taken to satisfy the standard of statistical significance.

Unsurprisingly, wealthy countries are more likely to be free from corruption (and countries free from corruption are more likely to be wealthy). Countries with a long experience of independence are less likely to be corrupt, and Latin American countries are more likely. There is no evidence that bigness diminishes corruption, as Madison predicted in his extended republic theory.

Of greatest interest here is the finding that the Presidential coefficient is strongly and significantly negative. Parliamentary regimes are relatively free from corruption, compared with presidential ones, a finding that is generally consistent with the empirical evidence on point.[3] The outlier among these studies is Persson and Tabellini, who found presidential systems to be significantly correlated with less corruption, as measured by the World Bank, when worse and younger democracies were excluded from the mix or when an inter-actor explanatory variable was added that multiplied the presidential dummy variable by a measure of the quality of democracy.[4] Excluding the inconveniently bad presidential systems comes rather close to cherry-picking, however, since one would expect more corruption in undemocratic countries, and when they dropped these techniques, Persson and Tabellini were unable to find that presidential govern-ments were correlated with less corruption, whether measured by Transparency International or by the World Bank, on normal stan-dards of statistical significance.

— Appendix B —

Fairness in Interstate Litigation Act: A Proposal

28 USC 1332 shall be amended to provide that:

(a) District courts shall exercise jurisdiction over any civil action in which the matter in controversy exceeds in the aggregate the sum or value of $100,000, exclusive of interest and costs, when the controversy is between:

(1) a state and any citizen of another state;

(2) any citizens of different states;

(3) citizens of the same state claiming lands under grants of different states; or

(4) a state, or the citizens thereof, and foreign states, citizens, or subjects.

(b) If such a controversy exists between any plaintiff and any de-fendant, the district court's jurisdiction shall not be defeat-ed by the presence of other parties to the action, and in any question concerning whether District courts shall exercise jurisdiction under this section, the party denying such jurisdiction shall have the onus of proof.

(c) Nothing in this statute shall be construed to authorize a district court to exercise jurisdiction over a suit against a state absent its consent.

Acknowledgments

I OWE THANKS to a good many people. I am very grateful for comments offered by Nick Capaldi, J. C. D. Clark, Chris DeMuth, David Keating, David Levy, Bradley Smith and Bob Tyrrell. I also thank Jack Abramoff, who shared with me some of his hard-earned lessons about how to rein in lobbyists. I presented some of my ideas at a talk at the Cato Institute and thank John Samples and Walter Olson for their helpful suggestions. I also presented a paper on corruption at a Liberty Fund program organized by David Schmidt, and benefited from comments at Hillsdale's Kirby Center, at the Manhattan Institute, and at IdeaCity and the Manning Center in Canada.

One person in particular deserves special thanks. Jim Wooton, the former head of the U.S. Chamber of Commerce Institute for Legal Reform, was the inspiration for the book. Over many messages and phone calls, and a good many bowls of phō, Jim gave me a highly sophisticated understanding of the issues, along with a sense of how much harm corruption does to a country he loved so dearly. Sadly, he passed away in 2016.

George Mason law student Robert Minchin provided excellent research assistance, and if you're a judge or a lawyer you'd do very well to hire him.

I also thank George Mason's Scalia Law School and George Mason's Mercatus Institute for their generous support. Cattelya Concepcion and Esther Koblenz at the George Mason Law Library were extremely helpful in getting interlibrary loans and finding online materials for me.

My thanks to everyone at Encounter Books, from the genial Roger Kimball to the production team of Heather Ohle and Katherine Wong to the incredibly able marketing team of Sam Schneider and Lauren Miklos. The book editor, Carol Staswick, was nothing less than superb. Dean Draznin and Anna Walsh helped spread the word far and wide about the book.

This book would not have been possible without the encouragement and invaluable organizational and editorial assistance offered by my wife, Esther Goldberg, whose help I cannot ever adequately acknowledge.

F. H. Buckley
Alexandria, Virginia
April 11, 2017

Endnotes

"Farrand" in the following notes refers to *The Records of the Federal Convention of 1787*, ed. Max Farrand, rev. ed., 4 vols. (Yale University Press, 1937).

Chapter 1: Our Machiavellian Moment

1   See John T. Noonan, *Bribes* (New York: Macmillan, 1984), 604–11. For the story as told by Melvin Weinberg, see Robert W. Greene, *The Sting Man: Inside Abscam* (New York: Penguin, 2013).
2   *Citizens United v. FEC*, 558 U.S. 310, 360 (2010).
3   *McCutcheon v. FEC*, 134 S. Ct. 1434 (2014).
4   Peter Schweizer, *Clinton Cash: The Untold Story of How and Why Foreign Governments and Businesses Helped Make Bill and Hillary Rich* (New York: Harper, 2015).
5   Nina Burleigh, "Meet Huma Abedin, Mysterious Clinton Confidante and Long-Suffering Spouse of Anthony Weiner," *Newsweek*, April 28, 2016.
6   Editorial, "Mrs. Clinton and Her Fixer," *National Review*, August 23, 2016.
7   Rosalind S. Helderman, Spencer S. Hsu and Tom Hamburger, "Donors Given Access to Clinton," *Washington Post*, August 23, 2016; Editorial, "Clinton's Colin Powell Excuse," *Wall Street Journal*, August 23, 2016.
8   David Sirota, "Emails Show Clinton Foundation Donor Reached Out to Hillary Clinton before Arms Export Boost," *International Business Times*, August 22, 2016.
9   James V. Grimaldi and Rebecca Ballhaus, "UBS Deal Shows Clinton's Complicated Ties," *Wall Street Journal*, July 30, 2015.
10 Stephen Braun and Eileen Sullivan, "Many Donors to Clinton Foundation Met with Her at State," Associated Press, August 23, 2016.

11 Jo Becker and Mike McIntire, "Cash Flowed to Clinton Foundation amid Russian Uranium Deal," *New York Times*, April 23, 2015.

12 Josh Voorhees, "New Hillary Scandal Checks All the Boxes on the Clinton Controversy Bingo Card," *Slate*, June 10, 2016.

13 Sarah Westwood, "Tech Firm Brags about Blocking FBI from Recovering Clinton Emails," *Washington Examiner*, August 26, 2016.

14 Robert Yoon, "$153 Million in Bill and Hillary Clinton Speaking Fees, Documented," CNN Politics, February 6, 2016.

15 Deborah Sontag, "An Award for Bill Clinton Came with $500,000 for His Foundation," *New York Times*, May 29, 2015.

16 Rosalind S. Helderman and Philip Rucker, "Plans for UCLA Visit Give Rare Glimpse into Hillary Clinton's Paid Speaking Career," *Washington Post*, November 26, 2014.

17 Isabel Vincent, "Charity Watchdog: Clinton Foundation a 'Slush Fund,'" *New York Post*, April 26, 2015.

18 Editorial, "Cutting Ties to the Clinton Foundation," *New York Times*, August 30, 2016.

19 Three remarkable historians—Bernard Bailyn, Gordon Wood and J. G. A. Pocock—may chiefly be credited for the revival of interest in republican virtue. See Bernard Bailyn, *The Ideological Origins of the American Revolution* (Harvard University Press, 1967), 34–54; Gordon S. Wood, *The Creation of the American Republic, 1776–1787* (University of North Carolina Press, 1998), 14–17; J. G. A. Pocock, *The Machiavellian Moment: Florentine Political Thought and the Atlantic Republican Tradition* (Princeton University Press, 2003), 466–67, 486–87. See also Daniel Lazare, *The Frozen Republic: How the Constitution Is Paralyzing Democracy* (New York: Harcourt, Brace, 1996), 23–35.

20 J. G. A. Pocock, *Virtue, Commerce, and History: Essays on Political Thought and History, Chiefly in the Eighteenth Century* (Cambridge University Press, 1985), 87–88.

21 Martin Gilens and Benjamin I. Page, "Testing Theories of American Politics: Elites, Interest Groups, and Average Citizens,"

Perspectives on Politics 12.3 (2014): 564–81. See Martin Gilens, *Affluence and Influence: Economic Inequality and Political Power in America* (Princeton University Press, 2012); Richard Hasen, "Citizens United and the Orphaned Antidistortion Rationale," *Georgia State University Law Review* 27.4 (2010–11): 989–1005.

22 Arthur Lupia, *Uninformed: Why People Seem to Know So Little about Politics and What We Can Do about It* (Oxford University Press, 2015); Bruce E. Cain, *Democracy More or Less: America's Political Reform Quandary* (Cambridge University Press, 2014).

23 Tamara Keith, "WikiLeaks Claims to Release Hillary Clinton's Goldman Sachs Transcripts," NPR, October 15, 2016.

24 Michael Walsh, "Leaked Emails Reveal Hillary Clinton's Life of Deceit," *New York Post*, October 15, 2016.

Chapter 2: Excusing Corruption

1 Alexis de Tocqueville, *Democracy in America* (University of Chicago Press, 2002), xvii.

2 For a penetrating study of Tocqueville's nuanced view of America, see S. J. D. Green, "Tocqueville's English Correspondence," *New Criterion*, November 2016.

3 Tocqueville, *Democracy in America*, 483–84.

4 Ibid., 486.

5 Jennifer Lawless, *Becoming a Candidate: Political Ambition and the Decision to Run for Office* (Cambridge University Press, 2012), 33, Table 3.1.

6 Elinor Ostrom, *Governing the Commons: The Evolution of Institutions for Collective Action* (Cambridge University Press, 1990); see also Robert C. Ellickson, *Order without Law: How Neighbors Settle Disputes* (Harvard University Press, 1991).

7 Robert Putnam, *Bowling Alone: The Collapse and Revival of American Community* (New York: Simon & Schuster, 2000).

8 Robert Nozick, *Anarchy, State, and Utopia* (New York: Basic Books, 1974), 12.

9 Marcel Mauss, *The Gift: The Form and Reason for Exchange in Archa-*

ic Societies, trans. W. D. Halls (New York: W. W. Norton, 1990); Lewis Hyde, *The Gift: Imagination and the Erotic Life of Property* (New York: Vintage, 1983).

10 Robert L. Trivers, "The Evolution of Reciprocal Altruism," *Quarterly Review of Biology* 46.1 (1971): 35–57; Robert Axelrod and W. D. Hamilton, "The Evolution of Cooperation," *Science* 211 no. 4489 (1981): 1390–96. See generally Robert Axelrod, *The Evolution of Cooperation* (New York: Basic Books, 1984); Susan Rose-Ackerman, *Corruption and Government: Causes, Consequences, and Reform* (Cambridge University Press, 1999), 96–110.

11 René Girard, *Celui par qui le scandale arrive* (Paris: Desclée de Brouwer, 2001).

12 Howard Kurtz, "Going Weak in the Knees for Clinton," *Washington Post*, July 6, 1998.

13 *The Last Word with Lawrence O'Donnell*, MSNBC, April 23, 2015.

14 I had my own little run-in with Media Matters, it seems, after I wrote a blog post about how Americans were tired of the divisiveness in public life. It was mocked by a "Jack London," and one of the readers identified the name as a pseudonym for a Media Matters troll who had been convicted on two counts of bestiality for molesting a black lab and a Rottweiler. My post was: "Bring Us Together," *American Spectator*, June 14, 2016.

15 "The White House Fires a Watchdog," *Wall Street Journal*, June 17, 2009.

16 See Editorial, *New York Times*, March 9, 2016.

17 Blaise Pascal, *Pensées* 667, in *Oeuvres complètes* (Paris: Gallimard, 2000), vol. 2: 817.

18 Bill Bishop, *The Big Sort: Why the Clustering of Like-Minded America Is Tearing Us Apart* (New York: Houghton Mifflin, 2008).

19 Carl Schmitt, *The Concept of the Political*, trans. G. Schwab (1932; University of Chicago Press, 2007), 26.

20 The statement was reported in "Florida: Anything Goes," *Time*, April 17, 1950. But the original sourcing is suspect, and there are reasons to doubt that Smathers ever said this on the stump.

Bonnie Taylor-Blake analyzed how the story emerged, in "Dirty Politics: Smathers, Pepper, and Quasi Malediction in American Political Folklore," *Spokelore*, September 20, 2009.

21 Maurice Merleau-Ponty, *Humanisme et terreur: Essai sur le problème communiste* (Paris: Gallimard, 1947), 3.

Chapter 3—Excusing Corruption

1 Quoted in David Cho, Steven Mufson, and Tomoeh Murakami Tse, "In Shift, Wall Street Goes to Washington," *Washington Post*, September 13, 2009.

2 Peter Schweizer, *Throw Them All Out: How Politicians and Their Friends Get Rich off Insider Stock Tips, Land Deals, and Cronyism That Would Send the Rest of Us to Jail* (Boston: Houghton Mifflin Harcourt, 2011), 78–80.

3 Malcolm S. Salter, "Crony Capitalism American Style: What Are We Talking about Here?" Harvard Business School Working Paper 15-025, October 22, 2014. See Timothy P. Carney, *The Big Ripoff: How Big Business and Big Government Steal Your Money* (Hoboken: John Wiley, 2006).

4 Rajhuram Rajan and Luigi Zingales, *Saving Capitalism from the Capitalists* (New York: Crown Books, 2003), 230.

5 Gordon Tullock, "The Welfare Costs of Tariffs, Monopolies and Theft," *Western Economic Journal* 5.3 (1967): 224–32. See also Gordon Tullock, *Rent Seeking* (Brookfield, Vt.: Edward Elgar, 1993); Robert D. Tollison, "The Economic Theory of Rent Seeking," *Public Choice* 152 (2012): 73–82; Robert D. Tollison, "Rent Seeking," in *Perspectives on Public Choice: A Handbook*, ed. Dennis C. Mueller (Cambridge University Press, 1997), 506.

6 Ran Duchin and Denis Sosyura, "The Politics of Government Investment," *Journal of Financial Economics* 106.1 (2012): 24–48.

7 Rodney D. Ludema, Anna Maria Mayda and Prachi Mishra, "The Political Economy of U.S. Tariff Suspensions," IMF Working Paper, September 2010.

8 Brian Kelleher Richter,, Krislert Samphantharak and Jeffrey F.

Timmons, "Lobbying and Taxes," *American Journal of Political Science* 53.4 (2009): 893–909.

9   Gene M. Grossman and Elhanan Helpman, *Special Interest Politics* (MIT Press, 2001).

10   Kevin Murphy, Andrei Shleifer and Robert Vishny, "Why Is Rent-Seeking So Costly to Growth?" *American Economic Review* 83.2 (1993): 409–14; Kevin Murphy, Andrei Shleifer and Robert Vishny, "The Allocation of Talent: Implications for Growth," *Quarterly Journal of Economics* 106.2 (1991): 503–30.

11   Jennifer L. Brown, Katharine Drake, and Laura Wellman, "The Benefits of a Relational Approach to Corporate Political Activity: Evidence from Political Contributions to Tax Policymakers," *Journal of the American Taxation Association* 37.1 (2015): 69–102.

12   George Stigler, "The Theory of Economic Regulation," *Bell Journal of Economics and Management Science* 2.1 (1971): 3–21.

13   James Bovard, "A Subsidy as Shameful as They Come," *Wall Street Journal*, May 25, 2016.

14   Henry Sender, "QE May Not Have Been Worth the Costs," *Financial Times*, April 10, 2015.

15   Benjamin M. Blau, "Central Bank Intervention and the Role of Political Connections," Mercatus Center Working Paper, George Mason University, October 2013.

16   Elizabeth Warren and Joe Manchin, "The Fed Needs Governors Who Aren't Wall Street Insiders," *Wall Street Journal*, November 18, 2014, A19. On the coalition between populist politicians and the major banks, see Charles W. Calomiris and Stephen H. Haber, *Fragile by Design: The Political Origins of Banking Crises and Scarce Credit* (Princeton University Press, 2014), 208; David Stockman, *The Great Deformation: The Corruption of Capitalism in America* (New York: PublicAffairs, 2013), 270–73.

17   When Nicholas von Hoffman complained about the cost of securities regulation in the 1970s, he called it "consumer protection for millionaires." That's billionaires, Dr. Evil.

18   Lee Drutman, *The Business of America Is Lobbying: How Corpora-*

tions Became Politicized and Politics Became Corporate (Oxford University Press, 2015), 29.

19 David Kocieniewski, "G.E.'s Strategies Let It Avoid Taxes Altogether," *New York Times*, March 24, 2011. See James Bailey and Diana Thomas, "Regulating Away Competition: The Effect of Regulation on Entrepreneurship and Employment," Mercatus Center Working Paper, George Mason University, September 2015.

20 Lee Drutman, "Companies That Lobby More on Taxes Pay Less in Taxes," Sunlight Foundation, November 21, 2011.

21 Mancur Olson, *The Rise and Decline of Nations: Economic Growth, Stagflation, and Economic Rigidities* (Yale University Press, 1982), 69–73; Steven M. Teles, "Kludgeocracy in America," *National Affairs* 17 (Fall 2013): 97–114.

22 Transparency International Corruption Perceptions Index 2010, Long Methodological Brief.

23 See John G. Peters and Susan Welch, "Gradients of Corruption in Perceptions of American Public Life," in *Political Corruption: Concepts and Contexts*, ed. Arnold J. Heidenheimer and Michael Johnston, 3rd ed. (New Brunswick: Transaction, 2002), 155–72; Michael Johnston, "Measuring the New Corruption Rankings: Implications for Analysis and Reform," in *Political Corruption*, 865. See generally Alina Mungiu-Pippidi, *The Quest for Good Governance: How Societies Develop Control of Corruption* (Cambridge University Press, 2015), 2–10, 27–33, 40–48.

24 Francis Fukuyama, *Political Order and Political Decay: From the Industrial Revolution to the Globalization of Democracy* (New York: Farrar, Straus & Giroux, 2014), 25.

25 Edward Glaeser, David Laibson, José A. Scheinkman and Christine L. Soutter, "Measuring Trust," *Quarterly Journal of Economics* 115.3 (2000): 811–46; Alberto Alesina and Eliana La Ferrara, "Who Trusts Others," *Journal of Public Economics* 85.2 (2002): 207–34.

26 See, e.g., Alberto Alesina and Eliana La Ferrara, "Ethnic Diversity and Economic Performance," *Journal of Economic Literature* 43.3 (2005): 762–800.

27 Measured in terms of purchasing power parity, which takes into account the relative cost of local goods and services.

28 Andrei Shleifer and Robert W. Vishny, "Corruption," *Quarterly Journal of Economics* 108.3 (1993): 599–607; Stephen Knack and Philip Keefer, "Institutions and Economic Performance: Cross-Country Tests Using Alternative Institutional Measures," *Economics and Politics* 7.3 (1995): 207–27; Rafael La Porta, Florencio López-de-Silanes, Cristian Pop-Eleches and Andrei Shleifer, "Judicial Checks and Balances," *Journal of Political Economy* 112.2 (2004): 445–70; Mushfiq Swaleheen, "Economic Growth with Endogenous Corruption: An Empirical Study," *Public Choice* 146.1 (2011): 23–41; Sutirtha Bagchi and Jan Svejnar, "Does Wealth Inequality Matter for Growth? The Effect of Billionaire Wealth, Income Distribution, and Poverty," Institute for the Study of Labor (IZA) Discussion Paper no. 7733, November 2013. For a review of the evidence, see Pranab Bardhan, "Corruption and Development: A Review of Issues," *Journal of Economic Literature* 35.3 (1997): 1320–46. But see Jakob Svensson, "Eight Questions about Corruption," *Journal of Economic Perspectives* 19.3 (2005): 19–42.

29 Noel D. Johnson, Courtney L. LaFountain and Steven Yamarik, "Corruption Is Bad for Growth (Even in the United States)," *Public Choice* 147.3 (2011): 377–93. But see Edward L. Glaeser and Raven E. Saks, "Corruption in America," *Journal of Public Economics* 90.6–7 (2006): 1053–72 (finding only a modest relationship between corruption and growth).

30 Craig A. Depken II and Courtney L. LaFountain, "Fiscal Consequences of Public Corruption: Empirical Evidence from State Bond Ratings," *Public Choice* 126.1 (2006): 75–85.

31 On the WJP methodology, see Juan Carlos Botero and Alejandro Ponce, "Measuring the Rule of Law," World Justice Project, November 30, 2011.

32 See Daron Acemoglu, *Introduction to Modern Economic Growth* (Princeton University Press, 2009), 123–40 ("the evidence . . . suggests that institutions are a major—perhaps the most signifi-

cant—fundamental cause of economic growth"). On the positive relation between economic growth and the rule of law, see Robert J. Barro and Xavier Sala-i-Martin, *Economic Growth*, 2nd ed. (MIT Press, 2004), 526–29.

33 World Bank, *Where Is the Wealth of Nations? Measuring Capital for the 21st Century* (Washington, D.C., 2006).

Chapter 4—Excusing Corruption

1 John Winthrop, "A Model of Christian Charity," in *American Sermons: The Pilgrims to Martin Luther King Jr.*, ed. Michael Warner (Library of America, 1999), 41–42.

2 Maximilien de Robespierre, "Sur les principes de morale politique qui doivent guider la Convention nationale dans l'administration intérieure de la République," Address to the National Convention, February 5, 1794, in *Oeuvres de Robespierre*, ed. A. Vermorel (Paris: F. Cournol, 1867), 295. On the rhetoric of virtue in revolutionary France, see Carol Blum, *Rousseau and the Republic of Virtue* (Cornell University Press, 1986).

3 Robespierre, "Sur les principes de morale politique," 301.

4 David Hume, "Idea of a Perfect Commonwealth," in *Hume: Political Essays* (Cambridge University Press, 1994), 222–33.

5 Farrand I.381 (Hamilton, June 22, 1787).

6 F. H. Buckley, *The Once and Future King: The Rise of Crown Government in America* (New York: Encounter Books, 2015).

7 Harold Laski, *Parliamentary Government in England* (New York: Viking, 1938), 119.

8 Dana Milbank, "On Health-Care Bill, Democratic Senators Are in States of Denial," *Washington Post*, December 22, 2009; Chris Frates, "Payoffs for States Get Harry Reid to 60 Votes," *Politico*, December 19, 2009.

9 See James L. Buckley, *Saving Congress from Itself: Emancipating the States and Empowering Their People* (New York: Encounter Books, 2014).

10 *Citizens United v. FEC*, 558 U.S. 310, 360 (2010).

11   *Buckley v. Valeo*, 424 U.S. 1 (1976).
12   *Morrison v. Olson*, 487 U.S. 654, 713 (1988) (dissenting).

Chapter 5—An Anticorruption Covenant

1   Thomas Jefferson, *The Anas*, in *Writings* (Library of America, 1984), 665. *The Anas* are Jefferson's political memoirs, written by the seventy-four-year-old former president in 1818.

2   Jefferson, November 14, 1786, in *The Papers of Thomas Jefferson*, vol. 10, ed. Julian P. Boyd (Princeton University Press, 1954), 531.

3   Jefferson, *Anas*, 666.

4   Ibid., 670, 671.

5   See, e.g., Farrand I.183 (Wilson, June 9); I.482 (Wilson, June 30); I.462 (Gorham, June 29); I.492 (Bedford, June 30)

6   Farrand I.530 (G. Morris, July 5).

7   Farrand IV.295 (Hugh Williamson to John Gray Blount, June 3, 1788). The acerbic Mason had a profound influence on the contours of the Constitution, which paradoxically he did not sign for reasons that have puzzled historians. Jeff Broadwater, *George Mason: Forgotten Founder* (University of North Carolina Press, 2006), 206–08.

8   Farrand I.82 (Franklin, June 2).

9   Farrand I.85 (Madison, June 2).

10   Gouverneur Morris, *A Diary of the French Revolution* (Boston: Houghton Mifflin, 1939).

11   Farrand III.236 ("sans moeurs, et, si l'on en croit ses ennemis, sans principes.").

12   Farrand I.513 (G. Morris, July 2).

13   Farrand I.584 (Madison, July 11).

14   Douglas Adair is credited as the person who first identified Hume as the source of Madison's thoughts on government. See Douglas Adair, "'That Politics May Be Reduced to a Science': David Hume, James Madison, and the Tenth Federalist," in *Fame and the Founding Fathers: Essays by Douglas Adair, ed. Trevor Colbourrn* (Indianapolis: Liberty Fund, 1998), 132–51.

15 Madison, "Vices of the Political System of the United States," in *The Papers of James Madison*, Congressional Series, vol. 9, ed. Robert A. Rutland and William M. E. Rachal (University of Chicago Press, 1975), 348–58.

16 Farrand I.50 (Madison, May 31). Besides Madison, other delegates subscribed to the idea of filtration as a method of countering corruption. Farrand I.133 (Wilson, June 6); I.136 (Dickinson, June 6); I.152 (Gerry, June 7); II.54 (G. Morris, July 19). Hamilton subsequently endorsed it in the New York ratifying debates. Hamilton, June 21, 1788, in *The Papers of Alexander Hamilton*, vol. 5, ed. Harold C. Syrett (Columbia University Press, 1962), 41.

17 Washington to James Madison, December 3, 1784, in *The Papers of George Washington*, Confederation Series, vol. 2, ed. W. W. Abbot (University Press of Virginia, 1992), 165–68.

18 Farrand I.48 (Gerry, May 31); I.51 (Randolph, May 31).

19 Farrand II.31 (Mason, July 17).

20 Farrand I.242 n.

21 Farrand II.20 (July 17).

22 In a letter written on the same day that the delegates voted to adopt Article II on the executive branch, Madison told Jefferson that "the plan . . . will neither effectually *answer* its *national object*, nor prevent the local *mischiefs* which everywhere *excite disgust* agst. the *State Governments*." Farrand III.77 (September 6, italics in original).

23 Farrand II.501 (Wilson, September 4).

24 Farrand II.28 (G. Morris).

25 Farrand II.29 (G. Morris).

26 Farrand II.52 (G. Morris, July 19).

27 Farrand II.56 (Madison, July 19).

28 Farrand II.171, II.185 (August 6).

29 Farrand II.399 (roll call 355).

30 Farrand II.404 (G. Morris).

31 Farrand II.399 (roll call 359).

32 Farrand II.501, II.500 (G. Morris, September 4). James Wilson

offered a similar explanation of the Constitution's method of choosing a president, as an anticorruption device, at the Pennsylvania ratifying convention in 1787. *Collected Works of James Wilson*, ed. Kermit L. Hall and Mark David Hall (Indianapolis: Liberty Fund, 2007), vol. 1: 267. Hamilton, too, observed in *Federalist* 68 that the Framers had sought to exclude the possibility of "cabal, intrigue, and corruption" in the election of presidents.

Chapter 6—What Corruption Meant to the Framers

1   Thoma David Hume, *The History of England, from the Invasion of Julius Caesar to the Revolution in 1688* (Indianapolis: Liberty Fund, 1983), vol. 5: 136–37.

2   Sir Lewis Namier, *The Structure of Politics at the Accession of George III*, 2nd ed. (London: Macmillan, 1957), 2.

3   David Hume, "Of the Independency of Parliament," in *Hume: Political Essays* (Cambridge University Press, 1994), 26.

4   John Adams, "Novanglus" no. 2, in *Revolutionary Writings 1755–1775*, ed. Gordon S. Wood (Library of America, 2011), 406–7. See Gordon S. Wood, *The Creation of the American Republic, 1776–1787* (University of North Carolina Press, 1998), 32.

5   So described in Moses Coit Tyler, *Literary History of the American Revolution* (New York: Putnam, 1897), vol. 2: 24.

6   John Dickinson, April 22, 1754, in H. Trevor Colbourn and Richard Peters, "A Pennsylvania Farmer at the Court of King George: John Dickinson's London Letters, 1754–1756," *Pennsylvania Magazine of History and Biography* 86.3 (1962): 241–86, at 286. See Bernard Bailyn, The Ideological Origins of the American Revolution (Harvard University Press, 1967), 83–92.

7   John Adams, "Novanglus" no. 5, in *Revolutionary Writings 1755–1775*, 458. On Adams's unbalanced and self-serving detestation of Hutchinson, see Bernard Bailyn's apology to the Loyalists in *The Ordeal of Thomas Hutchinson* (Harvard University Press, 1974), 2–3, 51, 163.

8   John Adams, June 13, 1771, in *Revolutionary Writings 1755–1775*, 204.

9   Farrand I.380 (Yates, June 22).

10 J. G. A. Pocock, *The Machiavellian Moment: Florentine Political Thought and the Atlantic Republican Tradition* (Princeton University Press, 2003), 507–17.

11 See generally William Howard Adams, *The Paris Years of Thomas Jefferson* (Yale University Press, 1997), 98–105; Warren Roberts, *Jacques-Louis David, Revolutionary Artist: Art, Politics, and the French Revolution* (University of North Carolina Press, 1989).

12 Jefferson to Mme de Bréhan, March 14, 1789, in *The Papers of Thomas Jefferson*, vol. 14, ed. Julian P. Boyd (Princeton University Press, 1958), 187.

13 Maximilien de Robespierre, "Sur les rapports des idées religieuses et morales avec les principes républicains et sur les fêtes nationales," Report of the Committee of Public Safety to the Convention, May 7, 1794, in *Oeuvres de Robespierre*, ed. A. Vermorel (Paris: F. Cournol, 1867), 308, 315. See George Rudé, *Robespierre: Portrait of a Revolutionary Democrat* (New York: Viking, 1975), 95–96.

14 Livy, *The History of Rome* I, bk. 2.3. (London: J. M. Dent, 1905).

15 F. H. Buckley, *The Once and Future King: The Rise of Crown Government in America* (New York: Encounter Books, 2015), 39–41.

16 Madison, "Vices of the Political System of the Unites States," April 1787, in *The Papers of James Madison*, Congressional Series, vol. 9, ed. Robert A. Rutland and William M. E. Rachal (University of Chicago Press, 1975), 348.

17 Robespierre, "Sur la constitution," in *Oeuvres de Robespierre*, 276, 278.

18 Farrand I.288 (Hamilton, June 18).

19 Farrand III.30 (Grayson).

20 Madison to R. H. Lee, July 7, 1785, in *The Papers of James Madison*, Congressional Series, vol. 7, ed. William T. Hutchinson and William M. E. Rachal (University of Chicago Press, 1971), 315.

21 Gordon S. Wood, *The Radicalism of the American Revolution* (New York: Vintage, 1991), 250.

22 Farrand I.168 (June 8).

23 Samuel Wales, 1785, "The Dangers of Our National Prosperity," in *Political Sermons of the American Founding Era, 1730–1805*, ed. El-

lis Sandoz, 2nd ed. (Indianapolis: Liberty Fund, 1998), vol. 1: 849.

24 Washington to Jefferson, Farrand III.31.

25 Washington to David Stuart, July 1, 1787, Farrand III.51.

26 Montesquieu, *The Spirit of the Laws* VIII.16 (Cambridge University Press, 1989), 124.

27 David Hume, "Idea of a Perfect Commonwealth," in *Hume: Political Essays*, 232.

28 Farrand I.136 (Madison, June 6).

29 Farrand 1.448 (Madison, June 28).

30 Bolingbroke, *The Idea of a Patriot King* (1738), in *Political Writings*, ed. David Armitage (Cambridge University Press, 1997), 257–58.

31 Sterne to Steven Croft, December 25, 1760, in *The Letters of Laurence Sterne to His Most Intimate Friends* (New York: J. F. Taylor, 1904), vol. 1: 188.

32 See *The Life and Correspondence of Rufus King Comprising His Letters, Private and Official; His Public Documents and His Speeches*, vol. 3, ed. Charles R. King (New York: G. P. Putnam's Sons, 1896), 545.

33 Madison, Virginia Ratifying Debates, June 20, 1788, in *Debates of the Several State Conventions*, ed. Jonathan Elliot, 2nd ed. (1836), vol. 3: 537.

34 Adams, May 27, 1778, in *Diary and Autobiography of John Adams*, vol. 4, *Autobiography, Parts Two and Three, 1777–1780*, ed. L. H. Butterfield (Harvard University Press, 1962), 118–19.

35 See Walter Isaacson, *Benjamin Franklin: An American Life* (New York: Simon & Schuster, 2003), chap. 13–14; Claude-Anne Lopez, *Mon Cher Papa: Franklin and the Ladies of Paris* (Yale University Press, 1990).

36 Adams, April 15, 1778, in *Diary and Autobiography of John Adams*, vol. 4: 58–59.

37 The Tribune, no. xvii, *South Carolina Gazette* (Charleston), October 6, 1766, in *American Political Writings during the Founding Era 1760–1805*, ed. Charles S. Hyneman and Donald S. Lutz (Indianapolis: Liberty Press, 1983), vol. 1: 92–93. See generally Wood, *The Creation of the American Republic*, 68–70, 109.

38 John Dickinson, January 21, 1755, in H. Trevor Colbourn and Richard Peters, "A Pennsylvania Farmer at the Court of King George: John Dickinson's London Letters, 1754–1756," *Pennsylvania Magazine of History and Biography* 86.4 (1962): 421.

39 Farrand I.402 (Pinckney, June 25).

40 Thomas Jefferson, *Notes on the State of Virginia*, in *Writings* (Library of America, 1984), 290.

41 Farrand II.344 (August 20). See, e.g., The Tribune, no. xvii, *American Political Writings during the Founding Era*, 95. Mason had likely taken his explanation of the link between luxury and corruption from *Cato's Letters* and from Bolingbroke. See John Trenchard and Thomas Gordon, *Cato's Letters, or Essays on Liberty, Civil and Religious, and Other Important Subjects*, ed. Ronald Hamowy (Indianapolis: Liberty Fund, 1995), vol. 1: 193; Bolingbroke, "A Dissertation upon Parties," in *Bolingbroke, Political Writings*, 183.

42 Farrand II.340 (roll call 319).

43 Farrand II.606 (Mason, September 13).

44 "Whether our countrymen have wisdom and virtue enough to submit to them I know not," said John Adams. "But the happiness of the people might be greatly promoted by them." John Adams, *Revolutionary Writings 1775–1783*, ed. Gordon S. Wood (Library of America, 2011), 55.

45 Isaac Samuel Harrell, *Loyalism in Virginia: Chapters in the Economic History of the Revolution* (Duke University Press, 1926). See also T. H. Breen, *Tobacco Culture: The Mentality of the Great Tidewater Planters on the Eve of the Revolution* (Princeton University Press, 1985), 128; Emory G. Evans, *"A Topping People": The Rise and Decline of Virginia's Old Political Elite, 1680–1790* (University of Virginia Press, 2009), 114–20.

46 Ron Chernow, *Washington: A Life* (New York: Penguin, 2010), 501.

47 Washington to Benjamin Harrison, January 22, 1785, in *The Writings of George Washington*, ed. Jared Sparks (New York: Harper & Bros., 1847), vol. 9: 83.

48 Jefferson to George Washington, July 10, 1785, in *The Papers of*

Thomas Jefferson, Digital Edition (University of Virginia Press, 2009–17), vol. 8: 279.See generally Gordon S. Wood, *Revolutionary Characters: What Made the Founders Different* (New York: Penguin, 2006), 44–45.

49 Washington to Edmund Randolph, July 30, 1785, in *The Writings of George Washington*, ed. Sparks, 9:116.

50 Montesquieu, *The Spirit of the Laws* XX.1, 338.

51 Farrand I.512 (G. Morris, July 2).

52 Quoted in Ruth Scurr, *Fatal Purity: Robespierre and the French Revolution* (New York: Henry Holt, 2006), 279.

53 Jonathan Edwards, "A Treatise Concerning Religious Affections," III.vi, in *The Works of President Edwards,* vol. 4 (Philadelphia: Edward Baines, 1808), 209. See generally Barry Alan Shain, *The Myth of American Individualism: The Protestant Origins of American Political Thought* (Princeton University Press, 1994), 106–7.

54 See Samuel Cooper, "A Sermon on the Day of the Commencement of the Constitution," Boston, 1780, in *Political Sermons of the American Founding Era*, vol. 1: 636.

55 John Witherspoon, "The Dominion of Providence over the Passions of Men," May 17, 1776, in *Political Sermons of the American Founding Era*, vol. 1: 536.

56 *Federalist* 55 (Madison). See Garrett Ward Sheldon, *The Political Philosophy of James Madison* (Johns Hopkins University Press, 2001), 20–25; Terence S. Morrow and Terence A. Morrow, "Common Sense Deliberative Practice: John Witherspoon, James Madison, and the U.S. Constitution," *Rhetoric Society Quarterly* 29.1 (1999): 25–47; Scott Horton, "Calvin and Madison on Men, Angels and Government," Browsings, *Harper's Magazine,* November 14, 2009.

57 Trenchard and Gordon, *Cato's Letters*, vol. 2: 802.

58 See *Political Sermons of the American Founding Era*, vol. 1: 204–6, 499–514, 603.

59 John Adams, "A Dissertation on the Canon and Feudal Law," 1765, in *Revolutionary Writings 1755–1775*, 115–16. On his impression of

the "poor Wretches" bowing and fingering their beads at a Catholic mass, see Letter to Abigail Adams, October 9, 1774, in ibid., 325.

60 John Adams, "Novanglus" no. 1, in *Revolutionary Writings 1755–1775*, 390.

61 The Quebec Act was a remarkable example of tolerance by an imperial power. See Sir Reginald Coupland, *The Quebec Act: A Study in Statesmanship* (Oxford University Press, 1925).

62 Alan Taylor, *American Revolutions: A Continental History, 1750–1804* (New York: W. W. Norton, 2016), 66–86.

63 See Charles H. Metzger, *Catholics and the American Revolution: A Study in Religious Climate* (Chicago: Loyola University Press, 1962), chap. 2.

64 See Adams, "Novanglus" no. 1, in *Revolutionary Writings 1755–1775*, 384.

65 James Madison, "Memorial and Remonstrance against Religious Assessments," *Writings* (Library of America, 1999), 32.

Chapter 7—The Promise of Virtuous Government

1 Farrand III.85.

2 Farrand I.83 (Franklin, June 2).

3 Gordon S. Wood, *Revolutionary Characters: What Made the Founders Different* (New York: Penguin, 2006), 50. See also Gordon S. Wood, *Empire of Liberty: A History of the Early Republic, 1789–1815* (Oxford University Press, 2009), 31; Louise Dunbar, *A Study of "Monarchical" Tendencies in the United States from 1776 to 1801* (University of Illinois Press, 1922), 60, 91. Conservatives such as Hamilton, Dickinson, and South Carolina's Charles Pinckney confessed their admiration of Britain's constitutional monarchy: Farrand I.299 (Hamilton, June 18); I.86–87 (Dickinson, June 2); I.398 (Pinckney, June 25). Only a republican system of government would do for the United States, said Virginia's Edmund Randolph; otherwise, he said, he might well be prepared to adopt the British system. Farrand I.66 (June 1). North Carolina's Hugh Williamson saw an American monarchy as inevitable.

Farrand II.101 (July 24). One less-than-reliable delegate wrote out a list of twenty delegates whom he said favored an American monarchy. Farrand II.191–92; III.306.

4   Farrand I.376 (Mason, June 22); I.379 (Butler, June 22).

5   After 1760, the amount became a fixed sum, voted on by Parliament, and over the course of George III's reign it became relatively smaller as control of the list passed to the prime minister. Jeremy Black, *George III: America's Last King* (Yale University Press, 2006), 53–54.

6   Quoted in Gordon S. Wood, *The Creation of the American Republic, 1776–1787* (University of North Carolina Press, 1998), 143–50. See Bernard Bailyn, *The Ideological Origins of the American Revolution* (Harvard University Press, 1967), 109–110.

7   Farrand II.42–43 (Madison, July 18); II.405 (Sherman, August 24); *Federalist* 69 (Hamilton).

8   *Federalist* 76 (Hamilton).

9   Hamilton, "Explanation," November 11, 1795, in *The Works of Alexander Hamilton*, ed. Henry Cabot Lodge (New York: G. P. Putnam's Sons, 1904), vol. 8: 128 (emphasis in original).

10   Farrand II.618 (September 14).

11   Farrand I.87 (June 2).

12   U.S. Const., art. I, sec 9, cl. 8. On the Emoluments Clause, see Zephyr Teachout, *Corruption in America: From Benjamin Franklin's Snuff Box to Citizens United* (Harvard University Press, 2014), chap. 1.

13   Charles Lee to Patrick Henry, July 29, 1776, in *The Lee Papers*, vol. 2 (New York Historical Society, 1873), 177.

14   Farrand II.550 (September 8).

15   Madison, "Method of Electing the President," [June 18], 1788, in *The Papers of James Madison*, Congressional Series, vol. 11, ed. Robert A. Rutland and Charles F. Hobson (University Press of Virginia, 1977), 154.

16   "Faithless Electors," Fairvote, at http://www.fairvote.org/reforms/national-popular-vote/the-electoral-college/problems-with-the-electoral-college/faithless-electors/.

17 The Supreme Court has upheld state laws that enforce the electors' pledges. *Ray v. Blair*, 343 U.S. 214 (1952).

18 Madison to Thomas Jefferson, August 12, 1786, in *The Papers of James Madison*, Congressional Series, vol. 9, ed. Robert A. Rutland and William M. E. Rachal (University of Chicago Press, 1975), 95.

19 James Wilson, *Lectures on Law*, II.2, "Of the Executive Branch," in *Collected Works of James Wilson*, ed. Kermit L. Hall and Mark David Hall (Indianapolis: Liberty Fund, 2007), vol. 2: 876.

20 Ibid., 877.

21 Farrand I.101 (Mason, June 1).

22 So William H. Riker argued in "The Heresthetics of Constitution-Making: The Presidency in 1787, with Comments on Determinism and Rational Choice," *American Political Science Review* 78.1 (1984): 1–16.

23 Farrand II.24 (roll call 169).

24 Farrand I.88 (June 2).

25 Farrand II.550 (September 8).

Chapter 8—How Did That Work Out?

1 Walter Bagehot, *The English Constitution* (Oxford World's Classics, 2001), 11.

2 This is a standard insight in the literature of public choice economics. See Mancur Olson, *The Logic of Collective Action: Public Goods and the Theory of Groups*, 2nd. ed. (Harvard University Press, 1971).

3 Jack Abramoff, *Capitol Punishment: The Hard Truth about Washington Corruption from America's Most Notorious Lobbyist* (Washington, D.C.: WND Books, 2011), 198.

4 On how stronger political parties reduce minoritarian misbehavior costs, see Philip Keefer and Stuti Khemani, "When Do Legislators Pass on Pork? The Role of Political Parties in Determining Legislator Effort," *American Political Science Review* 103.1 (2009): 99–112.

5 See Robert G. Boatright, *Interest Groups and Campaign Finance Reform in the United States and Canada* (University of Michigan Press, 2011), 36–37, 50.

6   Farrand II.500. See also II.512. Mason raised the figure to 98 percent in the Virginia ratifying convention, on June 18, 1788.

7   Ron Chernow, *Washington: A Life* (New York: Penguin, 2010), 540.

8   Lionel Casson, *Travel in the Ancient World* (London: George Allen & Unwin, 1974), 189.

9   Daniel Walker Howe, *What Hath God Wrought: The Transformation of America, 1815–1848* (Oxford University Press, 2009), 214. On travel in the early republic, see T. H. Breen, *George Washington's Journey: The President Forges a New Nation* (New York: Simon & Schuster, 2016), 78–81.

10   See Pauline Maier, *Ratification: The People Debate the Constitution, 1787–88* (New York: Simon & Schuster, 2010), 84.

11   See Jeffrey Jenkins and Brian Sala, "The Spatial Theory of Voting and the Presidential Election of 1824," *American Journal of Political Science* 42.2 (1998): 1157–79.

12   David S. Heider and Jeanne T. Heider, *Henry Clay: The Essential American* (New York: Random House, 2011), 141.

13   For an account of how Jackson become wealthy by forcing Native Americans out of Tennessee and then buying up their lands on the cheap, see Steve Inskeep, *Jacksonland: President Andrew Jackson, Cherokee Chief John Ross and a Great American Land Grab* (New York: Penguin, 2015).

14   Drew R. McCoy, *The Last of the Fathers: James Madison and the Republican Legacy* (Cambridge University Press, 1989), 192–98.

15   Louis Fisher, *Constitutional Conflicts between Congress and the President* (University Press of Kansas, 2007), 35.

16   Jean-Jacques Rousseau, *Of the Social Contract* III.2, in *The Social Contract and Other Later Political Writings*, ed. Victor Gourevitch and Raymond Geuss (Cambridge University Press, 1997), 84–85.

17   Edward Gibbon, *The Decline and Fall of the Roman Empire* (New York: Knopf, 1991), vol. 1: 136.

18   The leading study of the executive privilege doctrine concluded that its assertion during the Lewinsky scandal gave the administration time to blame it on the independent counsel, Kenneth

Starr, and save Clinton's presidency. Mark J. Rozell, *Executive Privilege: Presidential Power, Secrecy, and Accountability* (University Press of Kansas, 2010), 144.

19 See Torsten Persson and Guido Tabellini, *The Economic Effects of Constitutions* (MIT Press, 2003), 23–24.

20 See Mathew S. Shugart and John M. Carey, *Presidents and Assemblies: Constitutional Design and Electoral Dynamics* (Cambridge University Press, 1992), 44–45.

21 Johann Wolfgang von Goethe, "Annales de 1749 à 1822," in *Oeuvres complètes*, vol. 10, *Mélanges*, trans. Jacques Porchat (Paris: Hachette, 1863), 308.

Chapter 9—Federalism and Corruption

1 Farrand I.163 (June 8, roll call 34); II.24 (July 17, roll call 163); II.384 (August 23, roll call 349).

2 Farrand II.28 (G. Morris, July 17).

3 Farrand I.164 (June 8). See also I.447 (June 28); II.27 (July 17); II.110 (July 25); II.440 (August 28); II.589 (September 12).

4 F. H. Buckley, "The American Fresh Start," *Southern California Interdisciplinary Law Journal* 4.1 (1994): 67–97.

5 It required the ingenuity of federal judges to derive, from the grant of power to Congress to regulate commerce "among the several States" under the Constitution's Art. 1, § 8, cl. 3, a "negative commerce" clause under which an interstate commerce power was withdrawn from the states. See *C&A Carbone, Inc. v. Town of Clarkstown, N.Y.*, 511 U.S. 383 (1994) (Kennedy J.).

6 James M. Buchanan and Gordon Tullock, *The Calculus of Consent: Logical Foundations of Constitutional Government* (University of Michigan Press, 1962), 113–16.

7 James Wilson, Pennsylvania Ratifying Convention, November 26, 1787, in *Collected Works of James Wilson*, ed. Kermit L. Hall and Mark David Hall (Indianapolis: Liberty Fund, 2007), vol. 1: 188.

8 U.S. Const., art. I, § 8, cl. 2, 6, 10.

9 *C&A Carbone, Inc.*, 511 U.S. 383.

10 Edward Gibbon, *The Decline and Fall of the Roman Empire* (New York: Knopf, 1991), vol. 1: 90.

11 Ibid., 94.

12 Frederick Jackson Turner, *The Frontier in American History* (New York: Henry Holt, 1921).

13 Barry Weingast, "The Economic Role of Political Institutions: Market-Preserving Federalism and Economic Development," *Journal of Law, Economics, and Organization* 11.1 (1995): 1–13.

14 Thomas A. Garrett and Russell M. Rhine, "On the Size and Growth of Government," Federal Reserve Bank of St. Louis *Review* 88.1 (2006): 13–30.

15 Veronique de Rugy, "The Rise in Per Capita Federal Spending," Mercatus Center, November 12, 2014. On state spending, see Garrett and Rhine, "On the Size and Growth of Government."

16 *Wickard v. Filburn*, 317 U.S. 111 (1942).

17 U.S. Const., art. I, § 8, cl. 1.

18 Under *South Dakota v. Dole*, 483 U.S. 203 (1987), the amount in question cannot be so great that it can be considered coercive to the state's acceptance of the condition, but a 10 percent grant is often enough to get state officials to do the bidding of the federal government.

19 The NAFTA documents can be found at "The Loewen Group, Inc. and Raymond L. Loewen v. United States of America," U.S. Department of State, at http://www.state.gov/s/l/c3755.htm.

Chapter 10—The Mississippi Story

1 Howard Ball, *Murder in Mississippi: United States v. Price and the Struggle for Civil Rights* (University Press of Kansas, 2004), 84.

2 *U.S. v. Price*, 383 U.S. 787 (1966).

3 Douglas O. Linder, "Bending toward Justice: John Doar and the Mississippi Burning Trial," *Mississippi Law Journal* 72.2 (2002): 731–39.

4 Willie Morris, *The Courting of Marcus Dupree* (University Press of Mississippi, 1992), 155.

5 *Shelby County v. Holder*, 570 U.S. 2 (2013).

6   Taylor Branch, *Pillar of Fire: America in the King Years 1963–65* (New York: Simon & Schuster, 1999), 366–67.

7   Curtis Wilkie, *The Fall of the House of Zeus: The Rise and Ruin of America's Most Powerful Trial Lawyer* (New York: Broadway, 2012), 9.

8   Lloyd N. Cutler, "Using Morals, Not Money on Pretoria," *New York Times*, August 3, 1986.

9   Separately, Mississippi's broad culture of corruption prompted an FBI sting operation that investigated bribes paid to county officials throughout the state. See James R. Crockett, *Operation Pretense: The FBI's Sting on County Corruption in Mississippi* (University Press of Mississippi, 2003).

10 Wilkie, *The Fall of the House of Zeus*, 9–16.

11 Ibid., 16.

12 "Who's Afraid of Dickie Scruggs," *Newsweek*, December 5, 1999.

13 Michael Orey, *Assuming the Risk: The Mavericks, the Lawyers, and the Whistle-Blowers Who Beat Big Tobacco* (Boston: Little Brown, 1999), 255.

14 Peter J. Boyer, "The Bribe: How the Mississippi Lawyer Who Brought Down Big Tobacco Overstepped," *New Yorker*, May 19, 2008.

15 Wilkie, *The Fall of the House of Zeus*, 307.

Chapter 11—Designing a Virtuous Justice System

1   Farrand I.119 (Wilson, June 5).

2   Farrand I.120 (June 5).

3   U.S. Const., art. III, § 1.

4   See remarks of George Brown in *Canada's Founding Debates*, ed. Janet Ajzenstat (University of Toronto Press, 2003), 289.

5   Farrand I.125 (Butler, June 5).

6   "I declare that, in the Convention, the unanimous desire of all was to keep separate and distinct . . . the federal from . . . the state judiciary." Richard Spaight, Farrand III.349 (July 28, 1788).

7   As Sir Edward Coke ruled in Bonham's Case, 8 Co. Rep. 107, 77 Eng. Rep. 638 (1610).

8   Farrand II.173; II.186.

9   Roger Sherman letter, December 8, 1787, Farrand IV.288.

10 James Madison, Virginia Ratifying Convention, June 20, 1788, in *The Debates in the Several State Conventions on the Adoption of the Federal Constitution*, ed. J. Elliot (Philadelphia: J. B. Lippincott, 1891), vol. 3: 533.

11 *New State Ice Co. v. Liebmann*, 285 U.S. 262 (1932).

12 Roberta Romano, *The Genius of American Corporate Law* (Washington, D.C.: AEI, 1993). There is a further advantage to letting each state go its own way. By doing so, a federal country allows its citizens to settle in the state whose laws best match their preferences. When people can move easily (better still, costlessly) from one state to another, each individual will vote with his feet for the state that provides his desired level of goods and services. That's an application of Jack Sprat's Law, with fat lovers in one state and lean eaters in another, and it has come to be know as "Tiebout sorting," after Charles Tiebout's "A Pure Theory of Local Expenditures," *Journal of Political Economy* 64.5 (1956): 416–24.

13 Geoffrey P. Miller and Theodore Eisenberg, "Flight to New York: An Empirical Analysis of Choice of Law and Forum Selection Clauses in Large Commercial Contracts," *Cardozo Law Review* 30.4 (2009): 1475–512.

14 George Mason, Virginia Ratifying Convention, June 18, 1788, in *The Debates in the Several State Conventions on the Adoption of the Federal Constitution*, vol. 3: 26.

15 See Akhil Reed Amar, "Separating the Two Tiers of Federal Jurisdiction," *Boston University Law Review* 65 (1985): 205–72; "Marbury, Section 13, and the Original Jurisdiction of the Supreme Court," *University of Chicago Law Review* 56.2 (1989): 443–99; "The Two-Tiered Structure of the Judiciary Act of 1789," *University of Pennsylvania Law Review* 138.6 (1990): 1499–567. This was the solution proposed by Roger Sherman. Let the parties sue in state court, so long as this could be done "with safety to the general interest." Farrand II.46 (July 18).

16 Judiciary Act of 1789, ch. 20, § 11, 1 Stat. 73, 78–79. The restriction was upheld in *Sheldon v. Sill*, 49 U.S. (8 How.) 441, 448–49 (1850). Restrictions of this kind are expressly contemplated in the Constitution's Exceptions Clause of Article III, section 2: "the supreme Court shall have appellate Jurisdiction, both as to Law and Fact, with such Exceptions, and under such Regulations as the Congress shall make."

17 *Strawbridge v. Curtiss*, 7 U.S. (3 Cranch) 267 (1806).

18 *Louisville, C. &C.R. Co. v. Letson*, 43 U.S. (2 How.) 497, 555–56 (1844).

19 A narrower reading can be given to the *Strawbridge* decision. The defendants were all jointly liable, which meant that the Massachusetts plaintiff could have recovered the entire amount from a Massachusetts defendant, and there might have been no need to ask a Vermont court to get involved in collecting the award. Marshall himself explicitly limited his rule to cases "where the interest is joint" and stated that "the Court does not mean to give an opinion in the case where several parties represent several distinct [i.e., non-joint] interests."

20 Hilda Bankston, Testimony before the Judiciary Committee, U.S. Senate, July 31, 2002.

21 Robert A. Kagan, *Adversarial Legalism and American Government: The American Way of Life* (Harvard University Press, 2003). See also Robert A. Kagan, "On Surveying the Whole Legal Forest," *Law and Social Inquiry* 28.3 (2003): 833–72; W. A. Bogert, *Consequences: The Impact of Law and Its Complexity* (University of Toronto Press, 2002), 114.

22 See Mark Ramseyer and Eric Rasmusen, "Are Americans More Litigious? Some Quantitative Evidence," in *The American Illness: Essays on the Rule of Law*, ed. F. H. Buckley (Yale University Press, 2013), 69–99.

23 Michael Trebilcock and Paul-Erik Veel, "A Tamer Tort Law: The Canada-U.S. Divide," in *The American Illness*, 229.

24 Stephen P. Magee, "Lawyers as Spam: Congressional Capture Explains Why U.S. Lawyers Exceed the Optimum," in *The American Illness*, 100.

Chapter 12—The Silver Bullet

1   Class Action Fairness Act of 2005, 28 U.S.C. §§ 1332(d), 1453 and 1711–15.

2   See *Tanoh v. Dow Chem. Co.*, 561 F.3d 945 (9th Cir., 2009); *Scimone v. Carnival Corp.*, 720 F.3d 876 (11th Cir., 2014). But see *Corber v. Xanodyne Pharmaceuticals, Inc.*, 771 F.3d 1218 (9th Cir., 2014). See generally Charles J. Cooper and Howard C. Nielson, "Complete Diversity and the Closing of the Federal Courts," *Harvard Journal of Law and Public Policy* 37.1 (2014): 295–328.

3   I am indebted to the late Jim Wootton for the text of the bill and for his advice about crony capitalism in America.

4   *State Farm v. Campbell*, 538 U.S. 408 (2003). See also *Exxon Shipping Co. v. Baker*, 554 U.S. 471 (2008).

5   Michelle J. White, "Understanding the Asbestos Crisis," unpublished, May 2003, at 2, available at www.law.yale.edu/documents/pdf/white.pdf.

6   Bethany Krajelis, "2013 Asbestos Filings on Pace with Last Year at 793 Year to Date," *Madison–St. Clair Record*, June 27, 2013; Ann Maher, "Asbestos Filings in Madison County Down 20 Percent from Previous Year," *Madison–St. Clair Record*, January 12, 2015.

7   Forum shopping of this kind might also be coming to an end with the recent decision of the U.S. Supreme Court in *Bristol-Myers Squibb Co. v. Superior Court of California*, __ U.S. __ (2017).

8   The move to elected judges began, fittingly, in Mississippi, with an 1832 backwoods revolt against the state's economic elite. Jed Handelsman Shugerman, *The People's Court: Pursuing Judicial Independence in America* (Harvard University Press, 2012), 57.

9   Alexander Tabarrok and Eric Helland, "Court Politics: The Political Economy of Tort Awards," *Journal of Law and Economics* 42.1 (1999): 157–88.

10   Richard Neely, *The Product Liability Mess: How Business Can Be Rescued from the Politics of State Courts* (New York: Free Press, 1988), 4.

11   Steven J. Choi, Mitu G. Gulati and Eric A. Posner, "Professionals or Politicians: The Uncertain Empirical Case for an Elected

Rather than an Appointed Judiciary," *Journal of Law, Economics and Organization* 26.2 (2010): 290–336. See also Chris W. Bonneau and Melinda Gann Hall, *In Defense of Judicial Elections* (London: Routledge, 2009).

Elected judges who receive corporate support are more likely to side with defendants than merit-appointed judges. Michael S. Kang and Joanna M. Shepherd, "The Partisan Price of Justice: An Empirical Analysis of Campaign Contributions and Judicial Decisions," *New York University Law Review* 86.1 (2011): 69–130. That's just another way of saying that elected judges who don't get corporate support and depend instead on contributions from the trial bar are more likely to side with plaintiffs, and it doesn't mean anything unless you think plaintiffs should generally win. As long as there are two sides to a judicial issue, then, conservative and liberal judges will sort themselves out, and so will their supporters.

12   Conversation with Judge Kevin Duffy.

13   *Plessy v. Ferguson*, 163 U.S. 537 (1896).

14   Frank Sikora, *The Judge: The Life and Opinions of Alabama's Frank M. Johnson, Jr.* (Montgomery: Black Belt, 1992), 35–36. See Browder v. Gale, 142 F. Supp. 707 (M.D. Ala.).

15   *Gale v. Browder*, 352 U.S. 903 (1956).

Chapter 13—Bribes

1   Montesquieu, *The Spirit of the Laws* XI.6, (Cambridge University Press, 1989), 158.

2   Ibid., 157.

3   See *A Complete Collection of State-Trials, and Proceedings for High-Treason, and Other Crimes and Misdemeanours* (London: J. Walthoe, 1730), vol. 1: 353–65; "Passages in Parliament against Francis, Viscount St. Alban," in *The Works of Francis Bacon* (London: J. Johnson, 1803), vol. 4: 526–49. Nieves Mathews mounted a spirited defense of Bacon, in *Francis Bacon: The History of a Character Assassination* (Yale University Press, 1996), but few historians have been persuaded to depart from Macaulay's severe judgment of him: "That these

practices were common we admit. But they were common just as all wickedness to which there is strong temptation always was and always will be common." Thomas Babington, Lord Macaulay, "Lord Bacon," in *Critical and Historical Essays* (London: Longman, Brown, Green & Longmans, 1848), vol. 2: 280–429, at 361.

4   G. M. Trevelyan, *England under the Stuarts* (London: Folio, 1996), 96.

5   William Roper, "The Life of Sir Thomas More," in *Two English Tudor Lives*, ed. Richard S. Sylvester and Davis P. Harding (Yale University Press, 1962), 231–32.

6   Trevelyan, *England under the Stuarts*, 105. On the prosecution of Bacon, and Coke's role in it, see generally John T. Noonan, *Bribes: The Intellectual History of a Moral Idea* (New York: Macmillan, 1984), 334–65.

7   Sir Edward Coke, *Institutes of the Laws of England* III.68, 4th ed. (London: A. Crooke, 1669), 147, quoting Deuteronomy 16:19.

8   Citizens for Responsibility and Ethics in Washington, *Family Affair* (Washington, D.C.: 2012), 73.

9   Ecclesiastes 7:7.

10   Juvenile Law Center, "Lucerne County Kids-for-Cash Scandal," n.d.; William Ecenbarger, *Kids for Cash: Two Judges, Thousands of Children, and a $2.8 Million Kickback Scheme* (New York: New Press, 2012).

11   Juvenile Law Center, "Lucerne County Kids-for-Cash Scandal."

12   Larry Getlen, "Corrupt 'Kids for Cash' Judge Ruined More than 2,000 Lives," *New York Post*, February 23, 2014.

13   *U.S. v. Conahan and Ciaverella*, July 17, 2010 (Kosick, J.), in *Interbranch Commission on Juvenile Justice Report*, ed. John M. Cleland (Philadelphia, May 2010), 17.

14   *McDonnell v. U.S.*, __ U.S. __ (2016), rev'g 792 F.3d 478 (2015).

15   Under the federal bribery statute, public officials may not "corruptly" demand, seek, or receive anything of value "in return for . . . being influenced in the performance of any official act," with "official act" defined as "any decision or action on any question, matter, cause, suit, proceeding or controversy, which may at any

time be pending, or which may by law be brought before any public official, in such official's official capacity, or in such official's place of trust or profit." 18 U.S.C. §§ 201(b)(2), 201(a)(3). Several other federal criminal offenses piggyback on the bribery prohibition. The Supreme Court has held that the honest services wire fraud statute, 18 U.S.C. §§ 1343, 1346.16, which requires the government to prove that the defendant sought to carry out a fraudulent scheme to defraud a person of his intangible right to honest services, creates an antibribery offense. *Skilling v. U.S.*, 130 S. Ct. 2896, 2933 (2010). A second statute, the Hobbs Act, makes it criminal to commit extortion by obtaining property "under color of official right," 18 U.S.C. § 1951(b)(2), which again the Supreme Court has found comes down to taking a bribe. *Evans v. U.S.*, 504 U.S. 255, 260, 268 (1992).

16   *Howard v. United States*, 345 F.2d 126, 128 (1st Cir., 1965), f'lld. in *U.S. v. McDonnell*, __ F.3d __ (4th Cir., 2015).

17   18 U.S.C. § 201(c)(1)(A); 5 U.S.C. § 7353.

18   *U.S. v. Siegelman*, 640 F.3d 1159 (11th Cir., 2011).

19   See Adam Zagorin, "Selective Justice in Alabama?" *Time*, October 4, 2007.

20   Osmund Airy, *Charles II* (London: Longmans, Green, 1904), 149.

21   *U.S. v. Blagojevich*, __ F.3d __ (7th Cir., 2015), cert. den. __ U.S. __ (2016).

Chapter 14—The Republic of Defection

1   Editorial, "Decision of the Year," *Wall Street Journal*, June 27, 2016.

2   *Heartland Alliance National Immigration Justice Center v. U.S.*, __ F.3d __ (7th Cir., Oct. 21, 2016, per Manion C.J.); Nina Shea, "The U.S. and the U.N. Have Abandoned Christian Refugees," *Wall Street Journal*, October 7, 2016.

3   Editorial, "Loose Talk about Free Speech," *Washington Times*, December 6, 2015.

4   OECD, *Society at a Glance 2011: OECD Social Indicators* (2011), 91, Table A. The United States also ranked poorly on the World Val-

ues Survey when people were asked whether most people can be trusted. *World Values Survey 2010–2014*, Study # 906-WVS2010 (April 18, 2015), 42–43, Table V24.

5 Robert Putnam, *Bowling Alone: The Collapse and Revival of American Community* (New York: Simon & Schuster, 2000), 140. See also Pamela Paxton, "Is Social Capital Declining in the United States? A Multiple Indicator Assessment," *American Journal of Sociology* 105.1 (1999): 88–127.

6 Pew Research Center, "Beyond Distrust: How Americans View Their Government," November 23, 2015.

7 Dinesh D'Souza, *Stealing America: What My Experience with Criminal Gangs Taught Me about Obama, Hillary, and the Democratic Party* (New York: Broadside, 2015), discussing his prosecution for campaign finance violations; *Obama's America: Unmaking the American Dream* (New York: Threshold, 2014); *The Roots of Obama's Rage* (Washington: Regnery, 2011).

8 *Citizens United v. FEC*, 558 U.S. 310, 360 (2010).

9 *Wisconsin v. Peterson*, __ Wisc.2d __ (July 16, 2015). Since then, the Federal Election Commission has reportedly abandoned any effort to rein in coordination between candidates and donors. Matea Gold, "Less Is More for Super PACs," *Washington Post*, December 25, 2015.

10 Editorial, "Elusive Justice in Wisconsin," *New York Times*, March 10, 2015; Editorial, "The Revenge of Scott Walker," *New York Times*, October 27, 2015.

11 See Magnus Ohman, *Political Finance Regulations around the World: An Overview of the International IDEA Database*, International Foundation for Electoral Systems (Arlington, Va., 2014).

12 See Bradley A. Smith, *Unfree Speech: The Folly of Campaign Finance Reform* (Princeton University Press, 2001), 66–70; Chris W. Bonneau and Damon M. Cann, "Campaign Spending, Diminishing Marginal Returns, and Campaign Finance Restrictions in Judicial Elections," *Journal of Politics* 73.4 (2011): 1267–80.

13 See Bradley A. Smith, "Faulty Assumptions and Undemocratic

Consequences of Campaign Finance Reform," *Yale Law Journal* 105.4 (1996): 1049–91, at 1082–86.

14 See, e.g., Daniel H. Lowenstein, "On Campaign Finance Reform: The Root of All Evil Is Deeply Rooted," *Hofstra Law Review* 18.2 (1989): 301–67, at 335 (noting that President George H. W. Bush's 1989 campaign finance proposals favored Republicans and that congressional Democrats favored reforms that would benefit their party).

15 Ramsey Cox, "In First Speech Back, Reid Blasts Koch Brothers," *The Hill*, September 8, 2014.

16 See Jane Mayer, *Dark Money: The Hidden History of the Billionaires behind the Rise of the Radical Right* (New York: Doubleday, 2016).

17 See Kimberley Strassel, *The Intimidation Game: How the Left Is Silencing Free Speech* (New York: Twelve, 2016), 106, 120, 149.

18 Lauren French, "Two Democrats Call for Ethics Probe into J. Russell George's Work as IRS Inspector General," *Politico*, February 7, 2014.

19 Erik Wasson, "Obama: Not 'Even a Smidgen of Corruption' behind Internal Revenue Service Targeting," *The Hill*, February 2, 2014.

20 Editorial, "The Real Internal Revenue Scandal," *New York Times*, July 5, 2014.

21 On the politicization of criminal prosecutions in Milwaukee, see Strassel, *The Intimidation Game*, 283–95.

22 The case has now been dismissed by the Texas Court of Criminal Appeals, too late to save Perry's presidential ambitions. Ex p. Perry, PD-1067-15, Feb. 24, 2016.

23 See Jeffrey Toobin, "Casualties of Justice," New Yorker, January 3, 2011; Sidney Powell, *Licensed to Lie: Exposing Corruption in the Department of Justice* (Dallas: Brown Books, 2014). A special counsel reported that prosecutors in the botched prosecution of Senator Ted Stevens of Alaska had knowingly failed to comply with their duty to turn over exculpatory evidence, but declined to recommend that any of them be charged with contempt of court. Henry F. Schuelke, III, Special Report, D. D.C., 09-0198,

March 15, 2012. See Rob Cary, *Not Guilty: The Unlawful Prosecution of U.S. Senator Ted Stevens* (Thomson Reuters, 2014).

24 "Federal Agents and Prosecutors Routinely Break the Law and Violate Ethics Standards?" *Pittsburgh Post-Gazette*, November 22, 1998.

25 *U.S. v. Olsen*, 737 F.3d 625 (9th Cir., 2013) (Kozinski, C.J., dissenting).

26 Seth Apfel, "Prosecutorial Misconduct: Comparing American and Foreign Approaches to a Pervasive Problem and Devising Possible Solutions," *Arizona Journal of International and Comparative Law* 31.3 (2014): 835–73.

27 F. H. Buckley, *The Way Back: Restoring the Promise of America* (New York: Encounter Books, 2016), 258.

Chapter 15—Policing Crony Capitalism

1 *Citizens United v. FEC*, 558 U.S. 310, 360 (2010).

2 Federal Election Campaign Act Amendments of 1974, 88 Stat. 1263 (1974).

3 *Buckley v. Valeo*, 424 U.S. 1 (1976).

4 *Citizens United*, 558 U.S. at 366–71.

5 Correspondence with Bradley Smith.

6 *Abrams v. United States*, 250 U.S. 616, 630 (1919).

7 Richard Briffault, "Campaign Finance Disclosure 2.0," *Election Law Journal* 9.4 (2010): 273–303.

8 On the Media Matters strategy of revealing the names of corporate donors to conservative causes, and then organizing boycotts of them, see Kimberley Strassel, *The Intimidation Game: How the Left Is Silencing Free Speech* (New York: Twelve, 2016), 224.

9 James Surowiecki, "How Mozilla Lost Its CEO," New Yorker, April 4, 2014. Brendan Eich wasn't the only person who lost his job or suffered for his beliefs. See Bradley A. Smith, "In Defense of Political Anonymity," *City Journal*, Winter 2010; Strassel, *The Intimidation Game*, 344–49.

10 Stendhal, *Le rouge et le noir*, in *Oeuvres romanesques completes*, vol. 1, ed. Yves Ansel and Philippe Berthier (Paris: Gallimard, 2005), 354.

11 *Citizens United* thus put paid to "sham issue advocacy" ads that

sharply criticized or promoted a candidate but were neverthe-less permitted because they avoided the magic "for or against" words that, according to the *Buckley* Court constituted imper-missible express advocacy. All this has done, however, is shift campaign support from issue advocacy under a tax-exempt 501(c)(3) to express advocacy by Super PACs organized under section 501(c)(4) that do not coordinate with a candidate or qualify as a tax-exempt charity. See Michael S. Kang, "The End of Campaign Finance Law," *Virginia Law Review* 98.1 (2012): 1–65.

12 John Fritze, "National Organization for Marriage Donor List Leaked by IRS, Claims 'Traditional' Marriage Org's Chairman," *Huffington Post*, August 5, 2013.

13 California requires public disclosure of donor names when a (c)(4) takes sides in a voter initiative, as happened when the Nation-al Organization for Marriage's (c)(4) supported Prop 8's ban on same-sex marriage. Conservative (c)(4)'s argue that they should not be required to turn over their donor lists to the state, and have persuaded a district court judge to agree with them after he heard evidence about death threats to a donor. *Americans for Pros-perity v. Harris*, ___ F. Supp. ___ (2016). The Ninth Circuit Court of Appeals, in the absence of such evidence, has twice rejected arguments that a (c)(3) might refuse to disclose donor names to the state. Center for Competitive Politics v. Harris, 784 F.3d 1307 (2015), cert. den. 136 S. Ct. 480 (2015); and *Americans for Prosperity v. Harris*, ___ F.3d ___ (2015).

14 See Kenneth P. Vogel, "How the Koch Network Rivals the GOP," *Politico*, December 30, 2015.

15 Matea Gold, John Wagner and Abby Phillip, "Hacked Emails Show How Liberal Group Back-Channeled Advice to Clinton," *Washington Post*, October 16, 2016 (brackets in the original); Alex Shephard and Clio Chang, "How Neera Tanden Works," *New Republic*, October 28, 2016.

16 Avi Ben-Bassat and Momi Dahan, "The Regulation of Political Fi-nance and Corruption," *Election Law Journal* 14.3 (2015): 190–206.

17 Matea Gold and Tom Hamburger, "Political Parties Go after Million-Dollar Donors in Wake of Looser Rules," *Washington Post*, September 19, 2015.

18 *Citizens United*, 558 U.S. at 325.

19 *SpeechNow v. FEC*, 599 F.3d 686 (2010).

20 *Buckley*, 424 U.S. at 53.

21 Matea Gold, "How 'Ghost Corporations' Are Funding the 2016 Election," *Washington Post*, March 18, 2016.

22 Matea Gold and Anu Narayanswamy, "Bigger Role for Donors This Year," *Washington Post*, October 6, 2016.

23 Political parties have been weakened by the Bipartisan Campaign Reform Act of 2002 (McCain-Feingold) and the limits it has placed on soft-money contributions. Unlike hard money, which parties give directly to candidates, soft money is given to a party for party-building activities, get-out-the-vote drives, and issue ads. McCain-Feingold's limits on soft money contributions were upheld in *McConnell v. FEC*, 540 U.S. 93 (2003). See Raymond J. La Raja, *Small Change: Money, Political Parties, and Campaign Finance Reform* (University of Michigan Press, 2008).

24 Bradley Smith, "Kill the 'Money Buys Elections' Cliché," *Washington Examiner*, November 14, 2016.

25 Richard L. Hasen, *Plutocrats United: Campaign Money, the Supreme Court, and the Distortion of American Elections* (Yale University Press, 2016), 44–45.

26 See Samuel Issacharoff, "On Political Corruption," *Harvard Law Review* 124.1 (2010): 119–20.

27 Daniel Hays Lowenstein, Richard L. Hasen and Daniel P. Tokaji, *Election Law: Cases and Materials*, 5th ed. (Carolina Academic Press, 2012), 641; Tarini Parti, "FEC: $7B Spent on 2012 Campaign," Politico, January 31, 2013.

28 See Council of Economic Advisers, Economic Report of the President, January 1977 (U.S. Government Printing Office), 283, Table B22; and Economic Report of the President, March 2013, 361, Table B31.

29 Stephen Ansolabehere, John M. de Figueiredo and James M. Snyder, Jr., "Why Is There So Little Money in US Politics?" *Journal of Economic Perspectives* 17.1 (2003): 105–30.

30 Votes = .067*Spending. No. = 16, t = 6.73, adj. R-sq. = 0.75. See Jack Corrigan, "How Much Did Each Presidential Candidate Spend per Vote in the Primaries?" *San Jose Mercury-News*, July 29, 2016.

31 Nicholas Confessore and Sarah Cohen, "How Jeb Bush Spent $130 Million Running for President with Nothing to Show for It," *New York Times*, February 22, 2016.

32 Lee Drutman, "How Much Did Money Really Matter in 2012?" Sunlight Foundation, November 9, 2012.

Chapter 16—Three Reforms

1 Michael D. Gilbert and Benjamin F. Aiken, "Disclosure and Corruption," Election Law Journal 14.2 (2015): 148–64.

2 Bruce Ackerman and Ian Ayres, *Voting with Dollars: A New Paradigm for Campaign Finance* (Yale University Press, 2002). See also Ian Ayres and Jeremy Bulow, "The Donation Booth: Mandating Donor Anonymity to Disrupt the Market for Political Influence," *Stanford Law Review* 50 (1998): 837–91; Ian Ayres, "Should Campaign Donors Be Identified?" *Regulation* 24.2 (2001): 12–17.

3 *NAACP v. Alabama*, 357 U.S. 449 (1958).

4 See Charles Korte, "War of Words: Obama v. Koch Brothers," *USA Today*, August 26, 2015.

5 There are exceptions. When Pacific Gas and Electric was found to be behind a California initiative in which it had a financial stake, the measure was rejected by the voters. Bruce E. Cain, *Democracy More or Less: America's Political Reform Quandary* (Cambridge University Press, 2015), 49.

6 Christopher Weber, Johanna Dunaway and Tyler Johnson, "It's All in the Name: Source Cue Ambiguity and the Persuasive Appeal of Campaign Ads," *Political Behavior* 34.3 (2012): 561–84.

7 Full disclosure: when I was the executive director of the George

Mason Law and Economics Center's program for judges, we received about 10 percent of our support from the Charles Koch Institute. Never once did they tell me what programs I should put on or what lecturers I should hire.

8 "Senators Hit Back in Letter to Denial Front Groups," letter dated July 22, 2016, posted by Senator Sheldon Whitehouse at http://www.whitehouse.senate.gov/news/release/senators-hit-back-in-letter-to-denial-front-groups.

9 *Buckley v. Valeo*, 424 U.S. 1, 74 (1976). Adopted in *Citizens United v. FEC*, 558 U.S. 310, 367 (2010).

10 5 U.S.C. §§ 7321–26.

11 *United States Civil Service Commission v. National Association of Letter Carriers*, 413 U.S. 548 (1973).

12 The prohibition, which was incorporated into the Federal Election Campaign Act in 1976 (Pub. L. 94-283, sec. 112(2), § 322, 90 Stat. 475, 492–93), is limited to individual contractors, and does not extend to the executives, employees or shareholders of a corporate contractor, or to corporate-connected PACs. Code of Federal Regulations, Title 11, Federal Elections, Part 115. Corporations themselves, whether contractors or not, have long been banned from making direct political contributions.

13 52 U.S.C. § 30119(a)(1). See *Wagner v. FEC*, 793 F.3d 1, *cert. den. sub nom. Miller v. FEC*, __ U.S. __ (Jan. 19, 2016).

14 Id. at 22.

15 See Fred S. McChesney, *Money for Nothing: Politicians, Rent Extraction, and Political Extortion* (Harvard University Press, 1997); Peter Schweizer, *Extortion: How Politicians Extract Your Money, Buy Votes, and Line Their Own Pockets* (Boston: Houghton, Mifflin, Harcourt, 2013).

16 *Blount. v. SEC*, 61 F.3d 938 (D.C. Cir., 1995). In evaluating the rule, Judge Williams applied a strict scrutiny standard, under which restrictions on free speech must be based on a compelling government interest in curbing corruption and must be narrowly tailored to achieve that goal, but the *Wagner* court found

that a less exacting standard of review applied, since what was proposed was a limit on contributions, not expenditures.

17 Id. at 943.

18 Maureen Dowd, "Liberties; Revenge on the Nerds," *New York Times*, January 21, 1998.

19 Joel Brinkley, "U.S. v. Microsoft: The Lobbying," *New York Times*, September 7, 2001.

20 Frank Yu and Xiaoyun Yu, "Corporate Lobbying and Fraud Detection," *Journal of Financial and Quantitative Analysis* 46.6 (2011): 1865–91.

21 Brian Kelleher Richter, Krislert Samphantharak, and Jeffrey F. Timmons, "Lobbying and Taxes," *American Journal of Political Science* 53.4 (2009): 893–909.

22 "Money and Politics," *Economist*, October 1, 2011. See also Hui Chen, David Parsley and Ya-Wen Yang, "Corporate Lobbying and Firm Performance," *Journal of Business Finance and Accounting* 42.3-4 (2015): 444–81 (lobbying is positively related to accounting and market measures of financial performance); Jin-Hyuk Kim, "Corporate Lobbying Revisited," *Business and Politics* 10.2 (2008): 1–23 (lobbying firms tend to outperform the market average).

23 Michael J. Cooper, Huseyin Gulen, and Alexei Ovtchinnikov, "Corporate Political Contributions and Stock Returns," *Journal of Finance* 65.2 (2010): 687–724.

24 Rajesh K. Aggarwal, Felix Meschke and Tracy Yue Wang, "Corporate Political Donations: Investment or Agency?" *Business and Politics* 14.1 (2012): 1–40. Similarly, in a model that included lobbying expenses, Michael Hadani and Douglas Schuler found that corporate political contributions reduced firm value, except in regulated industries. "In Search of El Dorado: The Elusive Financial Returns on Corporate Political Investments," *Strategic Management Journal* 34.2 (2013): 165–81. See also Stephen Ansolabehere, James M. Snyder Jr. and Michiko Ueda, "Did Firms Profit from Soft Money?" *Election Law Journal* 3.2 (2004): 193–98, (no noticeable difference between firms that

gave large amounts of soft money compared to firms that gave no soft money).

25 Marcos Chamon and Ethan Kaplan, "The Iceberg Theory of Campaign Contributions: Political Threats and Interest Group Behavior," *American Economic Journal: Economic Policy* 5.1 (2013): 1–31.

26 See Natasha Singer, "Harry and Louise Return, with a New Message," *New York Times*, July 16, 2009; "Obamacare's Secret History," *Wall Street Journal*, June 13, 2012.

27 Quoted in Robert H. Sitkoff, "Corporate Political Speech, Political Extortion, and the Competition for Corporate Charters," *University of Chicago Law Review* 69.3 (2002): 1103–66, at 1115, 1136. See also Robert H. Sitkoff, "Politics and the Business Corporation," *Regulation* 26.4 (2003–4): 30–36.

28 Ansolabehere et al., "Did Firms Profit from Soft Money?" Another explanation for the curious finding that political contributions don't do much for firm value is that it might be a reflection of misbehaving managers. Executives might plunder the firm's treasury not to benefit their firm but rather to back the candidates they personally favor. It's not about the company, it's about the CEO. Politically active firms are in fact more likely to display the badges of management misbehavior: weak boards of directors, unusually high CEO pay, wasteful corporate acquisitions, the accumulation of surplus "free cash flow" in the corporate treasury for which the firm had no business use but which it declines to issue as dividends. See Aggarwal et al., "Corporate Political Donations."

29 Lee Drutman, *The Business of America Is Lobbying: How Corporations Became Politicized and Politics Became Corporate* (Oxford University Press, 2015), 93–94. See Jeffrey Milyo, David Primo, and Timothy Groseclose, "Corporate PAC Campaign Contributions in Perspective," *Business and Politics* 2.1 (2000): 75–88 (large PAC contributors spend 20 to 60 times more on lobbying expenses than they do on connected PAC money contributions).

30 Stephen W. Mazza, Raquel Alexander and Susan Scholz, "Measuring Rates of Return on Lobbying Expenditures: An Empirical

Case Study of Tax Breaks for Multinational Corporations," *Journal of Law and Politics* 25.4 (2009): 401–57.

31 Frank R. Baumgartner et al., *Lobbying and Policy Change: Who Wins, Who Loses, and Why* (University of Chicago Press, 2009). See also Frank R. Baumgartner et al., "Money Priorities and Stalemate: How Lobbying Affects Public Policy," *Election Law Journal* 13.1 (2014): 194–209.

32 FEC v. Wisconsin Right to Life, Inc., 551 U.S. 449 (2007). See generally Jay Alan Sekulow and Erik M. Zimmerman, "Weeding Them Out by the Roots: The Unconstitutionality of Regulating Grassroots Issue Advocacy," *Stanford Law and Policy Review* 19.1 (2008): 164. If organized under Internal Revenue Code section 501(c)(3), however, a charity is barred from spending a "substantial" amount of its budget on lobbying. As well, many states require grassroots lobbyists to disclose their expenditures to their donors. See Richard Briffault, "The Anxiety of Influence: The Evolving Regulation of Lobbying," *Election Law Journal* 13.1 (2014): 160–193, at 186–90.

33 See Nicholas W. Allard, "Lobbying Is an Honorable Profession: The Right to Petition and the Competition to Be Right," *Stanford Law and Policy Review* 19.1 (2008): 23–68, at 42–49 (describing the complex nature of the lobbyist's role as an informational intermediary).

34 The Lobbying Disclosure Act defines "lobbyist" as a person who (1) has made more than one "lobbying contact" for the client over the course of its representation and (2) spends at least 20 percent of his time for the client on "lobbyist activities." 2 U.S.C. § 1602(10). See generally William V. Luneburg and A. L. Spitzer, "The Lobbying Disclosure Act of 1995: Scope of Coverage," chap. 3 of *The Lobbying Manual: A Complete Guide to Federal Lobbying Law and Practice*, ed. William Luneberg et al., 4th ed. (American Bar Association, 2009). A "lobbying contact" is a simple communication with a congressman or staffer or with certain high executive branch officials, and "lobbying activities" include efforts in support of a lobbying contact. The definition of lobby-

ing extends to firms that conduct their activities in-house with their own government-relations departments, without relying on a third-party lobbyist. The ABA report concluded that the 20 percent threshold has proved too high and has permitted lobbyists to escape disclosure requirements. Within a lobbying firm, work might be divided between a partner who contacts a congressman but spends less than 20 percent of his time doing so, and an associate who spends all his time on the subject but doesn't contact an official. Instead of the 20 percent rule, the report suggested safe harbors for isolated or casual acts of soliciting contributions, and for lobbying activities that earn less than a *de minimis* amount.

35 Pub. L. 110-81, 121 Stat. 735, 2 U.S.C. § 1613.

36 Charles Fried et al., *Lobbying Law in the Spotlight: Challenges and Proposed Improvements*, Report of the Task Force on Federal Lobbying Laws, Section of Administrative Law and Regulatory Practice, American Bar Association (Washington, D.C., January 3, 2011); see also Joseph E. Sandler, "Lobbyists and Election Law: The New Challenge," chap. 36 of *The Lobbying Manual*, at 756–57.

37 The ABA committee also proposed a ban on contingency contracts, in which the lobbyist's fee is in part dependent on his success in promoting an earmark, tax relief or similar financial grant or loan.

38 *North Carolina Right to Life, Inc. v. Bartlett*, 168 F.3d 705 (4th Cir., 1999) (upholding a state ban on lobbyist contributions while the legislature was in session); Green Party of Conn. v. Garfield, 616 F.3d 189 (2d Cir., 2010) (disallowing a ban on lobbyist campaign contribution to state legislators). See Briffault, "The Anxiety of Influence," 174–80.

39 Richard L. Hasen, "Lobbying, Rent-Seeking, and the Constitution," *Stanford Law Review* 64.1 (2011): 191–253.

40 In *Preston v. Leake*, 660 F.3d 726 (2011), the Fourth Circuit Court of Appeals held that a North Carolina law that banned lobbyist contributions to state officials survived a strict scrutiny analysis under the First Amendment. The ban simply channeled lobbying support

into other avenues, "cutting off the avenue of association and expression that is most likely to lead to corruption but allowing numerous other avenues of association and expression." Id. at 734.

41 Thomas B. Edsall, "The Trouble with That Revolving Door," *New York Times*, December 18, 2011.

42 18 U.S.C. § 207, enacted as part of the Honest Leadership and Open Government Act.

43 Sunlight Foundation and Center for Responsive Politics, "All Cooled Off: As Congress Convenes, Former Colleagues Will Soon Be Calling from K Street," January 6, 2015, at OpenSecrets. org.

44 Quoted in Lawrence Lessig, *Republic, Lost: How Money Corrupts Congress—and a Plan to Stop It* (New York: Twelve, 2011), 123.

Chapter 17—The Heavenly City of the Enlightened Reformer

1 Francis Bacon, *Novum Organum* I.84 (New York: Collier, 1902), 61–62.

2 Robespierre, January 11, 1792, *Oeuvres de Maximilien Robespierre*, vol. 8, ed. Marc Bouloiseau et al. (Paris: P.U.F., 1954), 115.

3 Carl L. Becker, *The Heavenly City of the Eighteenth-Century Philosophers*, 2nd ed. (Yale University Press, 2003), 31.

4 Richard L. Hasen, *Plutocrats United: Campaign Money, the Supreme Court, and the Distortion of American Elections* (Yale University Press, 2016).

5 *Arizona Free Enterprise Club v. Bennett*, 564 U.S. 721 (2011).

6 Lee Drutman, *The Business of America Is Lobbying: How Corporations Became Politicized and Politics Became Corporate* (Oxford University Press, 2015), 56.

7 Nicholas O. Stephanopoulos, "Elections and Alignment," *Columbia Law Review* 114.2 (2014): 283–365.

8 *Buckley v. Valeo*, 424 U.S. 1, 48–49 (1976).

9 *Citizens United v. FEC*, 558 U.S. 310, 340–41 (2010), overturning *Austin v. Michigan Chamber of Commerce*, 494 U.S. 652 (1990).

10 Zephyr Teachout, *Corruption in America: From Benjamin Franklin's*

Snuff Box to Citizens United (Harvard University Press, 2014).

11 Charles Baudelaire, "De l'essence du rire," in *Oeuvres complètes*, vol. 2, ed. Claude Pichois (Paris: Gallimard, 1976), 532.

APPENDIX A

1 Andrei Shleifer and Robert W. Vishny, "Corruption," *Quarterly Journal of Economics* 108.3 (1993): 599–617; Stephen Knack and Philip Keefer, "Institutions and Economic Performance: Cross-Country Tests Using Alternative Institutional Measures," *Economics and Politics* 7.3 (1995): 207–27; Rafael La Porta, Florencio López-de-Silanes, Cristian Pop-Eleches and Andrei Shleifer, "Judicial Checks and Balances," *Journal of Political Economy* 112.2 (2004): 445–70; see generally Pranab Bardhan, "Corruption and Development: A Review of Issues," *Journal of Economic Literature* 35.3 (1997): 1320–46. Causation is likely to work in both directions here, since corruption makes a country poorer.

2 Torsten Persson and Guido Tabellini, "Democratic Capital: The Nexus of Political and Economic Change," *American Economic Journal: Macroeconomics* 1.2 (2009): 88–126.

3 See Alina Mungiu-Pippidi, *The Quest for Good Governance: How Societies Develop Control of Corruption* (Cambridge University Press, 2015), 102–3; Lorenz Blume, Jens Müller, Stefan Voigt and Carsten Wolf, "The Economic Effects of Constitutions: Replicating—and Extending—Persson and Tabellini," *Public Choice* 139.1 (2009): 197–225, at 212–14; Daniel Lederman, Norman V. Loayza and Rodrigo R. Soares, "Accountability and Corruption: Political Institutions Matter," *Economics and Politics* 17.1 (2005): 1–35; Jana Kunicova and Susan Rose-Ackerman, "Electoral Rules and Constitutional Structures as Constraints on Corruption," *British Journal of Political Science* 35.4 (2005): 573–606, (presidential systems interact with proportional representation voting rules to produce governments that are particularly susceptible to corruption).

Index

Tk

CPSIA information can be obtained
at www.ICGtesting.com
Printed in the USA
FFOW02n1833270917
40418FF